Narrowing the Achievement Gap for
Native American Students

There has been much talk and effort focused on the educational achievement gap between white versus black, Hispanic and American Indian students. While there has been some movement the gap has not appreciably narrowed, and it has narrowed the least for Native American students. This volume addresses this disparity by melding evidence-based instruction with culturally sensitive materials and approaches, outlining how we as educators and scientists can pay the educational debt we owe our children.

In the tradition of the Native American authors who also contribute to it, this volume will be a series of "stories" that will reveal how the authors have built upon research evidence and linked it with their knowledge of history and culture to develop curricula, materials and methods for instruction of not only Native American students, but of all students. It provides a framework for educators to promote cultural awareness and honor the cultures and traditions that too few people know about. After each major section of the volume, invited authors provide commentary addressing how the chapters and their approaches and activities can be applied to other populations, including Blacks, Hispanics, and minority and Indigenous groups in nations around the globe.

Peggy McCardle, Ph.D., M.P.H., is a former branch chief at *Eunice Kennedy Shriver* National Institute of Child Health and Human Development. In 2013 she received both an NICHD Mentor Award and the Einstein Award from The Dyslexia Foundation. She consults and writes about language development, bilingualism, reading, and learning disabilities.

Virginia Berninger is Professor of Educational Psychology at University of Washington, Seattle. Her research, teaching, and clinical work currently focuses on learning disabilities, diversity in learning, and translating research into educational practice.

Routledge Research in Education Policy and Politics

The Routledge Research in Education Policy and Politics series aims to enhance our understanding of key challenges and facilitate on-going academic debate within the influential and growing field of Education Policy and Politics.

Books in the series include:

Narrowing the Achievement Gap for Native American Students

Paying the Educational Debt

Edited by
**Peggy McCardle and
Virginia Berninger**

Routledge
Taylor & Francis Group

NEW YORK AND LONDON

First published 2015
by Routledge
711 Third Avenue, New York, NY 10017, USA

and by Routledge
2 Park Square, Milton Park, Abingdon, Oxfordshire OX14 4RN

First issued in paperback 2016

*Routledge is an imprint of the Taylor & Francis Group,
an informa business*

Library of Congress Cataloging-in-Publication Data

Narrowing the achievement gap for Native American students : paying the
   educational debt / edited by Peggy McCardle, Virginia Berninger.
      pages cm. — (Routledge research in education policy and politics ; 6)
   Includes bibliographical references and index.
   1. Indians of North America—Education.   2. Indian students—United
States.   3. Academic achievement—United States.   4. Educational
equalization—United States.   I. McCardle, Peggy D.   II. Berninger,
Virginia Wise.
   E97.N23 2014
   371.829'97—dc23
   2014011736

Typeset in Sabon
by IBT Global.

ISBN 13: 978-1-138-28669-6 (pbk)
ISBN 13: 978-0-415-72716-7 (hbk)

Dedication

The book is dedicated to **William Demmert and Denny Hurtado** for their distinguished leadership in demonstrating how evidence-based and culturally-sensitive education can be combined, and for their tireless dedication to Native students and quality education for Indigenous youth everywhere.

The late **William G. Demmert, Jr.**, of Tlingit and Oglalla Sioux heritage, received his doctorate of education in 1973 from Harvard University. A national leader in Indian Education, Demmert served as the first U.S. Deputy Commissioner of Education for the U.S. Office of Indian Education, in the Department of Health, Education, and Welfare, under the Indian Education Act of 1972 (Title IV of Public Law 92-318), legislation on which he had been hired to work with senate staff while still a doctoral student at Harvard. During his lifetime Demmert also served as Director of Education for the Bureau of Indian Affairs and Commissioner of Education for the State of Alaska, was a member of President Clinton's education transition team helping set the tone for Indian education during that administration, and worked closely with colleagues and collaborators on President Clinton's Executive Order 1998. Demmert was co-chair and primary writer for the influential report, *Indian Nations At Risk: An Educational Strategy for Action*, published by the U.S. Department of Education in 1991. As a founding member of National Indian Education Association (NIEA), his contributions led to his receiving a Lifetime Achievement Award in 2004.

Demmert's academic home was Western Washington University, Bellingham, WA, where he mentored and nurtured both Native and non-Native students, while maintaining a national presence in the education research community, always reminding us all not to forget Native students. Throughout his career he was dedicated to demonstrating the value of Culture-Based Education, and worked actively with groups such as the Northwest Regional Educational Laboratory in Portland, OR; the Center for Research on Education, Diversity, and Excellence (CREDE), UC Berkeley; the RAND Corporation; Educational Testing Services;

Haskins Laboratories in New Haven, CT; Kamehameha Schools, Hawaii; Arizona State University; and many schools serving Native students. In recognition of his work, he was honored by the formation of the *William G. Demmert Cultural Freedom Award* that recognizes "extraordinary and courageous work that celebrates the right to freedom of Native language, culture, and educational excellence" which was recently awarded to the Niigaane Ojibwemowin Immersion School. Demmert also was a convener of the Circumpolar North group, made up of ministers of education dedicated to the education of Indigenous persons from member nations (Norway, Sweden, Finland, Greenland, Russian Federation, Alaska, Nunavut Territory, Northern Quebec, and the Yukon Territory in Canada) and to the preservation of their languages and cultures. William Demmert was still actively engaged in conversations with close colleagues just weeks before his death in 2010, still seeking to ensure that his legacy of strong advocacy for Native students would continue. Our best tribute to him is to work to maintain and strengthen the focus on educating all students within a strong environment of respect for culture, language, and Indigenous heritage.

Denny Hurtado (of mixed Indigenous heritage: Pacific Northwest, Skokomish, Pacific Islander, and Filipino) also has been a leader and strong advocate for Native students of all ages. A descendant of Chief Seath for whom Seattle is named, Denny is recently retired from Evergreen College in Evergreen, Washington, where he served on the faculty and where he recruited, mentored, and guided both Native and non-Native students. In addition, to ensure that Native history and culture would be taught in Washington state schools, Hurtado in collaboration with Demmert and Magda Costantino, was a leader in the development of the Northwest Native American Reading Curriculum; these collaborators conducted studies on evidence-based, culturally sensitive early reading instruction for Native students in seven reservations in the Northwest, Southwest, and Hawaii, including work on response-to-intervention. Hurtado has been an active NIEA board member, and served for many years in the Office of Indian Education, Washington State Department of Education, always seeking to improve education for Native students. He was an influential Director of Indian Education for the State of Washington, and had an instrumental role in state and national legislation advocating for language and culture-based education. As Director of Indian Education, Hurtado played a critical role in getting Indian Education accepted into the general curriculum of Washington state schools through work on legislation (Washington House Bill 1495) and the development of the Sovereignty Curriculum, developed under his own and Shana Brown's leadership; the curriculum (*Since Time Immemorial*) is now freely available to educate students and both preservice and inservice teachers about the various tribes, their cultures, treaties, contributions and history. Hurtado is a gifted storyteller, and in fact chose that route for his contribution to this volume—an oral narrative that was written from his words. In addition, Hurtado is an accomplished photographer, who has exhibited photo essays of 20th and 21st-century Indian life; he graciously provided the photograph of William Demmert in the shadow of Demmert's ancestor, Chief Crazy Horse, included in this volume.

Figure 0.1   William G. Demmert, Jr.

Figure 0.2   Denny Sparr Hurtado (TacH mi acH t3n).

Contents

PART III
Diversity of Native American Student Populations, Instructional Approaches, and Research Applications

Figures

Tables

Preface

Listening to, and helping each other . . . Doing what one can for the next generation.

—Rosemary Ackley Christensen (February, 2014)

We listen to and learn from our Elders; we listen to and learn from those who are younger; together we seek to create equilibrium and a sense of steadiness, comfort, and safety that allows each of us as a living being to walk the 'good red road' until it becomes time to go home to join those who have gone before. Basically, it is one of the principles we live by, the *Principle of Balance*. The Elders teach seven principles, the others being: *Peaceful co-existence, Equality, Connectedness, the Circle, Sustenance,* and *Gratitude*. With each principle interrelated, we know the main elements must exist in harmony for each of us to live, continue to exist, and sustain each other (all living things), which means we must learn about, practice, and support or maintain balance with each other, seeking a way to interact with differences with respect. That is, we must look for and generate or produce balance.

Editors McCardle and Berninger, in their *Narrowing the Achievement Gap for Native American Students: Paying the Educational Debt,* work to provide a very stimulating 'look-see' or 'data bank' for understanding that incredibly important tool of balance, how to approach it relative to the education of children, all of our children. The child is a gift, the Elders say, and we must treat each as such. As I read through the chapters, I would get excited about the ideas as they are expressed and made into action by the young people working in education. The ideas are not new, but as we know, each generation does what it can, and each new generation works on what must be done according to the principles we live by.

I thought about 'back in the day' when my contemporaries worked with our Elders, and those younger, to help improve the educational environment for Indian children. I was on the Boarding School Evaluation Team for the U.S. Senate Indian sub-committee in 1968, from which a report was provided to the U.S. Senate (Subcommittee on Indian Education, 1969). What a learning event that was relative to how our children throughout the U.S. were 'educated'. During this work, and later as we went on to graduate school, some of us became friends and working-caring colleagues. Demmert and I both were at Harvard after we met at the First Convocation of American Indian Scholars, held at Princeton University, 1970, at the behest of Scholars/

Elders Jeannette Henry and Rupert Costo, American Indian Historical Society, California. We worked on organizing the founding of the National Indian Education Association, while at this conference with other Indian people we met there from around the country. We formed a bond then, and continued to work with others for many other things we did during our active working lives. What fun we had, while we used what we learned and knew to try to make a difference in Indian education for children.

I remember with fondness the article Demmert and I wrote for a class we took, later published (Christensen & Demmert, 1978) in a book edited by Tommy Thompson. We kind-of 'yell-around' in the article in discussing what *must* be done to improve Indian education:

> Tribal autonomy and controls over tribal affairs must lead to the recognition of the right of the tribal group to control education of Indian children. Indians ought to explore several areas that may be fruitful to this end. One of the most promising approaches is the avenue of customs and tradition. Indian people have values, customs, and life-styles different from the dominant cultural groups in the United States. (p. 141)

We went on to discuss what the dominant system does, what Indian people say about the schooling, and that Indian people continue to live their beliefs. We stated at the ending of one section that,

> Indians must help non-Indians see the need for tribal values and customs, for if non-tribal people wish to survive, they must adopt some of the values of tribal people. This country is rapidly destroying itself with its values of competition, conquest over nature, and material wealth at any cost. (p. 147)

We ended the article with a listing of 17 recommendations (pp. 151–152), prior to which we said this:

> In conclusion, the pivotal point in this investigation is repeated: Indians have autonomy within the context of treaties signed in good faith between tribes and the federal government. Further, court cases and congressional actions reinforce this doctrine. Indians, regardless of geographic location, have the right to autonomy unless they voluntarily chose to negate it. Indians are entitled to federal financing based on land wealth ceded to the government, an exchange for services for which the Indian paid in advance. The right to control education of Indian children is an inherent part of this doctrine. In order to implement Indian community control, the following actions are recommended. (p.151)

We, along with other colleagues, did a lot of work during those years, meeting wonderful, concerned, hard-working people, all interested in what we could do to help 'those coming after'. Plus, we had a lot of fun. I remember once we were all meeting somewhere in Demmert's 'territory', and his father, William George Demmert Sr., happened to come and visit, complete with his fishing boat, which he allowed us to board and look around while he explained his work on the boat and the water. Normally, when we got together like this, we would go out to dinner, and we would each take turns buying dinner. Demmert's father paid for dinner, and Demmert Jr. tried to claim he was taking his turn (while laughing, of course) since Wm. George Demmert paid the tab. We laughed back, and said, nope, that won't work. You still have to take your turn another time.

This tome obviously fits with the work we did, and it is such a joy to look at the three parts and note the excellent ideas and activities as well as the reinforcement of cultural norms. I love how in Part I, speaking toward instructional goals, Beltran and colleagues use and explain storytelling, something many of us grew up with as it was used by our elder scholars to teach us, while we were allowed as independent beings to understand the story as we saw it, depending on our age and learning mode. I still am amazed at how I finally got something that was told me by an Elder, and finally I understood and knew the teaching. I was allowed the time to absorb, understand and over time, finally 'know' what the teaching was. And of course the 'little rabbit story' in the Brown chapter is enjoyable and a learning device as well. Craig talks about cultural guides, which reminded me about our 'Elders in the classroom' use in our *Nibbin* (meaning summer, in Ojibwe) Minneapolis summer school. It was incredible how well it went, having fluent-speaking (of Tribal languages) Elders in the classroom with the children on a daily basis. We used an Elder also in the discipline schema, and it was so pleasing to come into that area and find a student sent there by a teacher being 'disciplined' by the rules put forth there. They worked beautifully, and students were not upset by the action. Parents loved *Nibbin*. I remember once looking out and seeing a staff member running down the sidewalk; I asked "what were you doing?" when he came back in. He said he was trying to catch up with an Elder who was walking with some kids, explaining how the air smelled when it was going to rain and explaining how the clouds looked when it was going to rain.

And of course the other chapters as well in Part I are so important and provide us with much to mull over and use to help, where we can, as we look toward the children's well-being: the use of the rubrics reminded me of when Demmert would send me a draft so that I (as well as others he asked) could review, comment, or make suggested additions. And needless to say, the work with language was always on the forefront for all of us—helping as needed, writing and working on legislation and procedures that might make a difference. The legislation procedures, processes, and work by Denny Hurtado and J P Leary tell an overwhelming story. Really, their work with Tribes, Sovereign nations we know and recognize, interacting with States, also fitting the sovereign model, seeking, advocating for, and moving toward a real balance between the needs, wants, and cultural-norm medium considered natural by each, although in some parts, immensely different, fits the notion of a sort of secretary of state role, or diplomatic task. Again, a task that works toward balance, something suggested long ago by our Elders who told us to go learn what that white man teaches in his school, and knowing it well, put it with our way, so both can work together. I did appreciate the statement by Hurtado regarding Lewis and Clark, true reciprocity/balance! And talk about the young people learning and using present technology is, or as the young ones say, 'awesome!' Speaking as someone who used to write on a typewriter, what a today-type thing to hire a web designer, eh? And the tribal interaction summarized in the table provided by Leary is such a delight to behold! It shows a picture of what indeed is possible in the education improvement realm we choose to work in, moving toward practice that can be proven in evidence recognized by the non-native world and take to our hearts the possibility that with hard work, the children are going to be okay!

In Part II the authors discuss an approach that seeks balance between cultural norm reality and evidence-based instruction, and they provide such interesting, stimulating, and real thought-provoking discussion that one sometimes thinks "Wow! I think I might be able to do that!" This book's use of commentators for each part is such an appealing notion. For example, the commentator for Part II, Rose, provides a very helpful review of what is provided. For instance the comment that reflects and defines balance regarding how languages can be used to "reflect on, and enhance the learning of the other" relative to Lockard and deGroat quoting Eilene Joe.

And of course Part III discusses the diversity of Indian populations, possible approaches and research ideas, and activities that are so informative, helpful for possible ideas, and engaging as stories, too. The potato experiment discussed by Yamauchi and colleagues was so clever! And it gave terrific learning results, too!

Back in the day, we worked closely with the Hawaiian friends we met, worked with them when we could be of help, and cheered with them as they put together the incredible Aha Pūnana Leo program. Namaka Rawlins, William Pila Wilson, Kauanoe Kamana and others we still see now and then. Sheehey and Jegatheesan provide an excellent review of what they will discuss, and the very informative, connective story about a caring mom and child with needs provides a focus that is not only helpful, but also it's a story that provides teaching illumination that will keep on shining. The commentator for Part III, Warner, points out that in *Indigenous cultures relationships trump individual acknowledgement.* What a simple yet profound, resounding statement!

Demmert was a hard worker his entire life. David Beaulieu and I went to see him (one last time) in January 2010. When we got to Bellingham, friends Namaka and Kauanoe were there discussing work they were doing with him. Demmert's wife Nora facilitated our interaction with Demmert in a way that was comfortable for him during his last days. We spent time with him talking about something he was very interested in. He wanted very much to see a history of Indian education written and organized by native scholars, and he spent time talking with us about it. We had discussed it during earlier times via email and phone calls sharing outlines and ideas. Beaulieu had come up with and organized the concept much earlier, had done some writing, discussed it with Demmert, and is continuing working on that effort, and he will finish it.

As Lakota friend Joseph Trimble, psychology professor at WWU, Bellingham, observed, "Cultural context needs to be understood if behavior is to be understood". He said that in Madison, Wisconsin, during a speech given in December 2002. Joseph of course was a close friend and colleague of Demmert, and as Linda Sue Warner speaks simply, yet profoundly, so does Joseph in this statement. In the end that is what must be understood, and put into the educational context if our children are to be educated the way our brilliant elders devised, using the seven principles that we must all live by, learn from, and exemplify in our lives so that as we walk the sacred road west, home, we will be greeted by those who have gone before, and be told: Come on in, you did a good job!

REFERENCES

Christensen, R. & Demmert. W.G. (1978). The education of Indians and the mandate of history (1978). In T. Thompson (Ed.) *The schooling of Native America.* American Association of Colleges for Teacher Education & Teacher Corps, U.S. Office of Education, Washington D.C., pp.138–152.

Subcommittee on Indian Education. (1969). *The education of American Indians: A compendium of federal boarding school evaluations.* Prepared for the Committee on Labor and Public Welfare, U.S. Senate, November 1969. U.S. Government Printing Office: Washington, DC.

Acknowledgments

This monograph is the result of an ever-widening circle, beginning with Peggy McCardle's early meetings with William Demmert and Denny Hurtado (TacH mi acH t3n), and their mutual conversations about culturally sensitive, evidence-based literacy instruction, and her introduction of Virginia Berninger to them. The circle widened as Demmert and Hurtado continued to introduce both co-editors to Native Americans involved in education and education research, and to others involved in Indigenous education and research. Now the intellectual offspring of these two men continues to build such relationships and grow the circle. Hopefully, readers will join these ever-widening circles, these ripples on the pond, and contribute in their way to this important effort inspired and informed by what Native Americans and others have already done. We wish to acknowledge not only the dedication and hard work of Demmert and Hurtado, but also of the authors who worked to meet deadlines and respond to queries, who were the ones who made this book possible.

In addition, we wish to acknowledge Dr. Magda Costantino, a Slovakian immigrant to the US who has dedicated her professional career to building bridges between countries, cultures, languages, and education, and played an instrumental role in Native education. She received the Thurston County Diversity Committee Lifetime Achievement Award for contributions in promoting human rights and cultural diversity in 2001 and the Washington State Historical Society David Douglas Award in 2005 for work on the Northwest Native American Reading Curriculum (NNARC). She was a collaborator with Denny Hurtado in the development and implementation of the NNARC (described in Chapter 6), and contributed significantly to the processes used in developing the Washington state Sovereignty curriculum.

Thanks, also to our editors at Routledge, in particular to Lauren Verity, who answered all the co-editors' many questions and guided us patiently, promptly, and with good grace; she was truly helpful.

We also wish to acknowledge the students who continue to seek an education that balances evidence-based practice with culturally sensitive and appropriate practices, enabling them to gain skills in the important academic areas of reading and writing, math and science, geography, and social studies, and to relate these to their own lives and cultures, to create their own stories. Ultimately this book is for them.

1 The Importance of Combining Culturally Sensitive and Evidence-Based Literacy Instruction

Virginia Berninger and Peggy McCardle

In the recent past, two independent traditions have greatly influenced educational practice. The first looks to research for evidence of effectiveness of instructional and intervention approaches. As in medicine, the scientific method generates a knowledge base that can serve as the evidence-based foundation for educational practice. This tradition draws on multiple disciplines (e.g., psychology, linguistics, learning science, instructional/intervention science, and neuroscience) to understand how children learn oral language, reading, written language, and math and other domain-specific content areas of the curriculum, and identify effective instructional and intervention practices for teaching them. Educators are increasingly encouraged to become knowledgeable about and apply to classroom practice the information that results from such research, that is, to become experts in translation science.

The second tradition—multiculturalism—has enhanced our awareness of the increasingly diverse student populations in our schools. And over the years, this tradition has increased our knowledge of the many cultural groups who have freely immigrated to the country in which their children are being educated as well as groups of involuntary immigrants (Native Americans and African Americans [Ladson-Billings, 2006]); see also e.g., Banks (2012), Banks & Banks (2011), Bill (1990), Gay (2010), Jones (2009), and Romero-Little, Ortiz, McCarty with Chen (2011). These groups are variously referred to, throughout the world, as First Peoples or Indigenous groups, or, in the United States, as Native Americans[1] because they were already there when European explorers arrived. Relatively less attention, even within the multicultural education field, has been devoted to these groups. Although educating educators about respecting all students' language and culture has been emphasized (Banks & Banks, 2010; National Urban Indian Family Coalition [NUIFC], 2008; Nieto, 2010; Romero-Little, Ortiz, McCarty with Chen, 2011), seldom is cultural sensitivity linked with evidence-based instructional and intervention practices. Yet, these two traditions can be reciprocally integrated to enhance student learning outcomes for all, especially First Peoples, Indigenous groups, and Native Americans (see Table 5.1), and thus ensure the Rights of Indigenous

Peoples (United Nations, 2008) to be educated with methods consistent with their cultures and languages (see Chapter 9). Our goals—to make a case for such an approach and illustrate how evidence-based, culturally sensitive practices have been implemented for Native Americans and could be for others—is timely given the Executive Order signed by President Obama committing the Federal Government to working closely with tribal governments to close the achievement gap between Indian and non-Indian students and to the preservation and revitalization of Native languages (Executive Order 13592, 2011).

A variety of research methods can be applied to developing, validating, and implementing evidence-based, culturally sensitive educational practices in general and specifically for Native Americans. These include descriptive (qualitative), correlational, and experimental, as well as mixed methods that combine two or more of these approaches. Throughout this book, authors draw on a variety of these and other research approaches to gather their evidence for specific educational purposes. Providing evidence-based, culturally sensitive education for Native Americans will narrow the current achievement gap and position Native students to pursue career choices and opportunities that will enhance their future life beyond schooling (see Part II).

This book has been written with a focus on Native Americans in the United States specifically but with, we believe, relevance for First Peoples/Indigenous groups throughout the world more generally. Although the chapters showcase Native Americans in the Northwest, Southwest, Midwest, or Hawaiian Islands, we consider them to have much broader relevance to other groups. As we consider Native students, who exhibit considerable diversity among themselves, we also call attention to the fastest growing group of Native Americans, Urban Indians, that is, , those who are no longer living on reservations. Rather, these Native Americans live in cities and sometimes in rural areas (National Urban Indian Family Coalition, 2008). Whether or not they live in cities, these non-reservation dwellers are often referred to as Urban Indians. In addition, the fastest growing "minority" or non-white group in the United States is of biracial or bicultural heritage. This includes Native Americans who historically and currently intermarry and have children with those from other races or cultures. Often, unfortunately, schools are not even aware that a student is Native American or of mixed heritage, although these cultural influences at home can significantly impact school learning and performance.

This book was conceived and written with respect for the cultural diversity of all peoples, and with the overarching goal of bringing together the two traditions of evidence-based practice and multicultural awareness and sensitivity, which have often developed independently of each other but can and should be integrated. This essentially includes all students; if our heritage is not that of an Indigenous group then it must be of an immigrant group at some point in each of our histories! This bringing together of these two traditions is addressed through chapters written—often in narrative story-telling style—to illustrate successes in implementing evidence-based or research-based,[2] culturally sensitive practices and to provide a model for classroom teachers, school administrators, and others who are in a position to implement culturally sensitive, evidence-based instruction and intervention for two sets of the 3 R's: (a) reading, writing, and arithmetic, and (b) respect, reciprocity, and relationships (see Chapter 7). Future directions for research and needed next steps are proposed to yield positive outcomes for Native students, families, and communities.

It is important that both educators and researchers develop a heightened awareness of Native Americans, who along with African Americans, have been targeted for narrowing the achievement gap in the United States (Ladson-Billings, 2006). Indeed many believe, as so ably articulated by Ladson-Billings, that there is an educational debt to be paid in acknowledgement of the trauma caused to earlier generations of Native students when they were taken from their homes, families, and culture and placed in boarding schools where they were not allowed to speak their native languages or share the oral traditions of the history of their peoples (Reyner & Eder, 2004). Currently many Native American children and youth are living in homes where grandparents remember the horrors of the boarding school and other historical trauma and discuss these with their children and their children's children (see Part I). At the same time, the hope is that what we have learned about narrowing the achievement gap for Native American students will also contribute to improving the education of students in mainstream and other cultures, living in poverty or other kinds of disadvantage or living in affluence. Additional goals are to situate the issues related to implementing effective evidence-based, culturally sensitive education practices in the global world of the 21st century, and to share and provide access to relevant technology-supported and other programs for educators.

The organization of the book provides a schema for those who wish to engage in research or educational practice related to the goals of the volume. Part 1 begins with two chapters on cultural sensitivity. Both Chapters 2 and 3 explain the role of story in Native American Culture. Story includes oral transmission of culture, but also of the past, which still affects today's children and youth. The next two chapters focus on the role of teachers and cultural guides in schools (Chapter 4) and the role of teacher education programs in preparing future teachers with a vision of how to narrow the achievement gap and what it will take to do so (Chapter 5). The last two chapters in Part I (Chapters 6 and 7) describe the roles of state government and legislation, education policy, community, curriculum development, and educational institutions in bringing about the changes that need to happen to narrow the achievement gap and pay the educational debt.

Part II offers a developmental model of evidence-based or research-based, culturally sensitive educational practices, beginning in the preschool (Chapters 8 and 10), continuing during K-1 transition and primary grades (Chapters 9 and 10) and middle and upper grades (Chapter 11 and Table 10.1).

Chapter 11, which includes a web link to a video conversation, models how technology can be used both to draw on the oral tradition of Native American Culture and on the ever evolving technology of the 21st century to help more Native American youth graduate from high school and gain access to higher education.

Part III features examples from both Native Hawaiians and American Indians in the Northwestern U.S., which highlight important issues in implementing evidence-based, culturally sensitive education to narrow the achievement gap and pay the educational debt. One explains the use of instructional conversation in teaching Native Hawaiians, developed and validated in university-school partnerships (Chapter 12). The next chapter deals with the challenges of helping Native students with special needs and their families (Chapter 13). The last chapter covers peer relationships among Native students and non-Native Students and school-community relationships; the model presented is already being scaled up and is an inspiration for what can be done to improve learning outcomes (Chapter 14).

Each major section of the book also contains a commentary, to examine the broader reach of these chapters, as they address issues relevant to Indigenous populations globally and to minority groups more generally. The commentary for Part I is written by Julie Washington, a scholar who addresses educational issues related to non-mainstream dialect within the US. The second is by David Rose, a scholar working with Indigenous groups within Australia. And the final commentary is by Linda Sue Warner, a Native scholar who works with Native students and who experienced mentoring by the late William Demmert and other scholars of his cohort and carries on this legacy.

Across the various sections of the book, authors provide examples of culturally sensitive, evidence- or research-based practices during early childhood, middle childhood, and even adolescence, both in and out of school. Some use technology, others use state of the art educational approaches without technology, but they merge these modern approaches with traditional practices and with all-important respect for and involvement of elders, family, and community. That is, they exemplify in their chapters our overriding goal to demonstrate that evidence and cultural sensitivity can and should mesh to produce the best education we can give our children, one in which they learn and achieve, are respectful of their own heritages and those of others, and are thus equipped to succeed in life, following whatever paths they choose.

NOTES

1. Here, the term 'Native Americans' is used as being inclusive of three groups: American Indians, Alaska Natives, and Native Hawaiians.
2. We make this distinction as some programs are based on available research but whose effectiveness has not yet been studied, or not studied with the particular group with whom they are being implemented.

REFERENCES

Banks, J. (2012). *Encyclopedia of diversity in education*. Thousand Oaks, CA: Sage Publications.

Banks, J., & Banks, C. (Eds.) (2011). *Handbook of research on multicultural education*. Flagstaff, AZ: Northern Arizona University.

Banks, J.A., & Banks, C.A.M. (2010). *Multicultural education: Issues and perspectives* (7th ed.). Danvers, MA: John Wiley & Sons, Inc.

Bill, Willard E. (1990). *From boarding schools to self-determination*. Olympia, WA: Office of the Superintendent of Public Instruction.

Executive Order 13592, 3 CFR. (2011). Improving American Indian and Alaska Native Educational Opportunities and Strengthening Tribal Colleges and Universities. Sec. 3, White House Initiative on American Indian and Alaska Native Education.

Gay, G. (2010). *Culturally responsive teaching: Theory, research, & practice* (2nd Ed.). New York: Teachers College Press.

Jones, J. (2009). *The psychology of multiculturalism in the schools: A primer for practice, training, and research*. Bethesda, MD: National Association of School Psychologists.

Ladson-Billings, G. (2006). From the achievement gap to the education debt: Understanding achievement in U.S. schools. *Educational Researcher, 35*(7), 3–12.

National Urban Indian Family Coalition (NUIFC). (2008) *Urban Indian America: The Status of American Indian and Alaska Native Children and Families Today*, The Annie E. Casey Foundation; National Urban Indian Family Coalition; Marguerite Casey Foundation; Americans for Indian Opportunity; National Indian Child Welfare Association, 2008. Online at http://www.aecf.org/KnowledgeCenter/Publications.aspx?pubguid={CCB6DEB2–007E-416A-A0B2-D15954B48600}

Nieto, S. (2010). *Language, culture, and teaching: Critical perspectives* (2nd ed.). New York: Taylor & Francis Group.

Reyner, J. & Eder, J. (2004). *American Indian education: A history*. Norman, OK: University of Oklahoma Press.

Romero-Little, M., Ortiz, S., McCarty, T, with Chen, R. (Eds). (2011). *Indigenous languages across generations—strengthening families and communities*. Tempe: Arizona State University Center for Indian Education.

United Nations. (2008). United Nations Declaration on the Rights of Indigenous Peoples. UN. 07–58681—March 2008—4,000. Retrieved from http://www.un.org/esa/socdev/unpfii/documents/DRIPS_en.pdf

Part I
Literacy Instruction for Native Americans

2   Digital Tapestry
Weaving Stories of Empowerment with Native Youth

Ramona Beltrán, Polly Olsen, Anastasia Ramey, Susanne Klawetter, and Karina Walters

"The truth about stories is, that's all we are"
—Thomas King (Cherokee Author)

For many Indigenous peoples (IP), storytelling is embedded into the tapestry of our lives. It is a way that we simultaneously learn historical knowledge and create new knowledge about our cultures and the complexities of daily life. Through and from story, we learn how to live in "right relationship" to our selves, each other, and complex webs of creation, from the cosmos above us to the insects below. It is our most fundamental form for expressing and transmitting cultural values, ethics, codes of conduct, and practical knowledge. In recent decades, social science research has shown the power of narrative in interrupting the transmission of intergenerational trauma in IP (Evans-Campbell & Walters, 2006; Lowery, 1999; Yellow Horse Brave Heart, 1999). That is, narrative can help mediate the effects of historically situated traumas that continue to produce responses impacting the conditions of daily life, including those that influence academic outcomes for Native youth. The process of creating and sharing narratives, or stories, is an important educational tool for reclaiming cultural knowledge and strengths despite legacies of colonization and ongoing discrimination. New digital technologies using video, photography, and audio combined with the availability of social networking sites and web-based interfaces are expanding the ways we can construct and share stories for healing in our communities. Digital storytelling (DS) is emerging as a particularly resonant practice that infuses traditional cultural aspects of oral tradition and storytelling with modern digital technologies (Benmayor, 2008).

This chapter presents findings of descriptive thematic analysis of digital stories completed by Native youth in the Pacific Northwest region of the U.S. Researchers from the Indigenous Wellness Research Institute (IWRI) at University of Washington (UW) worked together with the Center for Digital Storytelling (CDS) to facilitate DS workshops, which were integrated into the Native Youth Enrichment Program (NYEP), a science, technology, engineering and math (STEM) curriculum for Native youth in the Puget Sound region of the Pacific Northwest. Analysis of the stories suggests that DS may be a useful tool of educational empowerment for Native youth.[1] Though we cannot empirically link DS directly to improved education outcomes, thematic analysis reveals themes supporting an increase in confidence in cultural identity, which aligns with established evidence that does make connections between positive cultural identity and improved academic success.

HISTORICAL TRAUMA AND EDUCATION

It is well known that education in Indigenous communities is connected to complex histories of colonization and cultural stripping aimed at controlling and assimilating IP (Rehyner, 1992). From religious missions in South, Central, and North American Indigenous territories to Indian Boarding Schools in the U.S. and Canada, the effects have had wide-ranging deleterious impacts that continue to influence educational outcomes today. These historically situated colonial experiences have been shown to impact parenting abilities (Yellow Horse Brave Heart, 1999) and to lead to high rates of drug and alcohol abuse, depression, anxiety, somatization, suicide, and hypersensitivity to stress (Duran & Duran, 1995; Evans-Campbell, 2008; Walters & Simoni, 2002; Walters & Evans-Campbell, 2006; Yellow Horse Brave Heart, 1999, 2003); many of these problems are correlated with high dropout rates and low educational attainment (Zimmerman, Ramirez, Wahienko, Walter, & Dyer, 1994). The effects of this "historical trauma" (HT) (defined as a wounding from massive catastrophic events targeting a community, such as forced relocation, massacres, and boarding schools) are both personal and collective and can be experienced even generations after a particular event (Yellow Horse Brave Heart & Debruyn, 1998; Walters & Simoni, 2002; Evans-Campbell, 2008; Walters, Mohammed, Evans-Campbell, Beltrán, Chae & Duran, 2011). An important component in the definition of HT is its cumulative nature: historically situated traumas coupled with ongoing experiences of contemporary discrimination compound and create effects far more severe than exposure to an isolated traumatic event (Evans-Campbell, 2008; Walters et al., 2011).

Native students continue to face daily discrimination, both overtly and in the form of *microaggressions*: chronic, everyday injustices, the wear and tear of interpersonal and environmental messages to people of color that are denigrating, demeaning, or invalidating based on their racial affiliation (Sue et al., 2007; Sue et al., 2008; Walters et al, 2011). These include overt racial stereotypes (e.g., being called Pocahontas, Chief, Squaw), or seeing images of themselves as school mascots (e.g.,

Redskins, Braves), but also include more covert experiences of racism such as being made invisible (e.g., being told "you don't look Native") or completely dismissed (e.g., students not being called on for contributions in class, or others' eye-rolling when a Native student talks about topics relevant to her community). Additionally, current Western models of education, though improved from the injustices of Indian boarding schools and early missions, continue to alienate Indigenous ways of knowing, such as oral traditions, collective thinking, and holism (Pewewardy, 2002). These ongoing daily experiences can work together with the legacies of historically traumatic events to impose stress burdens on Native students that ultimately lead to poor educational outcomes.

INTERRUPTING HISTORICAL TRAUMA THROUGH CULTURE

Despite efforts to eradicate our communities and cultures, IP have survived and are thriving in many ways. Recent decades have seen a resurgence of Indigenous ways of knowing and culture, which have been found to positively impact educational outcomes (Zimmerman et al.; 1994; Whitbeck, Hoyt, Stubben, & LaFramboise, 2001) as well as reduce health and mental health burdens (Bals, Turi, Skre, & Kvernmo, 2011). According to the Indigenist Stress Coping Model (Walters & Simoni, 2002), strong connection to cultural identity and practice mediates the intergenerational transmission of trauma and its effects. For example, when Native students are actively exposed to and engaged in their traditional cultural practices such as language, ceremony, and art, they are more likely to achieve greater academic success (Whitbeck et al., 2001). Some programs seem to be realizing this phenomenon. In a recent review of field-based geoscience education for IP, Riggs (2005) found that successful earth system science education programs were those that linked directly to Indigenous cultural learning styles and traditional tribal earth science knowledge. (See also Semken, 2005.)

In a review of learning style theory, research, and models, Pewewardy (2002) found that American Indian and Alaska Native (AIAN) students are understood as learning in ways that are influenced by tribal culture, including language and heritage. He writes "AIAN students generally learn in ways characterized by social/affective emphasis, harmony, holistic perspectives, expressive creativity, and nonverbal communication" (Pewewardy, 2002, p. 22). He highlights kinesthetic, cooperative, and family and Elder roles in learning styles of AIAN and suggests that while there is much research yet to do on AIAN pedagogy, educators can begin by integrating culture-based education that appreciates tribal traditions, art, and Elder knowledge (Pewewardy, 2002). Storytelling in tribal communities is an ancient, sacred form that encompasses all three of these elements. Jo-ann Archibald (Q'um Q'um Xiiem) (2008) describes the oral tradition of storytelling as an important aspect of Indigenous knowledge systems that are not only meant to be expressed and passed down through generations but also are meant to be used as educational tools.

STORY FROM PAST TO PRESENT

> *"Story is medicine"*
>
> —Theda Newbreast (Blackfeet Activist)

Although there is a dearth of empirical literature measuring the impacts of storytelling on education and other outcomes for Indigenous youth, there is a body of literature that highlights the cultural importance of various forms of storytelling and oral tradition (Archibald, 2008; Basso, 1996). Oral tradition in Indigenous cultures remains one of the most important ways that IP preserve historical records, cultural traditions, and identities. It has been practiced in various forms throughout history and is seen as one of the most valuable tools for learning culture specific values and ethics, codes of conduct, creation stories, and practical knowledge associated with science (e.g., seasonal hunting and gathering, planting and harvesting, astronomy, and geography).

An important aspect of oral tradition, and storytelling in particular, is its dynamic nature. Though most tribal storytellers, often elders, uphold certain essential threads that maintain important lessons, or the spirit of the story, many details are shifted in relation to the particular time, place, context, and teller (Hopkins, 2006). Not only do stories emanate from a collective ethos and consciousness, but they also emerge from the unique individual voice of the teller. Stories have the freedom to shift and change according to the unique constellation of context and voice to promote multiple deeply contextualized "truths" (Hopkins, 2006) that together weave a singular cultural tapestry. Rather than accepting Western values of "historical fact" and written documentation, storytelling is more fluid and flexible. As such, oral tradition is allowed to bend like a tree in the wind according to context fostering opportunities to integrate creative and contemporary modes for communicating story.

In the early 1980s video emerged as a new terrain for Indigenous people to respond critically to historically inaccurate media that promoted stereotyped ideas of Indigenous life, partially because of what were seen as similarities between Indigenous oral tradition and the new technology (Hopkins, 2006). Though there has been debate about technology as a potentially dangerous territory built on Western capitalist principles, IP have had a great deal of success in creating and sharing our own media in our own way. This success may be attributed to "the degree to which [we] subvert the colonizer's indoctrination and champion Indigenous expression in the political landscape" (Masayesva, 2000, as quoted in Hopkins, 2006; p. 343). Bringing new technology for creating and sharing story into the hands of Indigenous communities expands the possibility, not only for "subverting indoctrination" but also for celebrating the strengths of our culture and expression. Digital storytelling is emerging as a particularly resonant community-based practice for IP as it integrates principles of oral tradition and contemporary technologies.

"Digital storytelling (DS) is the practice of combining still images and/or video with a narrated soundtrack including both voice and music" (Miller, 2009, p. 6). Digital stories are short videos ranging from 3–5 minutes, usually with a written script between 250–500 words that tells unique, often intimate personal stories. The term digital storytelling was coined by Joe Lambert, founder of the Center for Digital Storytelling, which "evolved out of the mixture of community arts practices, helping people make art for civic engagement, and the new media explosion of the late 1980's and 1990's (Lambert, 2007, p. 25). What makes DS unique is the attention to both individual and group process. A typical DS workshop is three to four days long, and includes an intensive 7-step process (as illustrated in Table 2.1) that combines social/relational, literacy, and technological skill development with a collaborative, supportive sharing of ideas. Each person in a story circle has a set amount of uninterrupted time to speak, then others share feedback and suggestions on how the story might be written and/or visualized. The process relies on supportive and skilled facilitation that allows for self-reflection and critical analysis of personal and social issues connected to story. The writing process is also collaborative, where others help the storyteller refine the script. This is followed by technical assembling and editing of the video where participants storyboard (i.e., create a visual or written outline), then upload digital and archive photos, video, music, and narrated voice to edit together a cohesive story. The final step involves screening stories and/or deciding what bounds and limits will be placed on public access to individual stories (Lambert, 2009); participants are not required to share their stories if they are not comfortable doing so. DS is more about process than product (Lambert, 2007), and can thus be seen as a therapeutic tool for healing storied traumas, an educational tool for learning concrete technical and literacy skills, a means of building health and resilience (Gubrium, 2009), and a cultural tool supporting the use of oral tradition and art to reflect on and relearn cultural knowledge.

Iseke (2011) describes Indigenous DS as a form of witnessing which facilitates healing. She writes "witnessing includes acts of remembrance in which we look back to re-interpret our relationship to the past in order to understand our present" (p. 311). DS also gives community members the opportunity for self-representation in media, which can work

Table 2.1   Center for Digital Storytelling 7-step Process

Steps:	Learning Areas and Technical Process
1. Owning your insight 2. Owning your emotions	Social/relational (story circle)
3. Finding the moment	
4. Seeing your story 5. Hearing your story	Literacy (script writing) Technological (photo, video, audio)
6. Assembling your story	
7. Sharing your story	Optional

to counter negative stereotypes often portrayed in mainstream media outlets (Pack, 2000). Like traditional storytelling, DS allows for the individual and collective voice to simultaneously and dynamically live and unfold.

The youth who participated in NYEP addressed topics of great cultural and personal significance, including health disparities, traditional foods, Indigenous identity and original cultural knowledge. Lambert (2009) notes, "If we had to sum up our learning, it would be that we see story work, and our work in particular, as only valuable when it is owned as a technology of healing by a local population" (p. xvi). The CDS process, whose value Lambert (2009) describes as a "technology of healing" (p. xvi), has elements that align well with community processes used by many IP. The talking circle is an integral part of the way many Indigenous communities pass on cultural knowledge. In it, they pay witness to each other's stories and give youth space to think critically about their personal and community narrative. The articulation of that narrative, too often silenced in their daily lives, encourages the participants to define themselves and their experiences. In the context of our project, the process allowed the youth to articulate their relationships to culture, health, and wellness for themselves and their communities.

NATIVE YOUTH ENRICHMENT PROGRAM

The Native Youth Empowerment Project[2] was a two-year (2009–2011) program working with 7th–12th graders from five Pacific Northwest school districts to establish (1) an innovative, culturally based 4-week summer intensive STEM career path program and (2) an enrichment program during the school year. Researchers worked with local area school districts to design and implement curricula that responded to the unique learning needs of Native youth and encourage STEM education and careers. Each program included a DS workshop conducted by CDS staff, with the goals of supporting students to develop communications and technology skills through the production of digital stories; develop self-identities that explored participants' heritage and cultures; extend social networks; expand educational and professional horizons; and gain confidence and leadership capacity. The underlying assumption of the NYEP approach was that students exploring their cultural heritage would gain a stronger sense of Indian identity, which would contribute to these goals.

Over the course of the two workshops 25 students produced 27 videos. Five of the videos were group projects and are not included in this analysis and two students declined public access of their videos and are also not included. Students were from diverse tribal[3] and racial[4] backgrounds and ranged from 7th through 12th grade with the majority enrolled in 9th or 10th grades. The digital stories themselves provide strong evidence of student engagement and experience during the workshops. They present personal stories of life experiences, exploration of sense of self and identity, and relationships with family members and tribes.

THEMATIC ANALYSIS OF DIGITAL STORIES

Descriptive thematic analysis of twenty individual digital stories yielded several themes associated with cultural identity. This chapter focuses on involvement in traditional cultural practices as a central theme, which has been identified as a protective factor connected to positive cultural identity and improved academic (Zimmerman et al., 1994; Whitbeck et al., 2001) as well as mental health outcomes (Bals et al, 2011). Throughout their digital stories, NYEP students poetically narrate the importance of cultural art forms, traditional food, and lessons from elders. Sometimes concretely and sometimes more nuanced, all of the stories involve narrative processes that culminate in a sense of positive cultural identity and pride.

TRADITIONAL CULTURAL PRACTICES

Music and Dance

For several students, music and dance was described as an important cultural practice and was also a way to transcend experiences of racism. For example, one student examined the frustration he feels when his family is treated disrespectfully because of their language skills. He used music and pictures of traditional Indigenous and folkloric dancers of Mexico, and his family religious altars to illustrate the beauty of his parents and their cultural heritage. He concluded his story by explaining, "*When I dance I feel the sound of every instrument . . . . This is why I am proud of who I am and of my culture.*" Another student described music and dance as a way that he fulfills his responsibility to preserve his cultural heritage for himself and others. In a confident voice, he said "*Ever since I was in the womb, I've been dancing in my grandparents dance group. . . and now I proudly sing in the dance group as the leader in training.*"

Beading

For two students, beading was illustrated as part of a process for understanding themselves as mixed race individuals. One student, who seemed to be questioning her cultural identity, began her story with expressions of doubt and confusion about the connection between her life and heritage. However, throughout her video she described the traditional beading she learned from her ancestors. While three generations sat together to bead, she narrated, "*I tell myself, loop over and under. . .over and under. Pull tight but not too tight. That's your heritage isn't it?*" She described feeling confused about her racial identity because of the assumptions of others and continued, "*I keep telling myself, loop over and under. . . over and under. Pull tight but not too tight. Grab another bead and do it again.*" She described a mist lifting as she finished her beading project. While showing a picture of beaded hair sticks and then a photo of her family, she said, "*I know that we make our own heritage and traditions. I am done. They are beautiful side by side. We are beautiful.*" Another student described beading as a family event, led by her grandmother, connecting her to her Native identity. "*I bead with my mom, my grandma, my aunties, my sister, and my cousin. Even my uncle bead[s] with us sometimes. . . I like it because it was part of my culture . . . I started beading when I was in the 4th grade because I wanted to learn more about my Native side. I see my Nana do it all the time.*"

Traditional Food

As students explored the meaning of "traditional food" in the context of health and wellness, they discovered ways that traditional food is directly connected to their identities as Native people. Eight students centered a particular traditional food in their stories. One student described how she was transported back to her Indigenous roots in Mexico as she touched tortilla masa (dough). While images of corn and rural Mexico faded in and out, she narrated the lessons her grandfather taught her, even though she didn't understand as a young girl. "*Every time I came down to El Rancho he would wake me up, and I would go with him to the corn factory and gather the corn and put it in the grinder and put the masa in plastic bags . . . he would tell me stories about the corn and how it'd be horrible if corn was to ever disappear.*" As she lamented her family move to the U.S. when she was 7-years-old and the abundance of processed food, she arrived at an understanding of her grandfather's teachings, "*as soon as I put my hands in the masa I realized what my grandpa meant . . . that people depended on him in that if they didn't make the masa for the tortillas, then it wouldn't just be the tortillas that would be gone, that our traditions would also be gone.*"

A student adopted from Guatemala by a non-Native family also articulated the importance of tortillas in his life as he explored his Indigenous identity in an adoptive family. He narrated, "*I have to eat tortillas everyday. Sometimes I wonder why . . . after reading [a book about] an Indian in Guatemala, I found out why I am hungry for tortillas. She says, 'making tortillas is a reflex that's thousands of years old,' and it answered my question of why I'm hungry for my culture.*" Weaving photos of himself as a toddler, Indigenous people of Guatemala, and Indigenous music, he recounted his adoption, which occurred because he required extensive medical care, and his birth mother had no choice but to leave him in the care of doctors. He concluded by showing pictures of himself with his non-Native family, expressed gratitude, and acknowledged the importance of his Indigenous culture in his life, "*I've never thought too much about why eating tortillas is so important to me, but I do know that there is something I'm missing. I also know that while I have a great family, I will always be hungry for my tortillas.*"

Three students created stories that explore the role of "frybread" in Native communities. One student described misconceptions about traditional food in her community. "*Traditional foods lift us up both spiritually and physically. But back home people hold the common misconception that only frybread, Indian tacos, salmon, and berries are traditional foods.*" She asserted, "*The first two [are] technically not traditional.*" Two other students told stories about the importance of frybread in their families, particularly as recipes are passed down from family and elders. While they centered frybread and Indian tacos in their narratives, each story highlighted the importance of family and elders in their understanding of tradition as the salient message. One student humorously illustrated his fondness for Indian tacos, "*They're kind of a big part of my family life. When we make them together, it's a way to bond. We're all in the kitchen: my mom, my grandma, my dad, and me. There's a lot of laughing and jokes.*" While self-composed ukulele music played in the background, he showed video of relatives and friends eating Indian tacos and giving "thumbs up". He added, "*I kind of learned on my own that Indian tacos aren't really traditional food. But, for me, tradition is when it brings everybody together.*" The other student described the special way his grandmother makes frybread and how he learns by watching. While he expressed that frybread isn't necessarily part of a traditional Indigenous diet, he asserted "*I know some people would think that frybread is not a serious enough food, but I think it's become a staple of Native American culture. If you don't think so, go talk to my grandma.*"

CULTURAL PRIDE

Throughout the digital stories produced by the NYEP students, exploring the role of cultural traditional practices in their lives was a powerful means to identify and articulate a sense of cultural pride. As the narratives progressed in each story, the overwhelming messages communicated appreciation, gratitude, and optimism for their Native heritage, families, and communities despite challenges associated with historical trauma. One student began his story articulating a sense of burden for his role in his culture but by the end of his story he realized this responsibility is a "*gift.*" He explained that it is in being part of the whole, a culture and a family, that he is stronger than by being alone.

DISCUSSION

DS is not only an educational tool teaching relational, literacy, and technical skills, but also a process that responds to unique learning styles of Native students by incorporating kinesthetic learning, collaboration and culture. Through the process of DS, students are encouraged to actively engage in hands-on learning with story, relationship, and technology in a context of shared space and reflective participation. This allows students to critically reflect on their individual narratives and arrive at their own critical analysis while also participating in the collective process. Additionally, DS allows production of media for self-representation that combats negative stereotypes and discrimination while supporting important lessons on cultural identity that seem to bolster an increased sense of pride, agency, and strength, all of which have been correlated with positive academic outcomes.

This data is a small contribution to an emerging dialogue supporting the incorporation of educational practices that respond to the unique cultural experiences and needs of Native youth. There are some limitations to this particular data as it is a small sample and there is no way to measure direct links between DS and improved education outcomes. Future research that explores these direct links and monitors them longitudinally is necessary to truly make connections to the DS process and academic success. As educators and practitioners working with Native youth continue to incorporate DS and other forms of media that accommodate important aspects of traditional culture and modern technology, opportunities will clearly arise. Continued content analysis (including both analysis of narrative and visual images) on already produced and widely accessible digital stories would also contribute to the increasing knowledge base.

While we have found DS to be an empowering process for Native youth, there are some issues that require continued consideration for educators and scholars related to process as well as protection of confidentiality. The solitude of the scripting and assembling process is a potential challenge for participants, as it is in stark contrast to the story circle, and requires that the storytellers place their stories in a particular context and moment in time. The fluid nature of storytelling in Indigenous communities is challenged by the fixed nature of a script; however, the use of sound/music and images allows storytellers to add complexity and nuance to their stories. Additionally, with the widespread and unbounded terrain of the web and social networking sites in particular, there are potential concerns for confidentiality. Though all participants and parents are informed and consent to participation and are also given control over the manner and extent to which their stories are shared, there are still many unknowns about access and dissemination through web-based platforms. As technology and web interfaces continue to develop and change, it is essential that educators, scholars, and communities participate in dialogue about the safekeeping of our stories.

Themes from the stories created by NYEP students demonstrate the power of narrative in articulating the importance of Indigenous identity and culture within a context of historically situated colonization, ongoing discrimination, and ultimately transcendence through cultural pride and strength. Individually they tell heartfelt stories that act as colorful strands that together weave a collective tapestry of a greater Indigenous narrative: one that is empowered and hopeful. As one student narrates while images of Puget Sound waters, Salish style canoes, and his grandparents fade in and out, "*Together we are a lot stronger than we are by ourselves . . . Now I know my culture is not my burden to carry but my greatest gift from my grandfather and grandmother, my path and my gift for future generations.*"

NOTES

1. While the majority of the students participating in NYEP identified as American Indian and Alaska Native, there were several who identified as Hispanic with Indigenous heritage from Mexico or mixed-race including Indigenous from Africa. For the purposes of inclusive language, participants will be described either as "Native" or "Indigenous".

2. The NYEP was funded by the American Recovery and Reinvestment Act (ARRA), NIH grant 5 RC1 MD 004387–02 to University of Washington, Indigenous Wellness Research Institute.
3. Tribal groups represented include Arapahoe, Blackfoot, Cherokee, Chippewa, Colville, Cowlitz, Haida, Tlingit, Kickapoo, Lakota Sioux, Lummi, Makah, Maya, Nisqually, Nu-Chui-Muth, Potowatomi, Pueblo, Shoshone-Bannock, Samish, Sioux, Tewa, Tlingit, Yakima, and Yurok. Note that some students had affiliation with more than one tribe, which is why there are more tribal groups than students.
4. In addition to being from mixed tribal backgrounds, many students indicated they were of mixed-race and tribal heritage. Multi-ethnic combinations included: AIAN and White; AIAN and African American; AIAN and Hispanic and White; and AIAN and African American and White. One student identified as Hispanic only.

REFERENCES

Archibald, J.A. (2008). *Indigenous storywork: Educating the heart, mind, body, and spirit.* Vancouver: UBC Press.
Bals, M., Turi, A.L., Skre, I., & Kvernmo, S. (2011). The relationship between internalizing and externalizing symptoms and cultural resilience factors in Indigenous Sami youth from Arctic Norway. *International Journal of Cicumpolar Health, 70*(1): 37–45.
Basso, K.H. (1996). *Wisdom sits in places: Landscape and language among the Western Apache.* Albuquerque, NM: University of New Mexico Press.
Benmayor, M. (2008). Digital storytelling as a signature pedagogy for the new humanities. *Arts and Humanities in Higher Education, 7*(2), 188–204.
Duran, E., & Duran, B. (1995). *Native American postcolonial psychology.* Albany: State University of New York Press.
Evans-Campbell, T. (2008). Historical trauma in American Indian/Native Alaska communities: A multilevel framework for exploring impacts on individuals, families, and communities. *Journal of Interpersonal Violence, 23*, 316–338.
Evans-Campbell, T., & Walters, K. (2006). Catching our breath: A decolonizing framework for healing Indigenous peoples. In R. Fong, R. McRoy, & C.O. Hendricks (Eds.) *Intersecting child welfare, substance abuse, and family violence: Culturally competent approaches* (pp. 91–110). Alexandria, VA: Council on Social Work Education Press.
Gubrium, A. (2009). Digital storytelling: An emergent method for health promotion research and practice. *Health Promotion Practice, 10*, 186–191.
Hopkins, C. (2006). Making things our own: The indigenous aesthetic in digital storytelling. *Leonardo, 39*(4), 341–344.
Iseke, J. M. (2011). Indigenous digital storytelling in video: Witnessing with Alma Desjarlais. *Equity & Excellence in Education, 44*(3), 311–329.
Lambert, J. (2007). Digital storytelling: How digital media help preserve cultures. *The Futurist 47*(2), 25.
Lambert, J. (2009). *Digital storytelling: Capturing lives, creating community.* Berkeley, CA: Digital Diner Press.
Lowery, C.T. (1999). A qualitative model of long-term recovery for American Indian women. *Journal of Human Behavior in the Social Environment, 2*(1–2), 35–50.
Miller, E.A. (2009). Digital storytelling: A graduate review submitted to the Elementary Education Division Department of Curriculum and Instruction in partial

fulfillment of the requirements for the degree of Master of Arts, University of Northern Iowa.

Pack, S. (2000). Indigenous media then and now: Situating the Navajo film project. *Quarterly Review of Film & Video, 17* (3), 273–286.

Pewewardy, C. (2002). Learning styles of American Indian/Alaska Native students: A review of the literature and implications for practice. *Journal of American Indian Education, 41*(3), 22–56.

Reyhner, J. (1992). American Indian cultures and school success. *Journal of American Indian Education,* 32(1), 30—39.

Riggs, E.M. (2005). Field-based education and indigenous knowledge: Essential components of geoscience education for Native American communities. *Science Education, 89,* 296–313.

Sadik, A. (2008). Digital storytelling: A meaningful technology-integrated approach for engaged student learning. *Educational Technology Research and Development: 56*(4), 487–506.

Semken, S. (2005). Sense of place and place-based introductory geoscience teaching for American Indian and Alaska Native undergraduates. *Journal of Geoscience Education Volume, 53*(2), 149–157.

Sue, D.W., Capodilupo, C.M., Nadal, K.L., and Torino, G.C. (2008) Racial micro aggressions and the power to define reality. *American Psychologist, 63*(4), 277–279.

Sue, D.W., Capodilupo, C.M., Torino, G.C., Bucceri, J.M., Holder, A., Nadal, K.L., & Esquilin, M. (2007). Racial microaggressions in everyday life: Implications for clinical practice. *American Psychologist, 62*(4), 271.

Walters, K.L. (2006). Dis-placement and dis-ease: Historical trauma and embodiment among Indigenous peoples. Presentation at University of Washington Place Matters Conference, October, 2006.

Walters, K.L., Beltran, R., Huh, D., & Evans-Campbell, T. (2011). Dis-Placement and Dis-Ease: Land, place, and health in American Indians and Alaska Natives. In L.M. Burton, S.P. Kemp, M. Leung, S.A. Matthews & D. T. Takeuchi (Eds.), *Communities, Neighborhoods, and Health: Expanding the boundaries of place.* New York: Springer.

Walters, K.L., Evans-Campbell, T., Simoni, J. M., Ronquillo, T., & Bhuyan, R. (2006). "My spirit in my heart": Identity experiences and challenges among American Indian Two-spirit women. *Journal of Lesbian Studies, 10,* 125–150.

Walters, K.L., Mohammed, S.A., Evans-Campbell, T., Beltrán, R.E., Chae, D.H., & Duran, B. (2011). Bodies don't just tell stories, they tell histories. *Du Bois Review: Social Science Research on Race, 8*(01), 179–189.

Walters, K.L., & Simoni, J.M. (2002) Reconceptualizing Native women's health: An Indigenist stress-coping model. *American Journal of Public Health, 92*(4), 520–524.

Walters, K.L., Simoni, J.M., & Evans-Campbell, T. (2006). *Substance use among American Indians and Alaska Natives: Incorporating culture in an "Indigenist" stress-coping paradigm. Public Health Reports,* 117(1), 104–117.

Whitbeck, L.B., Hoyt, D.R., Stubben, J.D., LaFramboise, T. (2001). Traditional culture and academic success among American Indian children in the upper Midwest. *Journal of American Indian Education, 40*(2), 48–60.

Yellow Horse Brave Heart, M. (1999).Oyate Ptayela: Rebuilding the Lakota Nation through addressing historical trauma among Lakota parents. *Journal of Human Behavior in the Social Environment, 2* (1–2), 109–126.

Yellow Horse Brave Heart, M. (2003). The historical trauma response among natives and its relationship with substance abuse: A Lakota illustration. *Journal of Psychoactive Drugs, 35*(1), 7–13.

Yellow Horse Brave Heart, M. (2007). The historical trauma response among Natives and its relationship with substance abuse: A Lakota illustration. *The Journal of Psychoactive Drugs, 35*(1), 7–13.

Yellow Horse Brave Heart, M. (2008). Gender differences in the historical trauma response among the Lakota. *Journal of Health and Social Policy 10*(4), 1–21.

Zimmerman, M., Ramirez, J., Wahienko, K., Walter, B., & Dyer, S. (1994). The enculturation hypothesis: Exploring direct and protective effects among Native American youth. In H. McCubbin, E. Thompson, & A. Thompson (Eds.) *Resiliency in ethnic minority families, Vol. 1. Native and immigrant American families* (pp. 199–220). Madison: University of Wisconsin.

3 The Creating of a Curriculum, or the Little Rabbit Who Became an Otter

Shana Brown

This chapter is the story of the development of *Since Time Immemorial (STI): A Tribal Sovereignty Curriculum,*[1] (which can be found online at http:// http://tribalsov.ospi.k12.wa.us/) and of my own development, which for me are tightly interwoven and carry many lessons. The curriculum name is drawn from our history:

> Since time immemorial, tribal sovereignty has been the life pursuit of Indigenous peoples throughout this great land. Since time immemorial, our life and times have been recorded through our oral histories, songs, and traditions, just as the trees have recorded their environmental growth and challenges in their rings. And since time immemorial, our spirit of sovereignty has enveloped our being, has permeated what we teach our children and—most importantly—**how** we have taught our children. (Brown & Pavel [CHiXapaid], 2010)

WRITING A CURRICULUM

Oh, God. I'm so ashamed.

As the hour passed 3:00 am, I went to sleep in a bed that matched my discomfort. After hours upon hours of designing, writing, and rewriting, I was still not close to a product I was proud of. It was like trying to fit into a dress that was two sizes too small: uncomfortable and embarrassing. But there I was nonetheless, poised to present the Tribal Sovereignty Curriculum (later to be named STI) to tribal leaders, tribal attorneys, tribal elders, the state attorney general, and the heads of the Washington State Librarians Association, Indian Education Association, and the State Association of Social Studies Teachers.

Earlier that year I had been charged with the task of writing Washington State's first (and probably only) tribal sovereignty curriculum. I tried to write what I'd always seen, a nice, neatly packaged binder full of activities and lessons for middle and high school. At the time, the Washington State

Superintendent of Public Instruction was Terry Bergeson, and she wanted to present a curriculum to reflect Washington State House Bill 1495 that strongly encouraged that tribal history be taught in the common schools. (See Chapter 6 in this volume by Hurtado for the story of that legislation, as well as Smith, Brown & Costantino, 2011.)

After my short, restless night, I somehow got through speaking. The presentation was a blur and then there was the deafening silence that followed. And there was that thought again: *Oh, God. I'm so ashamed.* In any other setting, I would hear an uproar of protest, like the kind in the musical "1776" when the Congressional delegates were asked if they had any additions or deletions after the reading of the Declaration of Independence. In any other setting, I would see furrowed brows and shaking heads. That was nothing compared to the reaction I actually received . . .

But before I share their reactions to my presentation, let me tell you how I came to this task.

MY PERSONAL JOURNEY

Since this is my story, but a collaborative one, I want to share who I am. My name is Shana Brown, and I'm a Yakama descendent and recovering "Indian Expert," born and raised on the Yakama Indian Reservation. My mother, an enrolled tribal member, married a white man, so my brother and I were lighter skinned than all our cousins, definitely lighter than the other Yakamas on the Rez. My brother found it fairly easy to fit in, going the cowboy route, but I didn't. I didn't like to get dirty, didn't like the dust, was distrustful of strangers, and introverted; none of this was good on a reservation. And I was afraid of all those tough Indian girls, even hiding behind my cousin at the local movie theater when I was young. I was small and as timid as a rabbit; these girls could take one look at me and see "lunch" not merely written on my little rabbit forehead, they'd see it on a big sandwich board with flashing neon letters. I learned how to melt into the wall.

I could be even more inconspicuous if I weren't there at all. So, I picked white friends, did "white" things like sleepovers, and found ways to avoid going to rodeos with my family. Attending a public school (the tribal school at that time was for those Indian kids who didn't fit in in the mainstream educational setting), I learned about ancient Greece and Rome, the Middle Ages, the Renaissance—white things. *That* was what was of value, I thought.

Now you might be thinking here, "Where's your family? Where's your tribal upbringing?" Indeed, where was it? My family never taught me to be ashamed to be Indian, to be sure, but those things that would or could make me proud were long gone. My mother's parents were products of Indian boarding schools, where they lost their language, and a good lot of their Indian identity. We didn't grow up traditional; we grew up Catholic. While others learned how to bead, I learned to crochet and embroider, just like my grandma had learned at St. George's Indian School in Tacoma, Washington. I avoided the summer programs designed to teach Indian kids about our culture and traditions, opting instead for watching TV alone.

I'm not telling you all this to excuse my shame, only to explain it. There were just as many children and grandchildren of boarding school kids who embraced traditional culture in spite of the cultural genocide experienced at those institutions. I'm very proud of my grandparents, Blanche (Hoptowit) and John Craig. My grandma worked for the tribe as a cook, first at Head Start, then for the tribal jail, and my grandpa worked construction, masonry, and concrete work. Not once did they or my mother ever negate their "Indianness." But there was always an explicit belief in my world, from all over the reservation, that white ways were superior.

LIFE ON THE RESERVATION

I should explain a little about my reservation. The Yakama Reservation is the largest in Washington State (probably one of the largest in the U.S.) but its land base is a "checkerboard." Through the General Allotment Act (1887; also known as the Dawes Act), land was divvied up among Indian families to establish individual ownership of tribal land, and thus divide and conquer. When the federal government ran out of enrolled tribal members to whom to allot land, the remainder of the reservation was declared "surplus," and then opened to non-Indian settlement. Moreover, Indian families were taxed on their property. Back then, it was easy to sustain your family in traditional ways of hunting and gathering; there wasn't a big need for cash. But as times changed, you needed lots of it to keep your land. Many Yakamas (like thousands of others) were forced to sell their property or have it foreclosed upon. This land was then offered up to non-Indian sale, and was purchased by non-Indian farmers and ranchers, including my husband's family. So there are large plots of land that are non-Indian owned within the borders of the reservation.

The voices that mattered were those of the business and property owners. And those are the only voices I heard. In my public education and therefore in my social world, there was no one who said or showed that traditional ways were anything other than the occasional spectacle at the All-Indian Rodeo or Treaty Days celebrations.

So remember that my little rabbit-self rabbited to everywhere Indians were not. In high school, going out to "cruise" on Saturday nights in Yakima, my best friend defended my acceptability by stating to a cute boy who accused me of being Indian, "It's okay; she's only half." I never joined the Indian Club, never went to visit the tribal family advocate hired by the district, and I continued to actively avoid any and all things Indian. One evening I overheard my aunties talking to my mother, "Shana's ashamed to be Indian." And in response my mother declared that I should be proud of who I am. I had no idea how.

"GO MY SON, GET AN EDUCATION"

And then there was high school United States History. My U.S. history teacher was an impressive man with an even more impressive belly: beloved by the community, this former coach absolutely exuded history. But not tribal history, even though he had a 9-foot totem pole in his classroom. His only mention of tribal history—let alone local tribal history—was the day he turned his metal classroom trashcan upside down and began beating it like a drum. He chanted, "Go my son, get an education! Go, my son, get off the reservation!"

That's exactly what this little rabbit did. At Western Washington University, they needed at least four Indian students to start an Indian Student Union. I was number four, but I remained silent. As I began the process of transferring to the University of Washington, I discovered that I could gain entrance through the Educational Opportunity Program. My white friends at Western resented my affirmative action entrance, and even when the BIA superintendent at the Indian Agency explained that it's not how you get there, it's what you do once you've arrived, I still felt a twinge of inferiority.

At the University of Washington, all of a sudden, I was introduced to Proud Indians. Active Indians, almost Militant Indians. What was I to do now? This whole idea of ethnic pride was utterly foreign to me, but I had gotten here because I was Indian. I had to do something, be something to prove to others that I was just like them, just as proud and just as vocal. I was still a rabbit, to be sure, but I wore a wolf's skin in those days.

And that camouflage got me to my first year in teaching. I'd found my calling, but . . . I'd always get the question, "What are you?" when I met new non-Indian people; though I could pass for something other than Indian, it was clear that I was not white. When I revealed that I was "Native American" I became the go-to gal for everything from peyote to dream catchers to "Just how authentic is *Dances With Wolves* anyway?" I, of course, was at a loss. So I faked it for a while, at the same time getting my hands on native legends books, anything to cram Indianness into my little rabbit brain. I was learning. Then my journey began in earnest while teaching in the Bay Area.

"IF I DON'T, WHO WILL?"

I realized that I could accept the reality of my past and what I wanted to do for the future, or spend my time getting angry for the ignorance of my colleagues, who seemed to expect a Plateau Indian to know about Plains or Southwestern tribes and traditions. How could they truly believe that an Indian is an Indian is an Indian? How presumptive. How rude. Well, I could stay there in that place, bouncing in place on my little angry rabbit feet, or I could do something about the cultural ignorance. I thought to myself, "If I don't teach them, who will?"

My journey, oddly enough, took me to the Bay Area. As you can well imagine, the urban Indian community in San Francisco is large and in charge. And proud. I volunteered at the family center, I went for a sweat in the East Bay (though it became too rainy that day), and I designed a course called "More Than Bows and Arrows" (taken from the documentary film I showed to my classes; Warriner & Engelstad, 1978) to teach about Northern California tribes as well as my own. I enlisted my Auntie Carol (the first in our family to graduate college; I was the second) who then worked at the Columbia River Intertribal Fish Commission to get me anything and everything about the Yakama tribe. She sent me a lot of my history (and by this time I could actually call it *my* history), full of who I was to become. The little rabbit didn't rabbit anywhere except to my home in Seattle. Not the reservation, but close. There I married my childhood sweetheart (whose non-Indian relatives owned hundreds of those checkerboard squares on my reservation), started my family, and continued my quest. I taught high school English and literature in a small suburban school district, brought my Auntie into town to speak to my classes about tribal tradition and the sacred salmon, and even received an education grant to include tribal perspectives in our social studies and English departments. I was gathering curriculum materials, but they were not valued by many others. In 2000 I met with the Multicultural Program Director at Shoreline Community College, who said something incredibly liberating and enlightening that explained why: "Introducing multiple perspectives into your classroom doesn't make things easier. It makes it harder. It makes it messy."

"WHEN MONDAY COMES"

I embraced that new maxim that doing something new is hard, and found new hope in my colleagues and my goals. I had to admit that I too had gone to many a conference, received a beautiful binder full of amazing curriculum only to find that when Monday comes, I'm in a crunch and choose to teach what I've always taught. It's easier, less messy, less time consuming. The rabbit had stopped rabbiting away from discomfort and shame, to be sure. But now it was time to rabbit toward something powerful, a place where I could make a difference as an Indian teacher.

I rabbited to the state Capitol, where I met with the then director of the Office of Indian Education, Denny Hurtado. I was his dream, because I volunteered to be on the committees no one else wanted to be on. I sat through meeting upon meeting, and then things started happening. Denny put me on a few different committees, then I found myself on the committee to help write the social studies standards for Washington State. We sent to the state legislature standards that required the inclusion of tribal government whenever teachers taught about any sort of federal, state, county, or municipal government. I don't know if they merely rubber stamped it, or even if they paid attention (with my faith in civics and government, I certainly hope they paid attention), but it was approved. Just that teeny phrase—tribal government. But it was teeny enough that no one noticed.

Washington State's educational system is based on "local control," meaning that local district governing bodies (usually school boards) are in charge of how state standards are delivered and what content is included in all the major disciplines, so we knew that enforcement would be an issue, but I was no longer alone. This little rabbit could make a difference. In fact, I no longer felt like a rabbit. More like an otter, industrious, playful, and, well . . . happy and proud.

THE COMMITTEE'S REACTION

Now jump back with me to the end of my presentation. Instead of this revered committee looking at me like I had just served them up a grilled cheese sandwich at a five star restaurant—as I expected and feared they would, they did what I can only describe as this: they held me, they held my energy and spirit and said, "Let's do this together." And we did.

To understand tribal sovereignty and tribal history one must accept this truth: *A tribe's history lives and breathes every day in the present and in the future.* How can one relegate that richness, that vibrancy, that sadness, that strength, that resilience into one or two beautifully packaged binders? You can't. We met again, this time in a sacred place, and were blessed with the presence of Billy Frank, Jr., a legend in these parts. In the 1970s he helped to lead the struggle for northwest tribes to exercise our treaty right to hunt and gather and fish in our "usual and accustomed" fishing grounds outside reservation boundaries. He gave us his blessing and a vision for tribal sovereignty. In trying to define tribal sovereignty for non-tribal people to understand, he said, one must understand the sovereignty of the trees, of the fish, of all that is living. It is our sacred trust and responsibility to all that is living, for all who are living, and for future generations. Our tribal sovereignty, then, is not merely self-governance or self-determination. We made a list of what was essential for everyone to know about tribal history and sovereignty—a page and a half, single-spaced. How the hell was that going to fit into a binder? It couldn't, so we made a list of the realities of the classroom of a typical public school: what is most taught is that which is most tested, which is not social studies; what matters is choice, because no one likes to be told what to do or how to do it. Our own realities were that tribal past, present, and future are inextricably linked to the history of our states and collectively to the history of the United States. Given all these competing agendas, we needed to be able to explain why we were placing tribal sovereignty at the front of the line.

All sorts of people wonder this. The more ignorant ask, "How come there's Native American History Month (ironically during the month of Thanksgiving)? African American History Month? Where's Caucasian History Month? Where's Italian History Month?" Tribes have a unique relationship with the American government. Our nations are recognized as sovereign by the United States, and reside within the boundaries of the U.S. As part of the treaties entered into with the U.S., our nations receive guarantees to health care, education, and other provisions, in many cases, in perpetuity (Canby, 2009; Hunn, 1991). No other ethnic group has this type of relationship with the federal government. No other ethnic group, then, impacts the remaining American population in quite the same ways that tribal nations do. (For further reading see Pevar, 2012).

The remaining questions that arose revolve around local control and teacher autonomy. The curriculum I was designing and presenting to them was in a vacuum. It gave one opportunity to teach tribal sovereignty, and it gave 3-, 4-, or 5-week units in which to teach it. If they missed it in their sole unit of study, then there were no more opportunities. I thought, *If what I say about tribal past, present, and future being linked to all other American history is true, then why am I giving a one shot deal as the only opportunity?* We needed a curriculum with broader reach, but in order for it to have that broader reach, we needed to make the units smaller, so that the teachers had some choice in what they had available to integrate into the overall education process. So, I started writing a lot more, a lot faster, and with a lot more choices. I liked the idea of a menu, and set out to provide one—more than a binder would be able to hold. It could not give teachers just one opportunity—five star restaurants were not open just one or two days a year. It could not be just in a single unit—five star restaurants did not offer only main dishes and nothing else. And it could not have an age restriction—even five star restaurants welcome all ages. Our curriculum had to offer a starter, a salad course, main dish, and dessert to everyone at the table. In Washington State there are 27 recommended units of study on the menu for elementary, middle, and high school students.

ABOUT THE CURRICULUM—SINCE TIME IMMEMORIAL

Three pedagogical bases—inquiry, place, and integration—anchor the curriculum, *Since Time Immemorial (STI): Tribal Sovereignty in Washington State.* When such practices are present, they furnish educators with a range of options. The result of *inquiry*, of grappling with and exploring concepts on one's own, is the self-reliance and engagement required for success of students with a wide range of cultural backgrounds and experiences. *Place* further engages students as they focus their time, energy and interests on issues that affect their lives and communities. They see, feel, and value the connection their educational experience has with their own communities. The opportunity for *integration* provides a powerful—as well as convenient and manageable—venue to design, implement, evaluate, and modify the curriculum as necessary. Because integration calls for us to share and infuse instruction within a culture of communities to go beyond the mere sharing of information, it brings tribal teachings into the mainstream where they belong, rather than in the margins where they so often reside. Together *inquiry, place,* and *integration* create a methodical and deliberate partnership, and a relationship that moves us towards common educational outcomes. An elder at a Salish potlatch once said, *There is a shared vision we all need to grasp and hold on to . . . to just grab is the easiest part, but to maintain your grip will be the most important.*

INNOVATION IN STI

Helping educators maintain their grip on our shared vision is paramount to the success of STI. There are tribal sovereignty units for every elementary, middle and high school unit in U.S. History, Washington State History, and Contemporary World Problems that Washington State's OSPI recommends. However, a teacher need not feel compelled or pressured to teach all of the material all at once. Regular OSPI social studies updates allow teachers access to materials they can integrate into units they likely will be teaching during that part of the school year. Within each STI unit are three levels of resources and lessons from which to choose, based on curricular needs and teaching time constraints. The teachers decide how much, to what degree, and how often they include issues of tribal sovereignty in the units and lessons that they already teach.

Inclusion and integration, therefore, are not a one-shot deal. Teachers have regular opportunities to integrate curriculum materials. If a teacher has only 30 minutes within a unit to introduce concepts and issues of tribal sovereignty, STI allows that. While it might not seem like a lot of teaching time, in most cases, it will be 100% more than what was taught previously. Moreover, in the months to come, there are other opportunities to include tribal sovereignty in upcoming units. It is our hope that, eventually, teachers will want to take it to the next level, that next time they will commit a few days to integrating tribal sovereignty lessons; the curriculum provides this latitude. Finally, if a teacher decides to make tribal sovereignty the focus of the unit, we have provided the means by which to accomplish this—as well as complete one of the state-required Classroom Based Assessments (CBAs), because each level builds upon the last, and thus all units culminate in the completion of a CBA. Everything is designed to accommodate the realities of teaching and to recognize the importance of teachers using their own strengths to ensure success.

Many essential common elements interact in the STI. It is designed to be collaborative, reliable, and seamless. Moreover, an emphasis on alignment to academic standards as well as tribal interests signifies much in the evolution of state and tribal governmental relations in Washington State. Critical to STI's implementation are the easy access and low cost—it's free! The overall manageability and integrated culture of STI ensure that classrooms function in a manner that cultivates engagement and results in increased levels of learning.

BRIDGING THE TRIBAL-PUBLIC EDUCATION GAP

Creating relationships between tribal and non-tribal communities and organizations is at the heart of how STI works, and these relationships ultimately result in a curriculum that can encompass all the tribal interests throughout the Pacific Northwest (and beyond should others choose to use it). While the goal is sustained symbiosis between tribal and non-tribal educational stakeholders, STI does not pretend that such an undertaking is easily or quickly acquired by schools wanting to improve academic achievement of Native students. Generations of institutional distrust weigh heavily on the shoulders of this burgeoning relationship. STI endeavors to acknowledge the pain and trauma of past and present educational experiences of tribal people in order to move forward and build a sustained relationship of trust, common interest, and understanding.

While the era of government boarding schools is over, tribal people today, especially school-aged children, bear the legacy of a destructive and cruel time in history. Just as STI hopes to incrementally combat the resentment and misinformation bred by generational ignorance and racism, non-tribal educational entities need to tread lightly and patiently on this remarkable, groundbreaking path. Tribes have waited patiently for mutual respect and understanding for over 500 years, and it should be no surprise to public education that the building of a worthwhile relationship takes time, patience, and diligence. STI works with such organizations as the Washington State School Directors' Association (WSSDA), Tribal Leaders Education Congress (TLC) and Washington Education Association (WEA) to foster skills that promote a true government-to-(tribal) government relationship that will result in the lasting relationships that will ensure the success of all students, tribal and non-tribal alike.

HOW STI IS ORGANIZED

The curriculum features five historical eras: Ancestral Teaching; Early Contact Period 1200–1500; Colonization Period and Indian Removal

1500–1855; Assimilation Period 1856–1970; and Self Determination & Self Governance 1970—present day, which correspond to OSPI-suggested unit outlines. Tribal sovereignty units and suggested CBAs address areas of emphasis while the state's Social Studies Grade Level Expectations, or GLEs, identify learning outcomes and are aligned to Common Cores State Standards. Lesson materials are listed along with essential questions that will be attended to while successfully implementing the curriculum.

ESSENTIAL QUESTIONS

There are five essential questions that educators and students will be able to answer when they have mastered the STI curriculum.

> 1. *How does physical geography affect Northwest tribes' culture, economy, and where they choose to settle and trade?*

We pose this question because physical geography can convey a sense of conservation and cohesion inherent in its earliest principles and cultivate our compassion for the environment inherent within Indigenous teachings. We are comfortable with teaching skill sets associated with measurement, hypothesis testing, mapping, models, and mathematics that serve as a foundation for understanding and utilizing knowledge of physical geography. With this sense of comfort also comes the choice of investigation of processes rather than mere description while telling our story, so current and future citizens of our state can better understand and appreciate how we are facing the future.

> 2. *What is the legal status of the tribes who negotiated or who did not enter into United States treaties?*

Many citizens in Washington State and elsewhere grow up not knowing that the Constitution of the United States vests our Congress with the authority to politically engage with tribes and that the Supreme Court recognizes that tribes retain inherent powers of self-governance. The interaction between the federal government and tribes is defined as a government-to-government relationship. Historical circumstances contributed to a variety of outcomes where some tribes entered into treaties with the federal government while other tribes were thwarted in their efforts to establish formal relations. Today, the tribes are still actively addressing the needs of their people, and each year it seems that mainstream political agendas challenge the existence of tribes while advocating regression to the assimilation strategies that have been so damaging to Indigenous peoples.

3. *What were the political, economic, and cultural forces that led to the treaties?*

In answering this question, it becomes important to understand and appreciate the factors that led to the treaties. Many Americans might believe that tribes were historically a threat to the U.S. However, in many circumstances Native lands were seized through military conquest, driven by an insatiable desire for natural resources to fuel the economy of a growing nation and to convert Native people to non-Native religious practices. The federal government and various state governments did negotiate with tribes, but many of these overtures were motivated by the desire to secure access to lands for non-Native settlement and were usually conducted by use of liquor, bribes, or physical threats.

4. *What are the ways in which tribes responded to the threats and outside pressure to extinguish their cultures and independence?*

The answer to this question begins to explain that our survival response no longer sees war as a legitimate strategy to confront opposition to our existence. On one hand, we seek resolution through the court system to ward off attack and to enforce the honoring of treaty obligations. On the other hand, tribal communities collaborate with other stakeholders to address prevailing concerns regarding the environment, economy, and education. Our desire is to work with other stakeholders throughout Washington to promote a better quality of life for all citizens.

5. *What have local tribes done to meet the challenges of reservation life? What have these tribes, as sovereign nations, done to meet the economic and cultural needs of their tribal communities?*

Embedded in the answer to this question is a basic request that citizens in Washington State understand that tribes have constantly sought avenues to ensure the health and vitality of their communities. This begins to explain why they continually practice their traditional cultures, speak their Native languages, and remember their magnificent histories. These efforts are complemented by economic and service programs that attest to the significant social hardships that many Native people experience every day in Washington State. The central meaning of sovereignty requires that tribes maintain their responsibility to ensure the survival of their people. To do anything less is to experience a sense of failure that adversely affects children and elders. Tribes will not accept such failure and there is a desire to possess the knowledge, compassion, and willingness to contribute to society that will help all citizens, Native and non-Native.

THE BIG FIVE LEARNING OUTCOMES: ELEMENTARY THROUGH HIGH SCHOOL

Within each grade level are five learning outcomes (shown in Table 3.1) that increase in depth and sophistication as students progress throughout their academic careers. These are the minimum that students ought to know– The Big Five (as the outcomes are referred to) are a baseline, not a ceiling, by no means limiting the unique academic goals of individual educators, schools, or districts.

Table 3.1   STI Major Learning Objectives for Washington State Students

By the end of elementary school, students will be able to:

- understand that over 500 independent tribal nations exist within the United States today, and that they deal with the United States, as well as each other, on a government-to-government basis;
- define *tribal* sovereignty as a way that tribes govern themselves in order to keep and support their cultural ways of life;
- understand that tribal sovereignty predates treaty times;
- explain how the treaties that tribal nations entered into with the United States government *limited* their sovereignty; and
- identify the names and locations of tribes in their area.

By the end of middle school, students will know the above, and be able to:

- understand that according to the US Constitution, treaties are the supreme law of the land, consequently treaty rights supersede most state laws;
- explain that tribal sovereignty has a cultural, as well as political, basis;
- understand that tribes are subject to federal law and taxes, as well as some state regulations;
- understand that tribal sovereignty is ever-evolving, and therefore levels of sovereignty and status vary from tribe to tribe; and
- explain that there were and are frequent and continued threats to tribal sovereignty that are mostly resolved through the court system.

By the end of high school, students will know the above, and will be able to:

- recognize landmark court decisions and legislation that affected and continue to affect tribal sovereignty;
- understand that tribal sovereignty works toward protecting tribes' ways of life and toward the development of their nations;
- understand that tribal, state, and federal agencies often work together toward the same goal;
- explain the governmental structure of at least one tribe in their community; and
- distinguish between federally and non-federally recognized tribes and explain the difference.

INTERNET AVAILABILITY OF MATERIALS

Because tribal sovereignty is viewed and practiced differently by different tribes, it is essential that the curriculum be regularly modified, updated, and refined. Tribal sovereignty can change daily, as tribal treaty rights are challenged, enforced, and clarified through the courts. STI is flexible, can be readily updated, and is designed to allow each tribe to share its own unique history, traditions, and experiences. While it is clear to many that tribal cultures are as vast and varied as the myriad of cultures on other continents, it may not be as clear that the more than 29 tribes that reside within Washington State are just as distinct. One tribe's history is not necessarily the same as another's, even if they share the same geography. While STI provides a basic framework for the teaching of tribal sovereignty within the context of typical mainstream social studies units, it is incumbent upon the stakeholders, tribal, and non-tribal alike, to tailor the lessons according to local tribal teachings and histories.

Our online format (found at http://www.indian-ed.org) allows for instant adaptation of materials and provides a clearinghouse for other educators to share curricula and materials they have developed. Through the support of OSPI, STI enjoys the latitude, not only of the instant updates that such subject matter requires, but also the inclusion of rich visual, kinesthetic and auditory materials required by the unique learning styles of Native learners. The consequence is a wealth of curricula suited for each district, each tribe, and each teacher. With the assistance of state library and media associations, we will eventually provide an online library and archive of materials and curricula already developed by tribes, but previously inaccessible because they were paper-based. Tribes can finally tell their stories in their own words, share with the educational community, and further trust that a lasting and invaluable relationship with non-tribal education communities is not only possible, it is imminent.

CONCLUDING THOUGHTS

In that state of Washington, we have all come together—Indian people, educators, even legislators—to make education of both our Native and non-Native students inclusive of information about tribal sovereignty, our history, our cultures, our governing processes, and to do so in a respectful and authentic way. The cornerstone of STI is that it doesn't pretend to be the definitive voice on any one tribe's history and definition of tribal sovereignty. STI compels its users to create and develop partnerships between school districts and tribes so that tribes can tell their own stories and begin trusting an education system that was hurtful at best and genocidal at worst. Tribes are tired of having schools teach about them rather than with them. STI's success depends on the success of this collaboration, this tribal and community involvement.

Our goals are lofty, idealistic, and rely on the assumption of good intentions. And yet, because we have experienced this extraordinary and wide-ranging convergence of cooperation and support, our goals are realistic *and will be realized.* Just as we have faith that in time, educators will teach about tribes with increasing respect, depth, inclusion, and sophistication, we have faith that in time, ours will be a model that is no longer the exception but the rule.

Otter is proud.

NOTES

1. The development of STI required the efforts of far more than one person, one tribe, or even one organization. Ours is a shared vision made possible by the following: The 29 Federally Recognized Tribes of the State of Washington; State Representative John McCoy; former Governors Gary Locke and Christine Gregoire; the Washington State Legislature and Offices of the Secretary of State and Attorney General; the Washington State School Directors Association; the Washington Library and Media Association; the Washington State Department of Education Office of the Superintendent of Public Instruction (OSPI), Indian Education Office, and former State Superintendent of Public Instruction Terry Bergeson; the U.S. Department of Education's Title Programs; and the pilot teachers, curriculum writers, parents, elders, ancestors, The Creator, and finally, those for whom we all labor and love, the children.

REFERENCES

Brown, Shana, & Michael Pavel, Ph.D. (ChiXapkaid). (2010). Washington State's tribal sovereignty curriculum initiative: Since Time Immemorial. *Journal of Educational Controversy.* Woodring College of Education, Western Washington University, 30 Sept. Retrieved from http://www.wce.wwu.edu/Resources/IASEC/docs/BrownCHiXapkaid.pdf

Canby, William C. American Indian Law in a Nutshell. 5th ed. St. Paul, MN: Thomson/West. (2009). Pp. lvii, 548. [Res. KF 8205.Z9 C36 2009]

CHiXapkaid (Pavel, M.), Banks-Joseph, S., Inglebret, E., McCubbin, Sievers, & Associates. (2009). *From Where the Sun Rises: Addressing the educational achievement of Native Americans in Washington State.* Pullman, WA: Clearinghouse on Native Teaching and Learning.

General Allotment Act of 1887. (or Dawes Act), Act of Feb. 8, 1887 (24 Stat. 388, ch. 119, 25 USCA 331), Acts of Forty-ninth Congress-Second Session, 1887. Retrieved from http://digital.library.okstate.edu/kappler/vol1/html_files/ses0033.html

Hunn, E.S. (1991). *Nch'i-Wana, the big river: Mid-Columbia Indians and their land.* Seattle: University of Washington Press.

Pevar, S. (2012). *The rights of Indians and tribes.* 4th Edition. New York: Oxford University Press.

Smith, B.L., Brown, S. & Costantino, M. (2011). *Since Time Immemorial: Developing tribal sovereignty curriculum for Washington's schools.* Retrieved from www.evergreen.edu/tribal/docs/sincetimeimmemorialcase.pdf

Warriner, G. & Engelstad (Directors). (1978). *More than bows and arrows* [Documentary]. United States: Camera One.

4 Classroom Teachers and Cultural Guides

Collaborating to Transform Teaching and Learning Through the Use of Traditional Tribal Knowledge

Anthony B. Craig

Much has been written about the experiences of American Indian communities in schools (Lomawaima & McCarty, 2006; Reyhner & Eder, 2006). Educational systems, from the time of colonization to the boarding school era to today, have for the most part failed to meet the needs of Indian students or communities. As an American Indian—and an Indian educator—I find these stories to be profound and overwhelmingly compelling. For me these stories do not exist solely in print, but in my own family, and my own experience. I also believe, though, that these stories are living today; the stories of American Indian communities continue to be written. While the horrors of history have been told and retold as a means of warning my relatives and me, we must also receive these stories as teachings, a call to action, and a strong reminder that we must continue to leverage the cultural and societal strengths of American Indian people to propel ourselves forward.

Educational systems and Native communities now must unite around ideas and practices that lead to realization of culturally-based schools that leverage powerful dynamic tribal cultures while providing high quality education to our youth. In this chapter, I review the theories underlying culturally-based approaches to education, a framework for their development and implementation, and a project our community conducted to use this information for our own school's improvement.

CULTURALLY-BASED EDUCATION

One of the major tasks facing Native American communities is to create lifelong learning opportunities that allow all the members to improve their quality of life, and to meet their tribal responsibilities through meaningful contributions to the local, national, and world communities in which they live and interact. The greatest educational challenge for many is to build learning environments that allow each of their young children to obtain an education that creates good people that are knowledgeable and wise.–(Demmert & Towner, 2003, p. 1)

In order to ensure academic and cultural successes that lead to successful, meaningful lives, tribal language, traditions, knowledge, and awareness of the tribal context must be the foundation for American Indian students (Demmert & Towner, 2003). Culturally-based education (CBE) requires that the community, youth and adults, must develop in a context that supports language and cultural customs; schools within tribal communities must work to develop such culturally based contexts. Based on years of assimilation, this charge is daunting and must be aspired to in a collaborative effort among tribal governments, school systems, and cultural experts within tribal contexts.

From a review of the research on culture in education, Demmert and Towner identified three major theories underlying CBE interventions: Cultural Compatibility Theory, Cognitive Theory, and Cultural-Historical-Activity Theory (CHAT). *Cultural Compatibility Theory* proposes that education is more efficacious when there is an increase in congruence between social cultural dispositions of students and social cultural expectations of the school. *Cognitive Theory* is the consideration of how "new" information is processed and used through the activation of prior knowledge; the theory states that in order for new learning to occur, relevant prior knowledge in long-term memory must be activated, or made accessible, and the new information must undergo some sort of processing. *CHAT* is a theory of development. According to CHAT, cultural activities among community members lead to internalization of knowledge, values, and cognitive routines. Because culture is created and recreated over generations through ceremonies and processes in daily life, traditional culture is more likely to contain repeated meaningful experiences leading to deeper understanding and authentic learning (Demmert & Towner, 2003). Therefore, CHAT places more emphasis on community-level elements for connectivity; based on this connected nature of members of a community, it is vital that schools—and other places of learning—recognize and leverage the collective experiences of the community in order to achieve new learning. This idea of community connectedness further implicates the need for community participation in the articulation of and planning for goals for student achievement.

All three theories presumably would agree that the basis of education is best built on the experience, values, and knowledge of the students and their families, both personal and community-based. This seems clear in Demmert and Towner's (2003) operational definition of CBE's six critical elements: (a) recognizing and using Native languages, (b) stressing traditional cultural characteristics, (c) using teaching strategies and curricula that are congruent with them, (d) recognizing the importance of Native spirituality and of adult-child interactions, (e) including community in planning and operation of the schools, and (f) respecting and using the community's social and political values and mores.

CONNECTING CURRENT REALITY TO
DEMMERT AND TOWNER'S DEFINITION

As educators serving Native students it is our responsibility to equip all students with the necessary skills to find success in life—academically, socio-emotionally, and culturally. Most (non-Native) teachers serving Native students are grappling with understanding the role of culture in teaching and learning in such classrooms. While there may be very few teachers who remain unconvinced that their teaching must be culturally based as an appropriate strategy to significantly improve student learning outcomes, an action plan toward that end has, thus far, seemed elusive. Michael Pavel (2007) points to research showing that Washington State teachers feel under-prepared to address the diverse needs of learners in their classrooms. Recognizing the need and having the will to transform practice are not yet coordinated with the skills to do so. Significant professional learning opportunities are called for to close the gap between current beliefs and practices and those described by Demmert and Towner.

PROFESSIONAL LEARNING FOR
TEACHERS OF NATIVE STUDENTS

We must create structured professional learning opportunities for teachers, offering the chance to access and acquire knowledge specific to local tribal communities, to enable them to understand how culture affects the way in which they view students and how they can develop pedagogical frameworks that are culturally responsive and increase overall achievement of students. To accomplish such transformation, we must motivate teachers and support them through the complexities of learning about culture and its impacts in the classroom. We must also develop and maintain strong partnerships with local cultural experts/community members who can offer guidance and support to educators and school systems.

PROFESSIONAL LEARNING: PROMOTING INTRINSIC
MOTIVATION & THE MOTIVATIONAL FRAMEWORK
FOR CULTURALLY RESPONSIVE TEACHING

Understanding why people do what they do lies in understanding motivation. For teachers, understanding what motivates students will help them ensure that they are creating the conditions under which students strive to excel (Ginsberg, 2011). For the purposes of this project, and for the overall school turnaround work I lead, I have adopted the *Motivational Framework for Culturally Responsive Teaching* (Ginsberg & Wlodkowski, 2000; 2009) to support teachers in instructional improvement efforts. I have also found this framework applicable for helping ensure that I create and maintain motivating conditions for educators as they participate in professional learning.

The framework includes four conditions (Ginsberg & Wlodkowski, 2009, p. 386):

Establishing Inclusion: Respect and Connectedness
How does this learning experience contribute to developing as a community of learners who feel respected by and connected to one another and to the teacher?

Developing a Positive Attitude: Volition and Personal Relevance
How does this learning experience offer meaningful choices and promote personal relevance to contribute to a positive attitude?

Enhancing Meaning: Challenge and Engagement
How does this learning experience engage students in challenging learning that has social merit?

Engendering Competence: Authenticity and Effectiveness
How does this learning experience create students' understanding that they are becoming more effective in authentic learning they value?

In interpreting and using the framework, one must also consider culture—one's own culture and the culture(s) of learners—in order to ensure motivation. Why we do what we do is also influenced by culture. As Ginsberg and Wlodkowski point out, what is culturally and emotionally significant to a person evokes intrinsic motivation (2000). As I designed learning opportunities that included the ideas of tribal culture in contrast to middle-class white cultural norms, it was critical to create plans that allowed all to be motivated and allowed us to consider, as a diverse group of learners, the predominant culture of the student body in my tribal community—Coast Salish. Recognizing the cultural differences between the adult learners' (teachers) and the students' cultures is an aspect of this kind of learning that is enhanced by the framework developed by Ginsberg and Wlodkowski; through the conditions of the framework we can develop a common language and collective way of asking questions and reaching understanding. By ensuring all four conditions are established, participants will be more likely to engage in learning that is truly transformative. In general terms, I have found culture, intrinsic motivation, and transformative learning to be inseparable.

COLLABORATING WITH COMMUNITY AND TAKING ACTION

One important step of collaborating with community is to hear stories, or counter-narratives, of local tribal members in order to transform teachers

(Rogers & Jaime, 2010). Beyond that, an important next step I have found is to empower community members by seeking their cultural expertise in learning situations; our systems are in need of such collaboration with "cultural guides." By asking cultural guides to participate in professional learning situations, these community members are offered a meaningful place in the school. Not only do we ask for guidance in overall school improvement and daily lesson improvement, we also ask for ongoing, genuine relationships between educators and cultural guides. Instead of hearing stories and then interpreting them through our own lenses, we are asking them to tell their stories and giving them the opportunity to act upon their knowledge *in the moment*—leading to deeper learning. As one cultural guide indicated, "By having us—tribal members—at *this* table, with teachers and principals, we are being empowered. By having us sit here you show you recognize that we care and have something to offer."

In this particular study, the action taken was a lesson study for teachers. Lesson study has the ultimate goal of helping teachers improve teaching and learning through improved lesson design (Ginsberg, 2011). This lesson study included the expertise of members of the tribal community, that is, cultural guides, who could join teachers in planning, teaching/observing, debriefing, and setting goals for next steps beyond this experience. Lesson study (and the collaborative experience itself) allows teachers exposure to the ancestral knowledge cultural guides carry as a step to improve their own instructional practice.

The lesson study process for this cycle followed specific steps. First, we articulated the focus for lesson study, including (a) developing tribal-specific culturally responsive teaching practices; (b) engaging struggling students in new/innovative ways; and (c) building collaboration between teachers and cultural guides to establish relationships around teaching and learning. Second, we selected participants. Because part of this project was to reveal the connection between teaching and learning in traditional tribal contexts and classroom contexts, participants were selected based on their interest in furthering this inquiry for their own practice, and in order to contribute to the tribal community. As Margaret Kovach (2009) proposes, participant selection in Indigenous research should not be random, or a random sample, but should, instead be based on relationships—between the researcher and participants, among participants themselves, and between participants and the inquiry question. I found this idea helpful in this context given the need to study both the use of ancestral knowledge in a professional learning context and the structure through which that ancestral knowledge is accessed and utilized (in this case, lesson study). The teachers participating in this research have been mired in ideas of what it means to be "culturally responsive" and in how such pedagogy can contribute to the successful development—cultural and academic—of their students. They have been involved in professional development focused on the *Motivational Framework for Culturally Responsive Teaching* (Ginsberg & Wlodkowski, 2000,

2009). Cultural guides for this project are each considered cultural leaders in the community.

When considering who would make a successful cultural guide for this research, I considered what the strengths of cultural traditions in the tribal community are, how those traditions are perpetuated and strengthened, and who is responsible for the transmission of those traditions. The cultural guides selected are leaders in the Tulalip Canoe Family who are responsible for the canoe traditions and protocol for the tribe, leaders in the Tulalip First Salmon Ceremony who are responsible for the revitalization and strengthening of the main harvest ceremony of the year, or a member of the Makah Nation (another regional tribe) who is a leader in the annual Makah Days celebration potlatch and coastal gathering and in the Tulalip education community and a parent who raises her children amongst the Tulalip Tribes. All cultural guides use traditional (ancestral) ways of teaching and are seen by learners (children) as elders (those who hold knowledge and must be respected). Given the successful teaching and learning evident from their work in ceremonial contexts, I was driven to access that ancestral knowledge in order to transform teaching practice within the school context. These participants also expressed a willingness to contribute to school/instructional improvement efforts from a tribal culture standpoint, in an attempt to infuse the schools with culture.

The third step was to select, adapt, or create tools anchored in an instructional framework to guide lesson study planning, implementation, and reflection (Ginsberg, 2011). This lesson study utilized a planning template based on the *Motivational Framework for Culturally Responsive Teaching* (Ginsberg & Wlodkowski, 2000; 2009). Fourth, we taught or observed lessons and gathered data and insights about our lesson study focus. The planned lesson was taught by a teacher with colleagues and cultural guides observing and taking notes (gathering data) to help the team think about the lesson study focus. Then the team reflected on the lesson as implemented and on the process. For reflection, questions from Ginsberg (2011) were adapted to our context; these questions included what was learned from the first round of lesson study and how that would be applied to each person's teaching, which parts of the process were most engaging, how they might improve the process, what supports would be needed to make this process more effective, and how it might best contribute to our school improvement process.

Our final step was to make plans for the next lesson study cycle or other collaborative learning. Based on the need to continually explore questions and ideas as they emerge, it is important for all participants to continue learning in a cycle; no one experience can uncover answers to "solve" our problem of practice. Based on the learning in this lesson study, teachers and cultural guides, through a common experience, now had more refined, rich questions to guide their learning in another cycle of lesson study.

AFTER THE LESSON STUDY WITH CULTURAL GUIDES:
WHAT TRANSFORMED IN TEACHER THINKING/PRACTICE?

From data gathered from teacher comments, reflections on the lessons study process, and walkthroughs conducted after the lesson study, evidence of transformation in teacher thinking and practice is emerging. One main focus of the lesson study cycles was the need to develop culturally responsive strategies for engaging students who remain disengaged from learning situations. Teachers reported and demonstrated renewed thinking about the possibility of engaging students who have baffled, even frustrated them, all year.

One key idea learned from our cultural guides is that in learning settings in the tribal community, every student knows his or her role. In the classrooms of participating teachers, one problem of practice had been engaging all students—particularly those who regularly avoid participation. With the insights of cultural guides, ideas of how to engage those disengaged students began to take shape in meaningful, culturally responsive ways. The idea of giving students a specific role or job in each lesson, while seemingly basic, motivated students in that lesson, and in lessons throughout the following weeks. The correlation between meaningful roles in tribal ceremonies, such as being a drummer, and meaningful roles in classrooms, in this case, being the "page turner" during a literacy lesson, changed how teachers thought about participation. This transformation in teachers' thinking about participation went from ideas of uniformity—in which all students participated in the exact same ways—to ideas of all students having their individual needs met *and* each student playing a role that contributes to the classroom community. Students who originally balked at the idea of sitting motionless and silent are now active book-holders or page-turners who enthusiastically fulfill their roles and participate in class reading and discussion.

Another challenge for teachers was how to engage students who were not passively disengaged, but were chronically disruptive. Teachers expressed concerns during the lesson study goal setting and planning phase about students who quickly escalate from disengaged to disruptive. These students have become behavior concerns in the classrooms, are not learning, and often keep others from learning. Cultural guides and teachers collaborated around a traditional value of inclusion and respect. While disruptive students seemed to be neglecting the cultural norm of giving respect to all others at all times, it is possible that their behavior was a result of a feeling of being unsafe in the classroom. Teachers reported learning two important ideas during lesson study: (a) if students know they can be removed from the learning (which is a typical consequence for disruptive behavior), it is likely they develop insecurity about their belonging in the classroom, or fear about the belonging of classmates and relatives in the class; and (b) teachers may spend significant time working to punish children who are struggling to display expected behaviors, when they would be better served trying to develop a strong relationship to problem-solve with students. This is not to suggest that struggling or disruptive students are not complex, or in need of complex sets of strategies to support their behavior; rather, it is possible that teachers have resorted to simply removing students from class, and are in need of innovative, more relevant strategies.

Cultural guides shared stories of children (and adults) in traditional contexts who are disruptive, or counterproductive, to the work of a ceremony; in those cases it is common practice for the community to literally circle around the individual who is struggling in order to determine solutions together, and ensure the person feels a sense of belonging and responsibility to the group. While no fixed set of solutions was generated for supporting disruptive students in the classroom, teachers noted that their thinking had shifted to being focused on the need to support students in a different way, rather than send them to the office for discipline. This problem of practice shared by teachers is of particular interest given that during this one lesson study no absolute direction for a change in instruction was set, but cultural knowledge was shared and new questions or ideas for inquiry arose. This is a powerful illustration about how such collaboration can be both supportive and generative, and can lead to transformation in practice.

Another significant transformation in teacher thinking and behavior that resulted from the lesson study was the active relationship between cultural guides and teachers. In the months following the lesson study, teachers regularly referred back to ideas shared at the lesson study table. Further, communication—phone calls, email exchanges, and informal conversations—continued to take place; teachers and cultural guides had developed a relationship around culture and learning that lasted well beyond the lesson study. The transformation in thinking was evident in how teachers spoke about cultural guides as reliable resources for issues large and small. Prior to the lesson study, teachers noted, they never would have considered reaching out to community members, simply because they did not know any in the way that they now know the cultural guides. Teachers reported feeling safe in exposing vulnerable parts of their practice as a result of the lesson study process. Teachers also reported that they have been invited to community events with the families of the cultural guides and were looking forward to getting into the community to learn. What before may have remained a suggestion on paper—learning from participating in community events—is now a reality for these teachers based on the work of lesson study. This transformative experience continues to drive teacher thinking and practice and continues to drive the learning needed to become culturally responsive through the accessing of ancestral knowledge.

WHAT WAS REVEALED ABOUT THE GOALS OF TEACHERS AND COMMUNITY MEMBERS TOWARD THE IMPROVEMENT OF TEACHING AND LEARNING?

A main theme that emerged from this research project was the overwhelming willingness of teachers and cultural guides to be open, vulnerable, and incredibly generous in a collaborative effort to contribute to the school and community. Mutual respect was shared between participating teachers and cultural guides as thinking and feelings were shared. As important as the respect shown between participants, though, was the immense level of respect paid to the culture and the cultural knowledge being shared. While there is sometimes a fear in open sharing of ancestral knowledge in contexts that include non-tribal members, in this case because the goals of the work were made clear, and relationships of trust and respect were established, many ideas founded in traditional knowledge were developed and have served to strengthen teaching and learning in this context.

I have found the best way to share the learning from this inquiry cycle is by framing the ideas in the conditions of the motivational framework. There are four main sets of ideas to consider: (a) How are cultural guides thinking about the learning of teachers as they transform practice to be more culturally responsive? (b) How are cultural guides thinking about the learning of students in classrooms? (c) How are teachers thinking about their own transformation and the transformation of their colleagues? That is, what do teachers need to learn in order to best serve this tribal context? (d) How are teachers thinking about culturally responsive teaching given this experience of collaborating with cultural guides? Based on the complex, but generative, nature of this work it is important to continue the learning in meaningful, collaborative cycles—in lesson study and/or other learning structures. Listed below are the themes from the lesson study cycle:

HOW ARE CULTURAL GUIDES THINKING ABOUT THE LEARNING OF TEACHERS AS THEY TRANSFORM PRACTICE TO BE MORE CULTURALLY RESPONSIVE?

Theme of Establishing Inclusion: Respect and Connectedness

In order to show respect and connect to us as a people, you must make an effort to understand the cultural context of our tribal community. Cultural guides said: Realize where you are and who you are serving; learn our Indigenous ways as it will benefit you in many ways; you should want to know about us—know our history and culture. Family is everything and family equals culture. Understand what family means to us as individuals and as a tribe; we are all connected. Family is not just siblings, or parents, or even grandparents. To know ourselves, we must know our lineage. To know us, you should know that, too.

Theme of Developing a Positive Attitude: Volition and Personal Relevance

Maintain a learning stance about the community you are serving. Cultural guides said: Be a learner! If you want to call yourself a teacher of tribal students, you had better know who they are! Know, this isn't just another teaching job in any other school. This is what we like to say is *our* school. We are Indian here; we don't think we are better than other people, but we are proud of who we are. This is our *home*! We are unique and want to be served like we are unique.

Theme of Enhancing Meaning: Challenge and Engagement

To learn about the culture you must be around it—that is the only way. Cultural guides said: You need to be around us to get to know us; we can't tell you; you have to feel it for yourself and experience our kids "feeling" it. Build relationships with students by being around them in the community. Sit at a ceremony, a basketball game, a meeting and just be there. Educators must remember that school is one place our kids learn; it is not *the* place for learning. We raise them in "the culture," too, and place great value on that learning. Educators must listen, observe, experience—over and over. This is how we learn culture, too.

Theme of Engendering Competence: Authenticity and Effectiveness

Involve us in goal setting for our children's education and development; we are all connected in our community and we plan together. Cultural guides said: You are investing in a community—a people, not just students. We need students to succeed for us all to succeed. Additionally, non-Indians live in our community and we need them to understand our culture, too. That can happen in school and benefit all of us in the future. These are our future leaders and they will know each other on a deeper level and can really change society. Solutions will be long-term and educators must be prepared to stay; we have over 150 years to undo and overcome. Looking ahead at our future, we need learning from both school and strong culture to thrive.

HOW DO CULTURAL GUIDES THINK ABOUT THE LEARNING OF STUDENTS IN CLASSROOM?

Establishing Inclusion: Respect and Connectedness

To make sure students are learning you must have a genuine relationship with them that develops over time. Cultural guides said: Love and safety will allow our kids to learn from you and you will learn from them. Show love and let students make mistakes; don't make us afraid of failure—we've had enough of that. Encourage us when we are down, tell us when we are doing well. Don't kick us out or disregard us. When students misbehave, they must know they won't be sent away; this will damage any relationship you have built.

Developing a Positive Attitude: Volition and Personal Relevance

Make sure what students are learning matters to them—because it matters to the community. Cultural guides said: Teachers must ask, how will reading, writing, and math make life better for a student's grandma? Will the student use this math in his job someday?

Enhancing Meaning: Challenge and Engagement

Make sure students know what they are expected to do. Cultural guides said: Make your expectations clear. Don't make students guess—they won't try unless you make it clear what you want. In our way of teaching and learning, demonstration and practice—with lots of support—are our main ways of teaching. We show, not just tell, and we let them try it with us right there; teachers should do that, too. Remember, repetition, repetition, repetition; if something is important enough to learn, it will take lots of practice and you will have lots of mistakes.

Engendering Competence: Authenticity and Effectiveness

To ensure students are clear about what they are learning, tell them when they are growing and learning, and encourage approximations. Cultural guides said: Make learning meaningful and keep expectations high. Students will be excited to show the teacher what they have learned or figured out. Students will know when they've been successful because the teacher has already shown them how it should look.

HOW ARE TEACHERS THINKING ABOUT THEIR OWN TRANSFORMATION AND THE TRANSFORMATION OF THEIR COLLEAGUES TO BEST SERVE THIS TRIBAL CONTEXT?

Establishing Inclusion: Respect and Connectedness

Build relationships by "getting into" the community. Teachers said: Build relationships first and ask who their family is; relationships are the only way to reach students. Relationships must be with those beyond the student, so get into the community and show your face. This will allow you to recognize how the student is connected to others and will remind you that you are serving a family, a tribe, a community—not just a student. One teacher revealed, "I used to think students were just making small talk when they would point out their cousins and siblings or talk about their family. Now I know they were introducing themselves—really telling me who they were. I pay attention now and really listen to what they are telling me."

Developing a Positive Attitude: Volition and Personal Relevance

Becoming culturally aware is our job. Teachers said: Be a flexible, open learner; it is a teacher's job to know student/community culture—it is one way for us to show respect and ensure we are strong, effective teachers.

Enhancing Meaning: Challenge and Engagement

We must get to know how teaching and learning work beyond our classrooms and school. Teachers said: Expectations and roles are clear in the community. Everybody knows what to do and what everybody else should be doing. Teachers must watch and listen; figure out how to get your questions answered without being presumptuous or overbearing. As learners, pay attention to how kids behave, learn, participate in community settings.

Engendering Competence: Authenticity and Effectiveness

Over time we will become more effective at teaching here. We must not think we can ever know everything . . . but we can become better and more knowledgeable. Teachers said: We need to recognize, as teachers, that we are part of a larger, connected community. However, we must accept being an "outsider" initially, but work at building a network over time. This network starts with one person, then one family, and they "sponsor" you to other people. We have a role in this community, which is to teach our students so they can serve their family and community.

HOW ARE TEACHERS THINKING ABOUT CULTURALLY RESPONSIVE TEACHING GIVEN THIS EXPERIENCE OF COLLABORATING WITH CULTURAL GUIDES?

Establishing Inclusion: Respect and Connectedness

Build relationships with students. Show respect by trying to be connected to them in authentic ways. Teachers said: We must find subtle, but clear, ways to show students that we care about them. Love is necessary in the classroom. We can build relationships around learning; we must offer students one on one time to talk about family *and* about content—reading, writing, math. One important practice is to ask about family . . . and then actually listen. Perhaps most important, remember to laugh with your students and let them joke with you; it is a sign of mutual respect and love.

Developing a Positive Attitude: Volition and Personal Relevance

Content and delivery of lessons should be culturally relevant. Teachers said: topics we cover in class should not be disconnected from student life. We might not know how to connect everything in deep ways, but we should know enough about their lives to connect some things. Additionally, students should feel comfortable in working on assignments in class because it fits what they need.

Enhancing Meaning: Challenge and Engagement

Allow for and encourage multiple ways of participation. Teachers said: Participation can look different in different contexts. We should provide several ways for students to participate. If talk is not working, ask what else might we try?

Engendering Competence: Authenticity and Effectiveness

Be clear about purpose so students know what you expect. Teachers said: set clear expectations by modeling, supporting, and reinforcing for students what we expect and how they will know they are learning and improving. We cannot just talk at students—we must find meaningful ways to make expectations explicit through modeling and experiences.

HOW DID THE LESSON STUDY WITH CULTURAL GUIDES CONTRIBUTE TO TEACHERS' AND COMMUNITY MEMBERS' THINKING?

Through this experience, participants began to imagine how such collaborative efforts could play a significant role in school improvement. The cultural guides and teachers began discussing next steps for their relationships and a more defined role for how and when the cultural guides and teachers might collaborate. Ideas shared include the potential of teachers joining certain community events/ceremonies with the cultural guides to "sponsor" them, that is, introduce them, show them around, develop a network for them with other community members. Additionally, teachers may contact cultural guides regarding questions about teaching and learning or student needs, and in turn, teachers can act as a liaison for cultural guides with questions or concerns about the school. Cultural guides can visit classrooms regularly, participate in professional learning (such as lesson study), and can offer perspectives, ideas, and guidance in school improvement efforts.

For participating teachers, ideas about transformation to culturally responsive practitioners began to take shape. Before participating in this cycle of inquiry focused on lesson study, teachers had a limited scope for *how* they would develop culturally responsive practices, how they might collaborate with cultural guides, and in what ways their thinking and practice might change. When debriefing the lesson study process, the central questions from teachers revolved around how soon, and in what ways, another opportunity to collaborate would occur. Based on the guidance of the cultural guides, participating teachers expressed an eagerness to attend community events and to have the cultural guides return to the classroom. Further, participating teachers began an informal dialogue with colleagues about the lesson study experience, spreading interest to others for similar opportunities.

CONCLUSION

What has allowed American Indians to survive is culture—a culture of strength—and that culture will continue to propel us forward. As educators we must seek answers to *how* we might leverage the culture in respectful, meaningful ways to change teaching and learning for the students of today and for future generations. By creating school systems that are more congruent with the cultural reality of our students, we will see the community thrive in school in ways that are much more aligned with the goals of the tribal community—which certainly include, but are not limited to, academic success. This must all be done through genuine school-community collaboration. In this chapter we have documented that not only can such collaborations be built and used in lesson study, but that they can have lasting impact on how teachers view the possibility and value of community participation in building culturally responsive approaches to problem solving within the classroom.

REFERENCES

Demmert, W.G.J., Towner, J.C., & Northwest Regional Educational Laboratory. (2003). A review of the research literature on the influences of culturally based education on the academic performance of Native American students. Final Paper. Portland, OR: Education Northwest.

Ginsberg, M.B. (2011). *Transformative professional learning: A system to enhance teacher and student motivation.* Thousand Oaks, CA: Corwin.

Ginsberg, M.B., & Wlodkowski, R.J. (2000). *Creating highly motivating classrooms for all students: A schoolwide approach to powerful teaching with diverse learners.* San Francisco: Jossey-Bass.

Ginsberg, M.B., & Wlodkowski, R.J. (2009). *Diversity and motivation: Culturally responsive teaching in college.* San Francisco: Jossey-Bass.

Kovach, M. (2009). *Indigenous methodologies: Characteristics, conversations, and contexts.* Toronto: University of Toronto Press.

Lomawaima, K.T., & McCarty, T.L. (2006). *To remain an Indian: Lessons in democracy from a century of Native American Education.* New York: Teachers College Press.

Pavel, D. M. [CHiXapKaid]. (2007). American Indian stories enrich intervention. *The ASHA Leader, 12*(1), 1, 26–27.

Reyhner, J., & Eder, J. (2006). *American Indian education: A history.* Norman: University of Oklahoma Press.

Rogers, C.A., & Jaime, A.M. (January 01, 2010). Listening to the community: Guidance from Native community members for emerging culturally responsive educators. *Equity & Excellence in Education, 43*(2), 188–201.

5 The Future of Indian Education
Research and Indigenous Perspectives

Kristen French and Leslie Harper

Stories are at the core of Indigenous learning—told in our home languages, based in rich, dynamic cultural traditions and shared by community members. Building on this tradition, Indigenous researchers (Brayboy, 2005; Archibald, 2008; Smith, 2012; Grande, 2004; Battiste, 2013) embody *storying* (Archibald, 2008) to weave together thoughts, experiences, and perspectives to cultivate knowledge and understanding. For this chapter our (Leslie's and Kristen's) stories—or critical personal narratives—build on our personal, professional, and community relationships, grounded in the honoring of Indigenous epistemologies, wisdom, and education through language and culture-based education. We have been guided and mentored by inspirational leaders, such as the late Dr. William G. Demmert, Jr. and Denny Hurtado, who have been tireless educational warriors keeping our peoples' stories, teachings, and languages alive. As we begin storying about the ways in which the past and present influence the future of Indian education and Indigenous perspectives, it is with humility and respect that we share our experiences in working with the Coalition for Indigenous Language and Culture-Based Education (CILCBE) and the National Indian Education Association (NIEA).[1]

The future of Indian education rests in collaborative, concerted efforts to cultivate, revitalize, and immerse children in their Indigenous languages and culture through education, provided with heart, love, care, and social justice. In this chapter, we discuss Dr. Demmert's ongoing legacy through the CILCBE, the impact this legacy has had on our own collaboration on decolonizing Indigenous education, and the current state of American Indian education and its complex and significant interconnections with multicultural education.

THE COALITION OF INDIGENOUS LANGUAGE AND CULTURE-BASED EDUCATION: ENDURING LEGACY OF DR. WILLIAM G. DEMMERT, JR.

Kristen's collaboration began with Dr. Demmert inviting her to join the Coalition in 2007 when she joined the Education faculty at Western Washington University. As his former student, Kristen cherished the opportunity to work with her mentor and support the Coalition. Leslie's connection with Dr. Demmert and the CILCBE naturally developed through the successful directorship and implementation of the Niigaane Ojibwemowin Language Immersion School. In 2003, on the Leech Lake Reservation, Leslie with a group of committed Ojibwe educators, elders, and community members imagined, created, and opened the doors to the school to revitalize Ojibwe language (Treuer, 2010). Niigaane is one of five language immersion schools, which along with four universities and one Regional Education Laboratory (REL Northwest) form the CILCBE partnership.[2]

The CILCBE was chaired by Dr. Demmert and founded in an American Indian educational movement built on profound public policy work and relationships with esteemed Indigenous scholars and educators, including David Beaulieu, Director of the Electa Quinney Institute for American Indian Education, and Namaka Rawlins, Director of Strategic Partnerships for the 'Aha Pūnana Leo, a non-profit Hawaiian language revitalization organization. In 2002, after Dr. Demmert and Dr. Beaulieu completed working on the Clinton Administration's Executive Order (Executive Order No. 13096, 1999), they initiated a research partnership that would eventually lead to the CILCBE (Beaulieu, 2011). Simultaneously, the Northwest Educational Regional Laboratory (now REL Northwest) surveyed Indigenous communities on the feasibility of "conducting experimental research on culture-based education" which led Demmert to gather a group "to discuss the development of assessments and research models for testing the effectiveness of culturally based education on academic performance" (Rawlins, Wilson, & Kawai'ae'a , 2011, p. 82). Subsequently, the CILCBE has met twice a year, in Portland at REL Northwest, and at the NIEA Convention through 2009; these groups still meet today to continue Demmert's research on language and culture-based education for the well-being of Indigenous children and communities.

Through years of co-constructed research, dialogue, sharing of resources, and collaboration, the CILCBE developed Indigenous Culture-Based Education Rubrics and a training manual (Demmert, 2001; Demmert & Towner, 2003; Demmert, 2008). Based on the six critical elements of culture-based education programs, Demmert and Towner (2003) define culture-based education as shown in Table 5.1. The CILCBE is currently working with Education Northwest to publish and make public the rubrics and manual to support the assessment and research of Indigenous culture-based programs. Within the last decade, the CILCBE led by Demmert, showed how Indigenous coalition-building generates much more than evidence of the academic and social success of language and culture-based programs; it has also demonstrated the power of solidarity across Indigenous language and culture-based communities. The CILCBE has historical "roots and routes" (Smith, 2012) in the NIEA (see this volume's dedication to Demmert and Hurtado). After the 2013 NIEA Convention, the Central and Pacific Regional Educational Laboratories (2013) organized a national forum to establish priorities for future education grounded in culture-based education for Indigenous languages.

Table 5.1   *Definition of Culture-Based Education* (Adapted from Demmert & Towner, 2003)

- Recognition and use of Native American (American Indian, Alaska Native, Native Hawaiian) languages (either bilingually or as a first or second language).

- Pedagogy that stresses traditional cultural characteristics and adult-child interactions as the starting place for education (mores that are currently practiced in the community, and which may differ from community to community).

- Pedagogy in which teaching strategies are congruent with the traditional culture as well as with contemporary ways of knowing and learning (opportunities to observe, opportunities to practice, and opportunities to demonstrate skills).

- Curriculum that is based on traditional culture and recognizes the importance of Native spirituality while placing the education of young children in a contemporary context (e.g., use and understanding of the visual arts, legends, oral histories, and fundamental beliefs of the community).

- Strong Native community participation (including parents, elders, other community resources) in educating children and in the planning and operation of school activities.

- Knowledge and use of the social and political mores of the community.

Ultimately, as Demmert and Hurtado expressed, the trust agreements among the United States and Indigenous sovereign nations have yet to be realized. A legacy of explicit colonization exists with educational systems from mission to boarding schools with a policy of "killing the Indian to save the man". In challenging neocolonialism, we (Leslie and Kristen) are currently collaborating to co-construct professional development for deeper understandings of and working toward an end to this insidious and enduring colonization.

DECOLONIZING INDIGENOUS EDUCATION WITH NIIGAANE OBJIWEMOWIN IMMERSION SCHOOL CO-AUTHORS' PARTNERSHIP

In December of 2012, Kristen traveled to Leech Lake Minnesota to collaborate with Leslie and the Niigaane Objiwemowin Immersion School educators on our Decolonizing Partnership and Professional Development Project. We had been working together since 2008 with the CILCBE. In honor of the school and faculty, the Center for Education, Equity and Diversity (CEED) has committed to assisting Niigaane team members in the development of a critical inquiry fellowship that examines ideas of decolonizing pedagogical practices to support and inform their three-year project objectives and share resources and promising practices. Together, the partnership hopes to strengthen the Niigaane team's integration of cultural practice, product, and perspective in curriculum objectives through a combination of in-person meetings and Skype contacts, online, email, and Canvas discussions held regularly throughout the school year, and at least two onsite visits.

Two sets of objectives are embraced by this collaborative team: The Nii-gaane school 3-year objectives are to teach all content areas in Ojibwemowin, document students' academic and social benchmarks, and create Ojibwe language assessments and document the developmental levels of Ojibwe language development in elementary-age Ojibwe language-immersion students. The team also has Decolonizing Partnership Objectives: With a decolonizing theoretical lens, which specifically focuses on the unique and urgent issues that Indigenous educators face, together we hope to create a space for critical dialogue that benefits the Niigaane School's immersion education site by (1) supporting a community of colleagues in a mutual learning and sharing of ideas and self-reflection, (2) developing common language on the Ojibwe community's definitions of academic, linguistic and social success, (3) developing explicit strategies to support each other and the students, (4) emphasizing decolonizing education from an Indigenous perspective, in our scholarship, and (5) acquiring and developing professional resources.

BRIEF BACKGROUND ON DECOLONIZATION THEORY AND ACTION

There are various perspectives on colonialism and neocolonialism as they pertain to Indigenous education, and many approaches to decolonization theory and practice (see for example Vizenor, 1994; Smith, 2012; Mishuah, 2003; Battiste, 2013). Indeed the very term Indigenous is sometimes used as an overarching description of people globally impacted by colonization or neocolonialism. The United Nations, however, offers the following as defining Indigenous: self-identification as Indigenous peoples individually and by the community; historical continuity with pre-colonial societies; strong links to the land and its resources; distinct social, economic, political, language, culture and belief systems; forming non-dominant groups of society and having a resolve to maintain and reproduce, as distinctive, their ancestral environments and systems (United Nations, n.d.). In writing about the response of Native Peoples to colonization and neocolonialism, Vizenor (1998) coined the term *survivance*, an active presence or an "active repudiation of dominance, tragedy, and victimry" (p. 15). Survivance, is therefore, the storying of Indigenous struggles including resistances to colonialism/neocolonialism, without relegating Native Peoples to a limited conceptualization as conquered victims of history. Instead, Native Peoples and their histories are embodied through personal, collective, and institutional movements of resistance and agency. Grande (2004), in addressing her Indigenous theory of subjectivity, includes the importance of place as it relates to sovereignty and self-determination; they do not seek to meld with the melting pot but to have their own unique cultures survive.

Indigenous education builds on these theories, and the theories have been reworked and redefined as Indigenous scholars seek to make clear the urgency of providing high quality education for Indigenous children (Smith, 2012; Grande, 2004). Developing and understanding these theories is a vital part of decolonization, just as reclaiming language and nationhood are (Battiste & Henderson, 2000). Indeed, the goal of a decolonization theory, according to Grande (2004), is to represent a multitude of Indigenous voices through both educational intellectualism and activism. It can and should provide a framework for education. Wilson (2005) believes that Indigenous people collectively need to create spaces in the process of decolonization to include words such as decolonization and critical consciousness. According to Wilson's research findings, a transformative praxis is as important as maintaining native languages. In this way Indigenous communities can "raise a new generation of Indigenous Peoples deeply committed to their tribal traditions but also deeply critical of the institutions of colonialism" (Wilson, 2005, p. 14). And this is what our collaborations have sought to do in terms of co-constructing educational practices, materials, experiences, and professional resources to educate our children, in collaboration with the community.

DECOLONIZING PEDAGOGY

Decolonizing pedagogy, according to Tejeda and Gutierrez (2006), acknowledges the hegemonic nature of curriculum design, instructional practices, assessments, and the sociopolitical structures of schools as reproducing and maintaining neocolonial domination and exploitation. Therefore, decolonizing pedagogy, methods, research and theoretical frameworks serves to provide a set of analytical tools to "excavate history and examine the present," repositioning Eurocentric mainstream views of history and highlighting the voices of targeted groups (Tejeda, Espinoza, & Gutierrez, 2002, p. 33; see also Mishuah & Wilson, 2004).

Investigations of neocolonial history and the reshaping of curricula to reflect better the neocolonial nature of U.S. schools and society do not preclude rigorous curriculum standards. Therefore, educators and students must examine American society through macro-level and micro-level theorizations, explicitly considering the larger picture of history and the sociopolitical contexts of neocolonial experiences of peoples in the United States, as well as the local experiences and realities of the students' immediate lives.

While Tejeda et al. (2002) provide a pedagogy larger in scope, to include all marginalized groups within the U.S. internal neocolonial context, Grande (2004) searches for a *red pedagogy*, or an emancipatory revolutionary pedagogy that privileges Indigenous intellectualism. Her specific concern is for American Indian youth, who have the country's highest dropout rates, lowest academic performance rates, and the lowest college admission and retention rates in the nation (American Council on Education, 2002, cited in Grande, 2004). Similar to the experiences of African American children (Ladson-Billings, 1998), American Indian students are tracked in high numbers in remedial courses, and subject to low teacher expectations and racism. American Indian educational scholars have found that schools that honor Indigenous language and culture have higher success rates with Indigenous students (McCardle & Demmert, 2006).

As a critical theorist, Grande (2004) envisions a form of democracy that sheds its "Western capitalist desires" and works for "both critical and Indigenous forms of education" (p. 7). According to her, the dreams of sovereignty and self-directed, self-determined communities are possibilities through red pedagogy because the ultimate goal is decolonization. Because the research honors both these positions by honoring Indigenous ways of knowing (which is provided by the theoretical framework of this research), the critical investigation of history, and the locally embedded perspectives and experiences of the lives and the communities students come from, a decolonizing pedagogy is an essential component to the sociopolitical and democratic movement toward emancipation and empowerment.

Storytelling has emerged as a powerful tool of decolonization. Smith (2012) adds that the alternative stories or counter-stories that contribute to healing, self-determination and sovereignty are "powerful forms of resistance which are repeated and shared across diverse Indigenous communities" (p. 2); in particular, the stories of emancipation or of the devastation of colonial histories do not alone change history. But the past, as told through our stories, as well as the present stories of our communities and our culture, our languages, and social practices have also become spaces not only of resistance but of hope (Smith, 2012).

The next steps involve action toward decolonization. Smith has inspired many Indigenous scholars and researchers such as Waziyatawin Angela Wilson to act and take on research agendas that explicitly ask who the research is for, whom it benefits, who conducts it, and who is responsible for developing the narratives and sharing the research. (See especially Wilson's [2005] decolonizing handbook with contributions by Indigenous scholars.)

What does this decolonizing action look like? Laenui (2000), incorporating Indigenous ways of knowing and practices, defines five distinct and dynamic phases of decolonization: rediscovery and recovery, mourning, dreaming, commitment, and action (Laenui, 2000, p. 152). Rediscovery and recovery create a space for embracing the traditions, beliefs, and values of precolonial cultures. Continuing to live in the victimization of colonization (or the mourning) does not change or transform Native lives; yet at the same time, it is necessary to understand the loss of language, culture and history at the hands of the colonizers, because the institutional practices that maintain these systems today must be stopped. Key concepts in the process of decolonization are commitment and action. Decolonization requires an "overturning of the institutions and systems that continue to subjugate and exploit Indigenous Peoples and our resources;" and this "must occur at the individual, collective and structural level" (Wilson, 2005, p. 192). This can happen individually, through a decolonization of the mind,collectively, through collaborations and education,and structurally, through the dismantling of institutional practices which refuse to acknowledge a decolonizing framework that must promote freedom and liberation for all.

After examining decolonizing theory through an Indigenous or American Indian lens, recognizing our own positionality, one as an enrolled tribal member and one as a multi-heritage Indigenous researcher, and the critical theories such as postcolonial, U.S. Third World Feminism, and Critical Race Theory, that inform a decolonizing theory, we have identified five key concepts relevant to teacher and student education for Indigenous populations. First, decolonizing theory can be defined in terms of the "cultural decentering of the [European] centered world system" (Bhabha, 1996). Second, it is a vehicle toward empowerment with the purpose of the cultural decentering of dominant paradigms of knowledge, which is the Western standard that is at the center of our U.S. public schools. Mohanty (2003) writes, "decolonization involves profound transformations of self, community, and governance structures. It is a historical and collective process" (p. 7). Therefore a decolonizing theoretical framework in education values the voices of the students' Indigenous backgrounds as bases of knowledge, making it imperative to collaborate and understand the common threads of oppression and strength that bind us.

Third, decolonizing theory is defined through internal neocolonialism. According to Tejeda et al. (2002), the oppression of colonized people in the United States must be seen differently today than it was in the 17th, 18th and 19th centuries. Forms of exploitation, domination, and oppression exist in government practices including school policies, which have colonized people of color in the 20th and 21st centuries. The ultimate goal is to move the issues of working class Indigenous people to the center and refuse to develop them into model oppressors; rather the goal is to create a collaborative space through social justice that honors the "integrity of the indigenous mind/body [as] the standard by which we measure the success of any decolonizing pedagogy" (Tejeda et al., 2002, p. 37).

The fourth key concept in the definition of a decolonizing theory informs the methodology of analysis in research. That is, storytelling—in all of its manifestations—has surfaced as an Indigenous or cultural way of knowing and expressing experiences and struggles, placing the voices of those most deeply affected by neocolonialism at the forefront. Finally, decolonizing theory is defined as dynamic, "as one goes through the phases of rediscovery and recovery, then mourning, next dreaming; it is at times helpful or even necessary to return to rediscovery and recovery to aid in the dreaming" (Laenui, 2000, p. 159). A decolonizing theory is not linear, but changes and accommodates the needs of the people who define it. Because our work with the Niigaane school and community is framed by the definition described, decolonizing theory is put into action through the research methodology, suggestions for praxis, analysis, and the overall thinking and writing of this document. Decolonizing theory is not simply an arm of postcolonial theory; instead it is based on critical mindfulness of the effects of colonialism of the past and the neocolonialism of today. It represents the conscious refusal of domination and power and the everyday resistance of these forces, particularly through sociopolitical and historical existences. It is a weighted history that cannot be forgotten or mistaken as no longer existing. It is a chance to reclaim the vision of a more equitable society where the possibilities of critical consciousness, sovereignty, self-determination, and freedom are possible.

THE CURRENT STATE AND FUTURE OF AMERICAN INDIAN EDUCATION AND RESEARCH

Through our partnership with CILCBE, NIEA, and the ongoing legacy of Dr. William G. Demmert, Jr.'s life work, we must situate our own activism and research in the current context of Native education. Many of the members of the CILCBE, including Leslie, have actively engaged in policy work in an effort to honor Indigenous languages and cultures and fulfill their essential place in Native education. In this section, we offer a brief overview highlighting Indigenous scholars and education agency recommendations regarding improved policy and practice for American Indian Education (Brayboy & Castagno, 2009; U.S. Department of Education, 2011; National Educational Association, 2011; Banks-Joseph et al., 2008). Brayboy and Castagno's (2009) review of the literature and current analysis of data on U.S. Indigenous youth suggest that community and culture-based education "best meet the educational needs of Indigenous children" (p. 31). They offer six recommendations (not an exhaustive list) for improved practice and policy through culturally responsive schooling. Brayboy and Castagno (2009, p. 49) recommend that (1) curricular materials be both relevant to and reflective of student's lives; (2) educators attend to how colonization, racism and power matter in educational settings, and work toward ways to help teachers understand and act as agents for greater social change and educational equity for Native students; (3) federal and state policies on education be consistent with treaties, tribal sovereignty and greater educational equity; (4) funding formulae enable communities, schools and teachers to enhance student opportunities and achievement; (5) assessments respond to locally and culturally developed standards; and (6) more Indigenous teachers be recruited, retained, and employed through collaborations among universities, tribal colleges, school districts and Native communities.

In 2009, President Obama initiated the first tribal consultations on education in U.S. History (U.S. Department of Education, 2011). Tribal leaders, community members, educators, and students testified to the inequities and challenges faced by U.S. Indigenous youth within the system of education. As a result of six official consultations, Native communities urged the department of education to (1) ameliorate the "failure of the education system to fulfill historic trust responsibility" (p. 6); (2) honor "more tribal control over education" (p. 8); (3) adhere to "regular, meaningful, and ongoing" government-to-government consultation (p. 10); (4) mandate greater tribal input on what would constitute appropriate standards, assessments, and curricula (p. 11); (5) improve the disconnection between federal, state and local governments as it pertains to Native education; (6) address the concerns for a lack of overarching education authority and, therefore, a lack of accountability; (7) provide adequate funding for notable deficiencies including lack of direct funding to tribes, lack of tribal grant writing capacity, subpar facilities and transportation, and inadequate instructional materials and lack of access to technology; (8) "Stress the need to recruit and retain highly effective teachers and leaders" (p. 28); (9) effectively collect and analyze student data; (10) provide comprehensive student supports to "address issues of poverty if future generations of American Indian students are to break the cycle of limited economic opportunity" (p. 34) and provide for a seamless cradle-to-career pipeline—from early childhood education to higher education.

Indigenous research (Brayboy & Castagno, 2009) and testimony (U.S. Department of Education, 2011) clearly outline Indigenous concerns and opportunities for change. Similarly, the National Indian Education Association (NIEA) has prioritized key provisions in the reauthorization of the Elementary and Secondary Education Act (ESEA). The ESEA expired in 2007. The 112th Congress has indicated its plans to advance ESEA reauthorization legislation and President Obama has stated that education reform is a top priority. The NIEA urges that ESEA "preserve and revitalize Native languages, strengthen Native participation in education, provide adequate resources to Native teachers, increase access to Native student records, encourage Tribal/State partnerships, and ensure parity for Native schools" (National Indian Education Association, 2013). Higher education also has an important role in preparing educators to implement new education legislation (see Leary, Chapter 7, this volume).

Educators interested in decolonizing mainstream education settings or Native schools have a multitude of Indigenous research to draw on; for instance, in Washington State a group of Indigenous educators wrote a comprehensive study of the local American Indian achievement gap (or opportunity gap). They outlined five recommendations including (1) a paradigm shift from test scores only to including relationship building; (2) provision of resources for pre- and in-service educators and stakeholders; (3) improved data collection and reporting and their applications; (4) development of partnerships with the NEA and other national groups concerned with education to improve their awareness of Native students' needs, and (5) increased state support and collaboration (Banks-Joseph et al., 2008). Accumulating evidence provides seeds of hope, as is demonstrated in the information reported in this volume on Washington State (HB 1495, see Chapter 6 by Hurtado; the WA Sovereignty curriculum, see Chapter 3 by Brown; and Wisconsin's Act 31, Chapter 7 by Leary, all in this volume).

As suggested in the Washington State Achievement Gap Study, *From Where the Sun Rises*, ally agencies, such as the National Education Association (NEA, 2011), provide educators with suggestions for what teachers and policy makers can do to support Native education. Educators must understand that Native students maintain a unique legal status as citizens of sovereign nations due to treaties signed with the U.S. government in exchange for vast tracts of aboriginal land. The education of Native children, who comprise over one percent of the U.S. student population, is a federal obligation and reflects this complex and multilayered relationship. While organizations work to improve the education of Native students nationally, concerned educators must take steps at the school and district levels to re-center Indigenous languages, culture, and knowledge. Ultimately, the paradigm shift toward relationship building will lead to collective actions of communities and allies for decolonization, self-determination and social justice.

NOTES

1. Acknowledgement: We write in recognition of the late Dr. William G. Demmert, Jr. who urged us to build relationships of learning through our languages and culture, to research, and to create and support policies for the healing and well-being of Indigenous communities. We write also to honor Denny Hurtado who consistently reminds us that "everything we do with our lives is about relationships" (see Hurtado, Chapter 6 in this volume).
2. Over time the CILCBE partnership has included these schools and institutional partners: 'Aha Pūnana Leo and Ke Kula 'o Nāwahīokalani'ōpu'u in Hilo, Hawai'i; Lower Kuskokwim School District (LKSD) in Bethel, Alaska; Tséhootsooí Diné Bi'ólta'in Window Rock, Arizona; Rough Rock Elementary School in Arizona; Niigaane Ojibwemowin Immersion Leech Lake, Minnesota; Piegan Institute, Inc., Three Rivers, Montana; Tulalip Elementary School, Marysville Washington; Education Northwest, Oregon; Kamehameha Schools, Hawaii; the Haskins Laboratories, Connecticut; Center for Research and Education, Diversity, and Excellence, U.C. Berkeley, California; Office of Superintendent of Public Instruction: Indian Education, State of Washington; and Western Washington University, Bellingham, Washington.

REFERENCES

American Council on Education. (2002). Nineteenth annual report on the status of minorities in higher education. Washington, D.C.: American Council on Education.

Archibald, J. (2008). *Indigenous storywork: Educating the heart, mind, body, and spirit.* Vancouver, BC: UBC Press.

Banks-Joseph, S.R., Inglebret, E., Sievers, J., Bruna, L., Galaviz, S., Anderson, A., Egan, E., Brownfield, S., Lockhart, M., & Grogan, G. (2008). *From Where the Sun Rises: Addressing the educational achievement of Native Americans in Washington state.* Clearing House on Native Teaching and Learning. Retrieved from http://www.goia. wa.gov/links-resources/nativeamericanachievementreport.pdf

Battiste, M. (2013). *Decolonizing education: Nourishing the learning spirit.* Saskatoon, Canada: Purich Publishing Ltd.

Battiste, M. & Henderson, J.Y. (2000). *Protecting Indigenous knowledge and heritage.* Saskatoon, Canada: Purich Publishing Ltd.

Beaulieu, D. (2011). The education policy work of William Demmert, Jr. *Journal of American Indian Education, 50*(1), 7–31.

Bhabha, H. K. (1996). Culture's in-between. In S. Hall & P. du Gay (Eds.) *Questions of cultural identity* (pp. 53–60). London: Sage Publications.

Brayboy, B.M.J. (2005). Toward a tribal critical race theory in education. *The Urban Review, 37*(5), 425–446.

Brayboy, B.M.J. & Castagno, A.E. (2009). Self-determination through self-education: Culturally responsive schooling for Indigenous students in the USA. *Teaching Education, 20*(1), 31–53.

Demmert, W.G., Jr. (2001). *Improving academic performance among Native American students: A review of the research literature.* Retrieved from ERIC database. (ED463917).

Demmert, W.G., Jr. (2008). *Indigenous culture-based education rubrics training manual.* Bellingham, WA: Western Washington University.

Demmert, W.G., Jr., & Towner, J.C. (2003). *A review of the research literature on the influences of culturally based education on the academic performance of Native American students: Final paper* (Rev. Ed.). Retrieved from Education Northwest website: http://educationnorthwest.org/webfm_send/196

Executive Order No. 13096. (1999) American Indian and Alaska Native Education. October 7, 1999. Vol. 64, Number 194. Pp. 54622–54624. Federal Register.

Grande, S. (2004). *Red pedagogy: Native American social and political thought.* Lanham, MD: Rowman & Littlefield Publishing Group, Inc.

Ladson-Billings, G. (1998). Just what is critical race theory and what's it doing in a nice field like education? *Qualitative Studies in Education, 11*(1), 7–24.

Laenui, P. (2000). Processes of decolonization. In Marie Battiste (Ed.) *Reclaiming Indigenous voice and vision* (pp. 150–160). Vancouver: UBC Press.

McCardle, P. & Demmert, W. (2006). Introduction: Improving academic performance among American Indian, Alaska Native and Native Hawaiian students. *Journal of American Indian Education, 45*(3), 1–4.

Mishuah, D.A. (2003). *Indigenous American women: Decolonization, empowerment, activism.* Lincoln: University of Nebraska Press.

Mishuah, D. & Wilson, A.C. (2004) *Indigenizing the academy: Transforming scholarship and empowering communities.* Lincoln: University of Nebraska Press.

Mohanty, C.T. (2003). *Feminism without borders: Decolonizing theory, practicing solidarity.* London: Duke University Press.

National Education Association. (2011). American Indians and Alaska Natives: Charting a new course for Native education. Retrieved from: http://www.nea. org/assets/docs/AIAnfocus2010–2011.pdf

National Indian Education Association. (2013). Standing for high quality Native education: Policy agenda. Washington, D.C.: NIEA. Retrieved from http://niea. org/data/files/policy/briefingbook2013_mobile.pdf

Rawlins, N., Wilson, W.P., & Kawai'ae'a, K. (2011). Bill Demmert, Native American language revitalization, and his Hawai'i connection. *Journal of American Indian Education, 50*(1), 74–85.

Regional Educational Laboratories. (2013). *Culturally based education for Indigenous language and culture: A national forum to establish priorities for future research* (Proceedings). REL Central, Northwest, and Pacific.

Smith, L.T. (2012). *Decolonizing methodologies: Research and indigenous peoples* (2nd ed.). New York: Zed Books.

Tejeda, C., Espinoza, M. & Gutierrez, K. (2002). Toward a decolonizing pedagogy: Social justice reconsidered. In P.P. Trifonas (Ed.*) Pedagogies of difference: Rethinking education for social change.* Pp. 10–40. New York: Routledge.

Tejeda, C. & Gutierrez, K. (2006). Fighting the backlash: Decolonizing perspectives and pedagogies in neocolonial times. In Pedro Pedraza & Melissa Rivera (Eds.) *Latino Education: An agenda for community action research* (pp. 257–290). Mahwah, NJ: Lawrence Erlbaum Associates.

Treuer, A. (2010). *Ojibwe in Minnesota.* St. Paul: MHS Press.

United Nations. (n.d.). Who are indigenous peoples? Indigenous Peoples, Indigenous voices fact sheet. United Nations permanent forum on Indigenous issues. Retrieved from: http://www.un.org/esa/socdev/unpfii/documents/5session_factsheet1.pdf

U.S. Department of Education, Office of Elementary and Secondary Education, Office of Indian Education, White House Initiative on Tribal Colleges and Universities. (2011). Tribal leaders speak: The state of American Indian education, 2010; Report of the Consultations With Tribal Leaders in Indian Country. Washington, D.C.

Vizenor, G. (1994). *Manifest manners: Narratives on postindian survivance.* Lincoln: University of Nebraska Press.

Wilson, A.C., & Bird, M.Y. (2005). *For indigenous eyes only: A decolonization handbook.* Santa Fe: School of American Research.

Wilson, W.A. (2005). *Remember this! Dakota decolonization and the Eli Taylor narratives.* Lincoln: University of Nebraska Press.

Figure 0.3 Since Time Immemorial: Tribal Sovereignty in Washington State Curriculum, logo representing the collaboration of the 29 Tribes.

6 A Model for 21st-Century Indian Education
A Story of State, School, and Community Collaboration

Denny Sparr Hurtado (TacH mi acH t3n),
as told to Peggy McCardle & Virginia Berninger[1]

HOW DID THE STATE OF WASHINGTON BECOME A MODEL FOR AMERICAN INDIAN EDUCATION?

I feel that that the Creator works in strange ways and that for some reason I was destined to be a part of this movement. I also acknowledge that everything we do in life is based on the relationships we have with Mother Earth, Father Sky, Trees, Plants, Animals and humans. I also want to acknowledge all our ancestors, because if it wasn't for their wisdom and bravery, we probably wouldn't be where we are today. To be honest, I think all the stars were aligned for this to happen between the tribes and the state.

Once I started working for the Office of Native Education (ONE) within the Office of the Superintendent of Public Instruction (OSPI), I was half-time Title I and half-time Indian Education, which really made it hard to focus just on Indian Education; however, we managed to continue to support the tribes, tribal education organizations, and students as much as we could. Our annual operating budget for the office was only $25,000 a year, but I was very fortunate to have one of the most dedicated people at OSPI to be my assistant: Joan Banker. We made a great team. I also had a boss who gave us the freedom to do the work at hand, and without her support it would have been difficult. I had good relationships with tribal leaders, state leaders, and the community. Those relationships were instrumental in getting the work done that had to get done. I was the director of the Upward Bound Program at the Evergreen State College, working on college readiness for first generation low-income students.

I was leaving Evergreen to go to work full time at OSPI. A week or two before I left, they moved me out of my office to move this lady, Dr. Magda Costantino, in there. But she didn't want to step on any toes or cause any trouble. One day I was leaving work, and I went out to the parking lot and there was this lady looking at me. She was all upset, apologizing. She had come to me earlier, saying, "I didn't really want to take your office. This wasn't my idea." I told her it was okay, I was checking out of here anyway.

So here she was in the parking lot, and she was actually apologizing to me and crying, and I was thinking "Who is this lady?" From that point, seeing her approach me like that, it showed me that she had a good heart. And at that point in time we started our relationship.

So I went off to ONE to start my new job, and Magda started her new job at Evergreen State College. Every so often I would go back, to visit people at Evergreen, and to see how Magda was doing. She had been doing some work for OSPI on bilingual migrant children and reading. She had just finished this report on bilingual migrant education. And I'm always thinking about how to make things better for Native students in school. So I looked at Magda's report on migrant kids and said that it would be great to do a report like that, but just for Native students. Magda said "Well guess what, Denny, I have ten thousand dollars left", and she used that to get this report underway. So she and I collaborated on this report, "Reading and the Native American Learner" (Bergeson & Hurtado, 2000). We needed to look at what the issues were. We were looking at the reading results for native kids, and they were dismal; our students were always in the bottom two quartiles for state testing. That report identified low reading levels as a key problem, based on cultural discontinuity, cultural differences, and underdeveloped communication skills (small vocabulary, 2000–5000 word vocabulary) (Chernoff, Flanagan, McPhee, & Park, 2007; Demmert, Grissmer, & Towner, 2000). For example, Native students had on average about 2500 word vocabularies by the time they got to kindergarten, and the non-Native middle-class kids had about 15–20,000 words. We know that reading is critical for students to succeed in our literate society. We know that prisons predict the number of beds they will need in the future by looking at the number of students not meeting grade level expectations in reading during 3rd grade. *Wow*, if we know this, then why don't we (the state, the nation) insure that all students know how to read by 3rd grade?

So, we asked the question, what do we do now that we know what the data show? We decided to develop some culturally responsive reading curricula for grades K–3. Magda was working at Evergreen State College and I was at OSPI/ONE. This is where our true partnership and collaboration began. We knew it would be labor intensive and expensive. We started looking for grants, and we found that the state Higher Education Coordinating Board was offering a grant focused on high school and college readiness, but we wanted to focus on younger students—kindergarten, 1st and 2nd grade. We said, well let's apply anyway, so we did. And lo and behold, we got funded, for $86,000. We used that money to start development of our Northwest Native American Reading Curriculum. This was the beginning of our journey with the State Department of Education (OSPI) focusing on curriculum and the needs of Native students, teachers, administrators, and communities. Our model was very inclusive of the tribes, tribal educators, and students. This is the model we also used for the development of the statewide curriculum: *Since Time Immemorial: Tribal Sovereignty in Washington State.*

WHY WAS LEGISLATION IMPORTANT
TO THIS EDUCATION EFFORT?

I knew the politics in Washington State. I knew that we needed legislative support for the curriculum to gain any traction. I met with the State Superintendent and talked about the importance of tribal involvement in the education of our students. The tribes were getting heavily involved in education issues in the state legislature. In 2003 OSPI and the Governor's Office Indian Affairs (GOIA) collaborated to co-host the first ever Washington State Tribal Education Summit, between the 29 Tribes and the State of Washington. This two day summit was a meeting among the powers that be: the tribal leaders, Governor Gary Locke, and State Superintendent Dr. Terry Bergeson. Many other educators and community members also attended.

The first day tribal leaders had a dialog with the governor, and then the second day tribal leaders had a dialog with the State Superintendent. The tribes explained to both of them that what they wanted was to work closely with the state and their local schools to develop curricula around our Indian history, language, and government. John McCoy, a Tulalip tribal member, had just been elected to the state House of Representatives in 2002; McCoy attended the summit and heard the tribes' concerns loud and clear. So in 2004, Representative John McCoy tried to get a bill passed to ensure that such a curriculum would be developed and implemented. The language in the bill talks about this. (See Table 6.1.) That first year, we were learning; didn't have our ducks in a line, and the bill didn't make it. But in 2005 we knew what to do. We had our team together, and we brought pressure on all the right players in the state—the governor, the State Department of Education, the Washington

Table 6.1   Excerpt from Substitute House Bill 1495 (Chapter 205, Laws of 2005)

It is the intent of the legislature to promote the full success of the Centennial Accord. . . . [which] will require "educating the citizens of our state, particularly the youth who are our future leaders, about tribal history, culture, treaty rights, contemporary tribal and state government institutions and relations and the contributions of Indian nations to the state of Washington." The legislature recognized that this goal has yet to be achieved . . . As a result, Indian students may not find the school curriculum, especially Washington state history curriculum, relevant to their lives or experiences. In addition, many students may remain uninformed about the experiences, contributions, and perspectives of their tribal neighbors, fellow citizens, and classmates. . . . Further . . . the lack of accurate and complete curricula may contribute to the persistent achievement gap between Indian and other students. . . . [T]here is a need to establish collaborative government-to-government relationships between elected school boards and tribal councils to create local and/or regional curricula about tribal history and culture, and to promote dialogue and cultural exchanges that can help tribal leaders and school leaders implement strategies to close the achievement gap.

Education Association, Washington State School Directors Association (WSSDA), and the State Board of Education. We had had tribal leaders, elders, students, parents, teachers, administrators and community members testify to help ensure passage. The education committee unanimously voted to approve passage of the bill. We were all elated and everyone thought it would pass without any changes.

So we had done all this, and then we waited to hear what the final committee's decision was. Then Ross Hunter, State Representative, came out and told us that some committee members couldn't agree to pass the bill because of one word. That word was "shall". The bill said the state "shall" work with the tribes—that one word, "shall", was holding up passage. Some members of the legislature wanted to change "shall" to "encourage" so it would say in section 4, "Each school district board of directors is *encouraged* (emphasis added) to incorporate curricula about the history, culture, and government of the nearest federally recognized tribe or tribes so that students learn about the unique heritage and experience of their closest neighbor," and in section 2, "the Washington State School Directors' Association *is encouraged* to convene regional meetings and invite the tribal councils from the region for the purpose of establishing government-to-government relationships and dialog between tribal councils and school district boards of directors." That would be the wording. But the tribal leaders had been really adamant about that "shall". And McCoy was looking at me, and he said "Denny, do you think we should do this?" And I thought about it for a minute, and I thought, yeah, we should do this, it was now or next year.

I knew there would be some flak, but we could explain and I felt like we could convince them this was the right thing. For the state legislature to at least say "encourage" I figured we would have a foot in the door. I was the only one standing there with John McCoy, waiting to hear what was happening when the bill was discussed. But I knew Washington State is a "local control" state, so the state Department of Education can't dictate to the schools what curricula they can use anyway. So we agreed to the change. They voted, and Substitute House Bill 1495 passed! That's where I understood that we had to do something to help students in the state of Washington, not just our Native students, but *all* students, to understand who we are and to learn about our sovereign Indian nations.

The passage of this bill, its implementation, and the overall work of everyone concerned about Indian education in the state of Washington, stand as a model of how to make an education system work; the tribes still hold annual meetings: OSPI, WSSDA, and tribal leaders hold a summit with the University of Washington president and trustees, and agree to work together and maintain a collaboration to support better education for Native students and to help all students in the state learn about

Native history, culture and government. (See, for example, the WSSDA/ TLC, 2012, progress report.)

That same year, 2005, the Tribal Leaders Congress on Education (TLC) made up of tribal leaders or delegates, who met monthly to talk about education, convened a special meeting of those who had played a major role in getting the legislation written and passed. They wanted to follow up and make sure that there was some action after this legislation, so that work on a curriculum would really happen. So with Representative McCoy they drafted a memorandum of understanding (MOU), to ensure that the policy would be followed. And then finally the 29 Tribes, OSPI, WSSDA, and the State Board of Education, all signed an MOU that they would work toward a curriculum on tribal sovereignty.

BUILDING BRIDGES AND DEVELOPING CURRICULA

Being a tribal Chairman for the Skokomish Tribe and having spent 17 years on a tribal council really helped me when I started working for OSPI/ONE. Already having good working relationships with many of the tribal leaders in the state gave me an advantage when meeting with them. Trust is a major issue with tribes; once you can gain their trust, then it is easier to work with the tribes and tribal people. It wasn't hard for me to go to them. So our office made a concerted effort to reach out to the tribes, educators, community members, and universities. One important factor in working with tribes is that you must involve them in the process from the beginning. Once they are vested in the process, then good work begins. This is also true in working with state staff. As I said earlier, *relationships, relationships, relationships—* this is so important in the work we do with Indian Education. The work was beginning on finding ways to implement the new law into the schools system in Washington State. This whole effort took the work of many people from the tribes and the state, and without this collaborative effort this project would have never happened. It truly was a great partnership.

Encounters—A History Curriculum

One curriculum, the Encounters curriculum, had already been developed for the Puyallup Tribe by an anthropologist named Llyn De Danaan (De Danaan, 2000). (See Table 6.2 for information on the three curricula discussed here.) Llyn was not satisfied with how Native history was being taught in Washington state classrooms, and began conversations with Magda and me. After reviewing the curricular materials currently available from the OSPI, Llyn proposed the development of a new one, to include critical thinking and authentic documents. I liked the Encounters curriculum, and asked her to develop a unit on the Point No Point Treaty. She did, and that one is now incorporated into the sovereignty curriculum.

Table 6.2   Native American Curricula Developed in Washington State

Since Time Immemorial: The Sovereignty Curriculum
http://www.indian-ed.org/

Seeks to build lasting educational partnerships between school districts and their
local tribes via elementary, middle, and high school curriculum on tribal sovereignty. The web site has tutorials for teachers, links to outside resources, videos,
a tribal directory and map, and other information. While it covers national level
(federal) treaties and legislation, it is set up in units for which local tribal information can be inserted.

Northwest Native American Reading Curriculum
http://www.evergreen.edu/k12outreach/ecei.htm[1]

A research-based, culturally-relevant supplemental reading curriculum for students
k-2, providing opportunities for students to read and write stories about their
own cultural heritage. While written for instruction in English, some communities
are translating the accompanying texts into tribal languages.

Encounters: Models for an Integrated Approach to Early Washington Territorial
and State History
http://www.evergreen.edu/k12outreach/ecei.htm[1]

A history curriculum originally developed for the Puyallup Tribe. The ideas and model
lessons address encounters between Native peoples and explorers-turned-colonists
in the context of social justice, politics and values of self and community and is
intended for use in humanities courses. It is meant to be integrated with studies of
geography, map reading, and the history of the western movement in the US.

Note: [1] The web link gives information on how to obtain the curriculum, which is not presented
in full on the internet.

Northwest Native American Reading Curriculum

Once our research report, "Reading and the Native Learner" (Hurtado &
Bergeson, 2000) had been completed, we concluded that we would focus on
developing a culturally relevant reading curriculum. This took several years
of development and implementation. Magda and I knew that one of most
important things we had found in reviewing the reading research was that
there were very few accurate books about tribes in Washington, especially in
literature for grades K–3. There was a little bit about other tribes, but very
little on the 29 tribes in Washington State. We commissioned several Native
authors and illustrators to write 21 books specifically for our curriculum.

The curriculum is based on research about Indian education as well as research on reading and culturally based education practices (e.g., Banks, 1997; Butterfield & Pepper, 1992; Carrell, 1983a, 1983b; Demmert & Towner, 2003). It addresses the legacies of boarding schools and the trauma suffered by Native students when removed from their homes in the name of education. The curriculum employs principles of practice that are sensitive to the cultures and traditions of the tribes of the Pacific Northwest, but sets a model for the development of reading materials produced by tribal members, and emphasizes the involvement of tribal members, elders, family and community. The curriculum is based on three thematic units: Hunting and Gathering, Canoes, and the Drum. To fulfill the commitment to using authentic documents, and to offer this as a model for others, Magda and I described the development, what it's based on, and the content of the curriculum in an article in the *Journal of American Indian Education* (Costantino & Hurtado, 2006).

Once the reading curriculum was completed, we pilot tested it with several schools in the state. One school, Wolfle Elementary, pilot tested it with their low level reading students. Half were Native students, half non-Native. The curriculum required the teachers to bring Native community members in to help with implementation of the curriculum, specifically the units on the Canoe. In our trainings, we always stress the importance of closely working and collaborating with the tribe, tribal community, or Indian education programs. For instance, if it was a unit on the canoe, teachers would ask their students if they knew of any canoe makers or carvers. This actually occurred. A teacher asked, "Does anyone know a canoe carver in the community?" One student said, "My grandfather is a canoe carver" so the teacher asked if the student would ask if his grandfather could come into the class and talk about the canoe. The grandfather agreed and so a relationship between the tribal community, the tribe, and the school was strengthened. This increased the community involvement and interest. It made for strong relationships and better scores for the kids. And it became pretty clear that the increased parental and community involvement was working. That was important. If the teachers using the curriculum don't understand that it has to connect to language, culture, and government *of the community they work in,* then there is a huge disconnect; family and community involvement is crucial. We have to be part of what's going on. With the success of that pilot, we were on the way to finalizing the Northwest Native American Reading Curriculum (NWNARC) and moving to implement it in more schools, and training teachers how to use it effectively.

You know, you give a good, culturally responsive curriculum to the teachers on a silver platter: the curriculum, the training and how to implement it, all for free. Some teachers just don't believe that culturally responsive curriculum and teaching are important. Teachers are forced to focus on the state tests. Social studies classes are not seen as that important. And if they don't care about who we are and what we're saying, if they just don't care, then we disengage. This is very important to our tribes and tribal communities because it's about who we are, our culture, language, history and government, and if they don't care about that, then our students, as well as all students, suffer. Schools look at their data on Native American students and wonder, what could they do better to help our students? Well, they could partner with their local tribes, they could implement more culturally responsive curricula in their schools, or they could continue to do what they have been doing for a hundred years, which does not work for our students. Our curriculum is based on solid research and tribal involvement.

Since Time Immemorial: Tribal Sovereignty in Washington State Curriculum

After the first tribal summit on education, it was clear what the tribes wanted: curricula about their own tribal nations. I knew that tribes were putting pressure on OSPI to start the development of a sovereignty curriculum for the State of Washington and at the signing of the MOU for HB1495, Dr. Terry Bergeson publicly made the commitment to develop a sovereignty curriculum. A year later we received $20,000 to start the process of developing one.

We knew the first thing we had to do was find someone to write the curriculum! Several years earlier I had had a call from a Native teacher wanting to get more involved with Indian education. I am a firm believer that we need to get more of our people involved in all aspects of education, especially these statewide education committees. This is where the action starts. So I recommended this young woman, Shana Brown (Yakama), a social studies teacher, to be on one of the state committees. This is how our relationship began. Through the years she has participated in many of the state committees, and has seen the curriculum developed for the *Seattle Times*. (She had partnered with the *Seattle Times* to develop a Native curriculum to be used statewide, which the *Times* published during November, Native American month). So I gave her a call and asked her if she was interested. She said she would discuss it with her family and get back to me. Not knowing what she/we were getting into, she called back and said yes.

Knowing the importance of always involving people, we formed the Tribal/State Sovereignty Committee. First, we established a larger group, a Tribal Sovereignty Advisory Committee, to ensure that this effort was a full, true partnership between the Washington tribes and the state; the committee was therefore half Native and half non-Native, and it was a mixed group in terms of expertise and knowledge, including attorneys, educators, elders, professors, educational organizations, tribal leaders, community members, etc. We wanted it to be clear that this was a true collaboration between the tribes and the state, and not an Indian-only thing. This group helped guide us through this journey we were taking. We originally planned one unit.

At the first meeting, there was a lot of talking about expectations and what the group wanted to do. At the very next meeting, they rolled up their sleeves and started writing. The flip chart sheets covered every wall; there was too much information, too many ideas. Tribal sovereignty is a hard concept. So we regrouped, wrote it all down, and Shana Brown became very ambitious. We were not paying her very much, but she was really working hard. She wrote a curriculum unit for social studies, one for world history, and one for world contemporary problems. We needed more money for them to keep working on this curriculum. What little money we had was running out, so I decided I would try and approach all the tribes to ask for financial support to help continue the sovereignty project. I decided I would first start with the tribes I had a good working relationship with. The first tribe I approached was the Muckleshoot tribe. The Chairwoman of the tribe had formerly been in Indian education for 40 years. I knew she supported Indian education 100%. I made a presentation to the tribal council asking for $20,000. Later that week we got a call from the chair saying they would give us $40,000. Wow! This was really a major stepping-stone for us. Now we could breathe a little deeper.

Then Shana suggested that we put the curriculum online, so that more people could access and use it more easily. Now we had the money to continue to pay Shana and hire a web designer. We hired a Native businessman, James Parker, to work with us. Always full of energy for the project, Shana next wanted to do more units. More people, more money. So we hired two more teachers to help us finalize all our units: Elese Washines, Yakama Nation Tribal School, and Jerry Price, a social studies teacher from the Yelm school district. Both of these teachers were also on our Tribal Sovereignty Curriculum Committee. These were the three core curriculum writers who developed all 23 units for the curriculum.

They called the curriculum *Since Time Immemorial* (STI): *Tribal Sovereignty in Washington State*, a web-based curriculum. Once it was completed, we decided to pilot test the curriculum. In 2009 we selected 14 schools to invite; we met with these schools and they all agreed to be part of the pilot. All schools participated in on-going training that we provided them on the curriculum. In 2010 we received a Gates Foundation grant to further develop STI. We focused on the feedback that we received from 14 pilots, for the continued development, and then continued pilots with four of the original pilot schools. Each school received $10,000 for planning and implementing the curriculum. As part of this, we developed a Trainer of Trainers model and trained teachers to be trainers of the curriculum. We have trained 600 or more teachers already.

The last component was that we aligned our curriculum with the Common Core State Standards (CCSS) (National Governors Association Center for Best Practices & Council of Chief State School Officers, 2010). Our curriculum is the first curriculum in the state to be aligned with common core standards. The Gates Foundation was adamant about the CCSS, and said they'd add $10,000 for us to align the curriculum to these standards. So we did. It was a tedious task, but the Title I staff and lots of people at the pilot schools helped. (See STI pilot project report, Office of Native Education, 2012). We learned a lot from the pilot studies, and it was clear that we needed technical support. Shana suggested we put the material on a wiki, to store a lot of information and let teachers share. We did that. There were issues of software compatibility, so it didn't work. Then we tried navigating through a MOODLE, and that didn't work, so we just put everything in our own dedicated server, and it is currently working well. After years of planning, development, and training, the curriculum has been implemented and used by many schools throughout the Pacific Northwest. The curriculum is now available on the web (http://www.indian-ed.org). It's set up for use not only in Washington state, but anywhere—tribes can insert their own local treaty information, policies, and cultural traditions within the overall modular curriculum framework.

IMPLEMENTATION OF HOUSE BILL 1495 AND THE CURRICULA

For success with our Native curricula, both awareness and training are critical to their implementation. They depend very much on community involvement, because Native culture is inclusive rather than individual. There are two videos that are part of the implementation of House Bill 1495, to educate students about our sovereignty and our history, culture and language. One, *A Shared History: The Story of HB 1495* (Longhouse Media, 2007), provides information about the bill itself and its passage, as well as why it's important for both Native and non-Native students to learn about Indian history in their state. The second, *The Northwest Native American Youth Leadership Summit: A Tribal Model* (Hurtado, 2008) shows how the tribal community works to develop leadership using education and experience. The video shows very well the importance for high school students of learning about their culture, their treaties and tribal governance, and leadership within a supportive group setting. We use youth from previous summits to help with the next one, and the students learn about tribal history and sovereignty.

Northwest Native American Literacy Curriculum

For the reading curriculum, ongoing training is offered to teachers, because we want them to use it. For example, the Office of Native Education asked Magda to come and introduce the NWNARC at the 2012 Washington State Indian Education Association meeting; she introduced it, discussed the research that has been done on it, what the curriculum is about, what it's intended to do, and why we chose the approach we did. At the same meeting, Linda Middlebrook, who has used the curriculum from the beginning, held a major session to tell teachers how she uses the curriculum to develop community involvement, one of the most important aspects of the curriculum. She explained that she has gone from almost no interaction between school and community to having nearly the entire tribe involved. As part of preparation for delivering this curriculum, teachers are also asked to read the research report, Reading and the Native American Learner (Bergeson & Hurtado, 2000), and to view the CD ROM that accompanies the curriculum (Costantino & Hurtado, 2002), which includes video clips and explanations for those using the curriculum.

Since Time Immemorial: The Sovereignty Curriculum

In using STI, a major part is professional development for teachers. What is emphasized in this professional development is that one of the most important things the teacher can do is to establish a good, firm relationship with the tribal community. Teachers should use whatever stories they have from the local community to implement the curriculum, to illustrate tribal sovereignty, using their own local tribes' court cases, history, language, and culture. The general definition of tribal sovereignty can be applicable nationally. Federal polices and court cases have had major impacts on tribes throughout history. For example, the Dawes Act of 1887 relates to all tribes. If they use this curriculum, we recommend that teachers use their own local tribes' stories and case law. There are federal issues as well, and the curriculum gives approaches to teaching and a framework. But talking about history and culture is local. Any Indigenous group could learn something from this curriculum, as it's really about telling our own history, and its being told by us.

WHY HAVE THESE EFFORTS WORKED?

Relationships, Relationships, Relationships!!! First it is always about the relationships we develop in our lives, and in our professions, and always about how we can make it better for our students and communities. Throughout the whole process, I had a vision to make this curriculum and education and learning better for ALL students in our state. I was asked by a friend, Julian Argel, to serve as chair of the Native American Advisory Board at the University of Washington (UW). I served on this board for many years. Because of my relationships with UW staff and students, we forged a partnership with the College of Education to better prepare teachers for our communities.

Teachers play a major role in the classrooms every day with our Native students. And we knew the teacher education programs in the state needed to be more responsive to the needs of our Native students; I met with them at the university, and spoke with them. I said, you need to rethink how you train your teachers, because you train them, and they come to the reservation; they mean well but just are not ready for what they will experience on the reservation. They have culture shock and don't last. In a few months they're gone. Then we have to start over again with new teachers. The same goes for administrators. They need more background, a better understanding of how these students learn, what our history is, how that history and our culture have shaped and continue to shape how we learn. And they responded. The university agreed to help develop the Indian Education certification efforts.

Now, at the University of Washington, the faculty has started development of a Certificate on Native Education. I met with the President of the University, the Dean of the College of Education, and other people at the university about the importance of this certificate. The plan is to use existing coursework that was already being taught at the university, with the exception of incorporating our STI curriculum into the Indian education course taught in the American Indian Studies Department, a 400 level course. This way we would not have to expend dollars for the development of specific curricula for the certification courses. There were classes already developed in many other departments at the university: anthropology, American Indian studies, and courses in the school of social work, the law school, etc. We offered the first class in 2012, and 30 educators participated in this on-line course. The feedback was very positive and plans are being made to further develop the certificate. Eventually, UW will offer a 15-credit, five-course certification program for Indian Education. The tribes are ready to hire teachers with these types of special certificates. The primary goal is to better prepare teachers, both Native but especially non-Native teachers on how to work with our students and communities.

Once again, relationships were key to making this idea become a reality. The University of Washington has finally broken ground for the new longhouse that is being built on campus. This has been a dream for many Natives and non-Natives in the Pacific Northwest, for the past 40 years. With the concerted effort of the Native American Advisory Board, we made it clear to the President of the college that the longhouse was a major priority of our Native community. Once the President understood the importance of this issue, he committed the UW staff to making this a reality. In October 2013, UW broke ground. This longhouse will be a gathering place for all students, but especially it will be a central meeting place for our Native students. It's a place where they will feel at home. Our children and youth don't like leaving home, and we need to support them in any way we can. They need to feel safe and connected. Having such a place will also help recruit Native students to the university. It's a place for Native students, Native research, Native academics to grow. It's a place to congregate, a place to showcase our history, culture, language and sovereignty.

And here is a great irony—the longhouse will stand in between the Lewis building and the Clark building on Stevens Street. Governor Stevens was the governor who negotiated the 10 Stevens Treaties in the Pacific Northwest in 1855–1856, and we all know who Lewis and Clark were. Now our students will learn true history of the Pacific Northwest!

NOTES

1. Authors' Note: This chapter is written in an oral storytelling style, as told by Denny Sparr Hurtado (TacH mi acH t3n), member of the Skokomish Indian Tribe, a resident of the Skokomish Reservation, and descendent of sPaX3 Headman/Chief of Hoodsport. He shared this information in an interview on July 25, 2013, and has edited the contents.

REFERENCES

Banks, J.A. (1997). Approaches to multicultural curriculum reform. In J.A. Banks & C. McGee Banks (Eds.) *Multicultural education: Issues and perspectives* (pp. 229–250). Needham Heights, MA: Allyn and Bacon.

Bergeson, T. & Hurtado, D. (2000). Reading and the Native American learner: Research Report. Prepared for the Indian Education Office, Office of Superintendent of Public Instruction, Seattle, WA. Available at http://www.evergreen.edu/k12outreach/docs/RdgNAlrner.pdf

Butterfield, R.A. & Pepper, F. (1992). Improving parental participation in elementary and secondary education for American Indian and Alaska Native students. In P. Cahape & C.B. Howley (Eds.) *Indian nations at risk: Listening to the people*. (Summaries of papers commissioned by the Indian Nations at Risk Task Force of the U.S. Department of Education) (pp. 47–53). (ERIC Document Reproduction Service No. ED 339 588).

Carrell, P.L. (1983a). Background knowledge in second language comprehension. *Language Learning and Communication*, 2(1), 25–34.

Carrell, P.L. (1983b). Three components of background knowledge in reading comprehension. *Language Learning*, 33(2): 183–207.

Chernoff, J.J., Flanagan, K.D., McPhee, C., & Park, J. (2007). *Preschool: First findings from the third follow-up of the Early Childhood Longitudinal Study, Birth Cohort (ECLS-B)*. Washington, D.C.: U.S. Department of Education, NCES 2008–025.

Costantino, M. & Hurtado, D. (2002). *Northwest Native American Reading Curriculum*. CD-ROM. Funded by the Higher Education Coordinating Board. Seattle, WA: Evergreen State College and the Office of Superintendent of Public Instruction.

Costantino, M. & Hurtado, D. (2006). Northwest Native American Reading Curriculum. *Journal of American Indian Education*, 45(2): 45–49.

Dawes Act of 1887. Also known as the General Allotment Act of Feb. 8, 1887 (24 Stat. 388, ch. 119, 25 USCA 331), Acts of Forty-ninth Congress-Second Session, 1887. Retrieved from http://digital.library.okstate.edu/kappler/vol1/html_files/ses0033.html

Demmert, W., Grissmer, D. & Towner, J.A. (2000). Review and analysis of the research on Native American students. *Journal of American Indian Education*, (45)3: 5–23.

Demmert, W. & Towner, J. (2003). *A review of the research literature on the influences of culturally based education on the academic performance of Native American students.* Portland, OR: Northwest Regional Educational Laboratory. Retrieved from http://educationnorthwest.org/webfm_send/196

Hurtado, D. (2008). *The Northwest Native American Youth Leadership Summit: A tribal model.* DVD. Seattle, WA: Office of Superintendent of Public Instruction.

Longhouse Media. (2007). *A shared history: The story of HB 1495.* Seattle, WA: Longhouse Media and the Office of Superintendent of Public Instruction.

National Governors Association Center for Best Practices & Council of Chief State School Officers (NGA/CCSSO). (2010). *Common core state standards for English language arts and literacy in history/social studies, science, and technical subjects.* Washington, D.C.: Authors.

Office of Native Education. (2012). Since Time Immemorial Curriculum pilot project: Office of Native Education Summary Report. 7/20/2012. Seattle, WA: State Department of Education, Office of Native Education.

Substitute House Bill 1495, Chapter 205, Laws of 2005, 59th Legislature, 2005 Regular Session, Seattle, WA. Tribal History—Common Schools. SHN 1495 has been codified as RCW 28A.345.070, RCW 28A. 320.170 and RCW 28A. 230.090.

WSSDA (Washington State School Directors' Association)/ TLC (Tribal Leaders Congress on Education representing Washington State Tribes). 2012. Teaching Washington State tribal history, culture, government and language: A progress report on SHB 1495 (Chapter 205, Laws of 2005). Author. Retrieved from http://www.wssda.org/Portals/0/Resources/Publications/HB1495%20-%20 Tribal%20Project%20Report-feb2012.pdf

7 The American Indian Studies Summer Institute
Professional Development for Culturally Responsive Teaching and Learning

J P Leary

Indian educators and their allies counted a significant victory on August 8, 1989 when Wisconsin Governor Tommy Thompson signed into law Senate Bill 31, the 1989—1991 Biennial Budget Act (Wisconsin Act 31, 1989), which included provisions creating new statutes related to instruction in the "history, culture, and tribal sovereignty of the federally recognized tribes and bands in the state". It was an important legislative victory because these new laws' specificity was unprecedented in Wisconsin, where traditions of local control of education and broad authority of locally elected school boards were points of pride.[1] This bill became known as 1989 Act 31 upon publication on August 20, 1989; and in Indian education circles, this remains the common name for the instructional requirements themselves. This chapter highlights the American Indian Studies Summer Institute (AISSI), an Act 31-focused professional development offering that embeds cultural responsiveness into the instructional design in order to expand opportunities for all students to receive accurate, authentic teachings about the eleven federally recognized tribes and bands in the state.

In the years since the passage of Act 31, there have been several important shifts in the policy landscape that have affected how educators and policy makers think about and implement its requirements. Initially, state policymakers sought to build greater public awareness of American Indian history, culture, and tribal sovereignty in order to address widespread public ignorance and violent protests over Ojibwe treaty rights. The policy focused on all students, and its goals were primarily social and long-term. By the late 1990s, as the state adopted standards-based reform, the Wisconsin Indian Education Association and others organized to ensure that this content would be included in the Model Academic Standards. As the No Child Left Behind Act (NCLB) Act of 2001 shifted national policy toward closing achievement gaps and high-stakes accountability measures, many schools serving large numbers of Native American students began to view Act 31 as a means to defend existing curricula against another wave of reforms. In many school districts, especially those struggling to close achievement gaps and reduce dis-proportionality in special education, Act 31 has become the basis for culturally responsive approaches intended to provide better educational experiences and outcomes for Native American students. Since 1997, the AISSI has been the premier tribal-state-university sponsored professional development program in Wisconsin.

Act 31 contained several provisions that sought to use the public schools to develop understanding of American Indian history, culture, tribal sovereignty, and related concerns. One provision required the State Superintendent to collaborate with the American Indian Language and Culture Education Board to develop appropriate instructional materials on the "Chippewa Indians' treaty-based, off reservation rights to hunt, fish and gather" by the end of the biennium (Wisc. Act 31, 1989, s.115). Other provisions, listed in Table 7.1, addressed broader issues related to race and human relations, and they required specific actions of Wisconsin school districts. The policy as designed was comprehensive and intended to address several aspects of student learning, but traditional school policies and practices can often be slow or resistant to change.

These requirements were essentially intended to address past education policy decisions that left the general public largely ignorant of historical, cultural, and legal aspects of contemporary tribal nations in Wisconsin. When the Seventh Circuit Court of Appeals ruled in 1983 that the Ojibwe people had retained the right to hunt, fish, and gather in an area roughly equivalent to the northern third of the state, the Voigt Decision caught

Table 7.1   Specific Requirements for Wisconsin School Districts, under Act 31 (Wisc. Act 31, 1989, s. 115-121)

- Develop a curriculum for grades 2-4 on the Chippewa Indians' treat-based, off reservation rights to hunt, fish and gather (s. 115.28(17)(d). Wis. Stats.)
- Provide learning opportunities for students to gain an "appreciation and understanding of different value systems and cultures" and "an understanding of human relations, particularly with regard to American Indians, Black Americans and Hispanics" (s.118.01(2)(c)7-8 Wis. Stats.).
- Ensure that those seeking a license to serve as a teacher, administrator, or pupil services professional in Wisconsin learn about "minority group relations, including instruction in the history, culture and tribal sovereignty of the federally recognized American Indian tribes and bands located in this state" (s.118.19(8) Wis. Stats.)
- "Provide adequate instructional materials, texts and library services which reflect the cultural diversity and pluralistic nature of American society," reflecting a multifaceted approach to transforming students' understanding of these issues (s. 121.02(1)(h)
- "Include instruction in the history, culture and tribal sovereignty of the federally recognized American Indian tribes and bands located in this state at least twice in the elementary grades and at least once in the high school grades" (s.121.02(1)(L)4 Wis. Stats.)

the state of Wisconsin "socially, politically, and educationally unprepared" (Osawa, 1999). The public reaction was a product of broadly shared educational experiences of generations of Wisconsin students, schooling that left them largely unaware of the history, culture, tribal sovereignty, and reserved treaty rights of their Ojibwe neighbors (Leary, 2013; Leary, 2012). They were effectively left, to paraphrase Bishop William Wantland (Brixley, 1990), ignorant of their own ignorance, a situation that fueled misperceptions, including ideas about "special rights" and other purported social advantages enjoyed by American Indian people. Media observers linked the violent protests to "the divisive class and racial animosities prevalent in the Reagan-Bush era" and to a lack of accurate information about Native people (Oberly, 1989, pp. 844–845). The protests themselves changed the perception of how outsiders viewed Wisconsin and forced Wisconsin residents to reconsider how they viewed themselves.[2]

Past curriculum policy decisions contributed to curricular absences and problematic presences for Native people, excluding tribal concerns altogether, or significantly misrepresenting reality through stereotypes and oversimplification. Even as curriculum policy began to shift to include ethnic studies in the 1970s and 1980s, Native people were most often considered simply another racial or ethnic group rather than citizens of sovereign nations. This left little opportunity for students to develop a true understanding of American Indian history, culture, and tribal sovereignty.

Act 31's proponents sought to counter the post-Voigt backlash, but it was not simply another example of using the public schools to address broader social issues largely external to the schools themselves. Americans have long sought to use schools to reform society itself, trying to accomplish through children the kinds of changes that are much more difficult with adults (Graham, 1995). Because the focus of social change is on the adults that our students will become, the best indicator of the success of policies like Act 31 is not student test scores or similar measures but "the behavior of our alumni" (Bauer, 1967). During the 1980s in Wisconsin, some of the alumni of our public schools were engaging in violent, racist protests on boatlandings, some were organizing opposition to those views and working in support of treaty rights, but most stayed disengaged. If we consider that these behaviors, and the racism and ignorance they reflect, are themselves outcomes of past education policy decisions, it becomes clearer why a policy solution based on the involvement of, and cooperation from, public schools was essential.

Initially, Act 31 appeared to be a source of hope for addressing the kind of racism and ignorance exhibited at Wisconsin boatlandings in the wake of the Voigt Decision. A number of challenges complicated early implementation efforts, including perceptions of a state imposition on school boards' authority, the absence of dedicated funds for school districts to carry out their new responsibilities, local racial politics, and state level political tensions. These challenges limited available resources locally and hampered the state's effort to provide professional development and techni-cal assistance. The absence of sanctions, aside from the political impossibil-ity of withholding 25% of state aid, further contributed to local resistance and uneven implementation. Subsequent developments in state and federal education policy also affected implementation in largely unintended and unforeseen ways.

Current conversations about Act 31 more often reflect great disap-pointment in its seemingly small impact. Initially, it was part of the 20 Standards, provisions in state law subject to monitoring by Department of Public Instruction (DPI) audit teams, but after the legislature eliminated funding for these accountability measures in 1995, there was little oversight of implementation. Act 31 enjoyed a short-lived boost after the Wisconsin Indian Education Association and others mobilized to ensure that the state's Model Academic Standards, adopted in 1998, included concepts related to Wisconsin Indian history, culture, and tribal sovereignty in the social stud-ies standards. Just three years later, local curriculum reforms ushered in by NCLB (2001) significantly eroded social studies as an instructional prior-ity by focusing federally required accountability regimes on student profi-ciency in reading and math (Center on Education Policy, 2007; Heafner & Fitchett, 2012). More recent shifts in federal policy present an opportunity to revitalize Act 31 implementation, particularly in those districts with a significant population of American Indian students.

Wisconsin's nearly 14,000 American Indian or Alaska Native students were not the policy focus of Act 31, but thoughtful implementation can serve to elevate levels of student achievement and attainment and expand learning opportunities and reduce the disproportionate identification of these students for special education. The policy goals were long term and social, rather than short term and academic, and focused on the entire student body rather than on Native students. Because the broad statu-tory language and local authority over curriculum policy frustrate efforts to evaluate compliance, the DPI has historically focused its efforts toward building local capacity to provide accurate, authentic instruction about the federally recognized tribes and bands in the state. It has developed instruc-tional resources, partnered with other entities, including the Wisconsin Historical Society Office of School Services and Educational Communica-tions Board to develop materials, and focused its efforts on professional development. The centerpiece of its professional development efforts is the American Indian Studies Summer Institute.

The American Indian Studies Summer Institute (AISSI) is an inten-sive, week-long workshop focusing on history, culture, tribal sovereignty, and contemporary status of the 11 federally recognized American Indian tribes and bands in Wisconsin.[3] Each year, it is held in partnership with one or more tribal communities who serve as hosts, contribute content, and serve as the focus of most of the examples provided. The Institute's aims are to improve teaching and learning in American Indian Studies, to build capacity to effectively serve American Indian students and families, to model partnerships with tribal communities, and to equip educators with the knowledge and skills necessary to adapt or develop new techniques best suited to their unique circumstances. The approach to Act 31 incorporates culturally responsive instructional content and forms, focusing on what transformed schooling might look like.

The AISSI began in 1997 as a follow-up to a series of workshops introducing *Classroom Activities on Wisconsin Indian Treaties and Tribal Sovereignty*, which the DPI published in fall 1996 (DPI, 1996). The first year, the event was headquartered at The University of Wisconsin-Eau Claire, the home campus of the guide's lead author, Dr. Ronald N. Satz, with a day spent in Black River Falls, the administrative headquarters of the Ho-Chunk Nation. In subsequent years, the Department of Public Instruction partnered with Menominee Nation (1998–2005), Stockbridge-Munsee Band of Mohicans, (1999, 2012–2013), and Oneida Nation (2000, 2006–2011). Each event takes held in a tribal community, which itself serves to demystify reservations for many participants. See Table 7.2 for a list.

The overall design of the AISSI is culturally responsive in both content and form (Castagno & Brayboy, 2008; McCardle & Demmert, 2006; Beaulieu 2006). We follow all of the appropriate cultural protocols of the host community, and two Elders—one man and one woman—serve as staff members for this purpose. They open the event in the appropriate manner,

Table 7.2 Partners and Locations for American Indian Studies Summer Institute by Year

	Location	Partner Tribe(s)	University
1997	UW-Eau Claire/ Black River Falls	Ho-Chunk Nation	UW-Eau Claire
1998	Keshena, WI	Menominee Nation	College of Menominee Nation/UW-Eau Claire
1999	Keshena, WI, Gresham, WI	Menominee Nation, Stockbridge-Munsee Band of Mohicans	College of Menominee Nation
2000	Keshena, WI, Gresham, WI	Menominee Nation, Oneida Nation	College of Menominee Nation
2001–2005	Keshena, WI	Menominee Nation	College of Menominee Nation, UW-Green Bay
2006–2011	Oneida, WI	Oneida Nation	UW-Green Bay
2012–2013	Gresham, WI	Stockbridge-Munsee Band of Mohicans	UW-Green Bay

with prayer (Ho-Chunk, Mohican), "words of encouragement" (Menominee), or the Thanksgiving Address (Oneida), and continue to provide traditional teachings throughout the week. The content shared throughout the week stresses multiple perspectives and privileges Native voices and experiences. The instructional methods bring tribal world forms into the classroom, modeling pedagogy that is both effective and similar to traditional teaching forms.

From the beginning, the instructional model has utilized community building, cooperative learning, knowledge constructing, role modeling from experienced Native and non-Native educators who exhibit cultural humility (Tervalon & Murray-Garcia, 1998; Terhune, 2006) and applied learning. The current instructional model bears a great debt to Rosemary Christensen, whose Shared Core Values of the Tribal World and Circle Teaching techniques helped to systematize the approach and brought a new degree of intentionality, beginning in 2000 (Christensen 2006). Christensen (2006) emphasizes personal sovereignty and non-interference within the "Three R's" framework of respect, reciprocity, and relationship. In oral teachings from Rosemary Christensen, as well as Linda Oxendine and the late William Demmert, Jr. (colleagues she identifies as using similar techniques), choices presented to and exercised by the learner are central to the process and reflect concern for personal sovereignty. The role of the teacher is to provide support without interfering with the learning process, and "correction" is minimal, reflecting the learners' need to identify and master what is of value to them in their own time and manner. Further discussion with Demmert both by telephone and in person helped to clarify the role that the teachers' tribal culture, gender, and personality play in shaping their approach. These teachings inform the practice of all staff members involved, particularly those responsible for leading the event and those working closely with the small groups.

The culturally relevant approach and the alignment between the Institute's content and the Model Academic Standards exposes the false choice between rigor and relevance as is often presumed by those who support measuring student achievement solely through large-scale assessments. After the opening ceremony, the first morning focuses on building a learning community through experiential education activities, and participants form small groups to be used for interactive activities, discussion, and group reflection. As part of the community building process, the staff introduces Christensen's Core Values of the Tribal World (Christensen 2006): respect, reciprocity, relationship, and responsibility, concepts that guide interactions throughout the week. The sessions in the first afternoon establish a common base of basic knowledge about Wisconsin tribes to allow the group to move forward together. The structure of the afternoon session reinforces cooperative learning by approaching the participants as knowers and actively soliciting their knowledge and experience. Beginning at the end of the first afternoon, small groups of participants, supported by a staff member who joins them for the week, engage in an exercise called Clarify and Apply. Their task is to discuss the content, ensuring that all group members understand the key ideas, and to help each other identify opportunities to apply this knowledge in their own school, classroom, or other context.

The second morning problematizes prior knowledge through an interactive workshop called "Bias is a Four Letter Word," led by Dorothy Davids, a Mohican Elder, and Dr. Ruth Gudinas, one of the pioneers in multicultural education in Wisconsin. In this session, participants analyze various stereotypical items collected by the facilitators, build skills related to evaluating instructional materials, and learn about authentic resources. The host community selects the content for the afternoon, and it typically features presentations on their history and aspects of their culture. In past years, these sessions have provided a general understanding as well as more focused teaching related to termination, restoration, and sustainable forestry (Menominee); the Iroquois Confederacy and wampum belts (Oneida); and migration, removal, and cultural recovery (Mohican). The second day once again concludes with a facilitated Clarify and Apply session.

The third day features a reservation tour, with guides, routes, and destinations defined by the host community. This provides participants with the opportunity to experience an insider's view of the community and to learn about local cultural geography and tribal institutions. By now, participants have had the lens through which they view tribal communities challenged and adjusted or rebuilt to a degree where they are able to understand and accept new perspectives. The afternoon session has traditionally focused on tribal sovereignty and treaty rights, and has been led by Andrew Gokee (Red Cliff Ojibwe), former tribal judge and active spearer,[4] and David Raasch (Mohican), former Chief Justice of the Stockbridge-Munsee Band of Mohicans. Concepts of sovereignty and jurisdiction are considerably more concrete and real after the tour.

On Wednesday, institute staff introduce what Christensen (2006; 2013) often terms the "fourth R," responsibility, and expand the process begun with Clarify and Apply through the Vision into Action process. This component uses a backward mapping process adapted from LeaderShape (www. leadershape.org), and it helps participants identify their long range goals and plan how to use the remaining days toward that end. Between Wednesday afternoon and Thursday morning, every participant develops a long-term goal, writes it on large easel pad paper, and then it is hung on the wall. For example, a 4th-grade teacher might write "My social studies curriculum infuses accurate, authentic content about Native peoples of Wisconsin on all topics and in all time periods covered." During the gallery walk which follows, all members of the learning community, participants and staff, read the vision statements and make specific, constructive comments intended to help identify instructional materials and resource people, and otherwise provide input intended to refine the idea and develop effective strategies for implementation. This process engages the entire learning community and creates a sense of investment in others' success.

The fourth day features a high degree of differentiation as participants pursue their own course of learning related to the vision they created. Institute staff members identify and offer a range of optional learning stations, mini-workshops, and spaces for participant-initiated informal consultation and collaboration based on the vision statements and participant feedback from daily evaluations. This reflects the value of choice in Indigenous teaching and learning models, reinforces the importance of collaboration, and demonstrates how teachers can balance the need to provide a set curriculum with the benefits of learner-centered project-based learning.

The last day centers on developing a sound strategy for realizing the vision using backward mapping. In their small groups, participants assist each other in identifying steps and milestones for moving toward the realization of the vision as well as re-entry points should the process get derailed. Because the groups tend to become quite close during the week, this process introduces an element of relational accountability as participants share their vision and the process for realizing it. The three R's of respect, reciprocity, and relationship, which have characterized the week, are joined by the fourth R, responsibility, as participants prepare to leave the learning community and return to their home community of practice.

The AISSI is a professional development opportunity that models a culturally responsive approach to Act 31. Cultural forms, which serve as the means through which culturally relevant teaching and learning take place, thereby transform a state-level education policy from a mechanism intended to promote broader understanding of Native people into a means to engage and empower Native students. By introducing practices that validate and build upon tribal communities' knowledge and norms, teachers become positioned to implement practices that show strong promise for closing existing gaps in achievement and attainment.

Since 1997, the Institute has served over 750 participants, including professional educators in PK-20 public, tribal, and private schools, colleges and universities; officials in tribal, federal, and state education agencies; library and museum staff; multimedia producers and curriculum developers; social services providers; and authors, among others. Many individuals and institutions have made significant investments in their faculty, staff, and students' professional development. There are many examples of individuals who have attended as many as five and six times, representing a depth of commitment from the individual or institution. Several districts and educational institutions repeatedly sent teams to the event, representing breadth of commitment.

Nearly half of the participants, 327 of 764, came from public school districts. Twenty five of the thirty-five public school districts receiving Indian Education formula grants under Title IX of Improving America's Schools (IASA, 1994) or Title VII of NCLB (2001) sent a total of 280 participants.

Seventeen of the twenty-six districts participating in the state's American Indian Student Achievement Network (AISAN) sent a total of 235 participants.[5] These districts tend to be involved in efforts to close achievement gaps and to reduce disproportionality in special education, and culturally responsive education is a sound, research-based strategy for addressing both issues. A review of participants' professional roles suggests that because many did not have Act 31-related instructional responsibilities, the culturally responsive nature of the event was an important draw. In several cases, a school or district's efforts to provide a more comprehensive, culturally responsive educational program is evidenced by participation from guidance counselors, social workers, psychologists, and nurses, in addition to administrators and instructional staff. This is particularly true of Menominee Indian School District, which sent 64 participants, and Seymour School District, which sent 50.

The three tribally controlled schools were well-represented among AISSI participants, suggesting that they recognize and value the culturally responsive approach. A total of 22 staff members from Menominee Tribal School attended the Institute, including one who attended 5 times. Oneida Nation School System, whose Turtle School served as the host site from 2006–2011, sent 32 staff members, including four who attended multiple years. Lac Courte Oreilles School sent 18 people, including 5 who attended multiple events. The school systems on the host reservations particularly appreciated culturally responsive professional development focused on their own culture and community.

Colleges and universities, particularly teacher education programs in Wisconsin, are very well represented. Over the years, UW System institutions sent a total of 127 participants, including 44 faculty, 47 staff, and 34 students. The most significant investment in faculty development was at the University of Wisconsin-Oshkosh, which sponsored a total of 14 faculty members, three of whom attended multiple years. The state's flagship institution, the University of Wisconsin-Madison, primarily invested in academic staff and graduate students in its efforts to provide more culturally responsive admissions and student services programs. College of Menominee Nation, the host institution from 1998–2005, sent 12 faculty, staff, and students, including faculty in its new teacher education program.

Professional development opportunities related to culturally responsive education that are themselves culturally responsive can be important tools for closing achievement gaps, lowering rates of disproportionality in special education, student discipline, suspension, and expulsion, and raising student attainment levels. The American Indian Studies Summer Institute, offered in partnership between the state's Department of Public Instruction, one or more tribal host communities, and one or more universities, is a sound example of such an event. Its content and form owe a significant debt to the late William Demmert, Jr., to Rosemary Christensen, and to other Native Elders and educators.

NOTES

1. State-level Leadership responsibilities for public education in Wisconsin are vested in the State Superintendent, an elected, non-partisan official whose duties are defined in the state constitution. This official serves as the head of the Department of Public Instruction, the state education agency. Unlike many states, Wisconsin does not have a state school board, which means that local school boards possess broad discretion over education policy. An increasing federal role in education, particularly since the passage of the Improving America's Schools Act (IASA) of 1994, and its successor, No Child Left Behind (NCLB) Act of 2001, has significantly eroded local authority. These policy shifts have created a new context for the implementation of Act 31.
2. For more information on Chippewa/Ojibwe treaty rights and the post-Voigt backlash, see Satz (1991), Whaley & Bressette (1994), Nesper (2002), and Loew & Thannum (2011).
3. The addition of the phrase "and current status" reflects the Model Academic Standards for Social Studies. See History: Time, Continuity, and Change, standards B.4.8, B.8.10, and B.12.12. (The Social Studies standards can be accessed at http://standards.dpi.wi.gov/stn_ssintro where links can also be found to other content area standards.)
4. This term refers to those Ojibwe people who exercise their reserved right to harvest fish using headlamps and spears at night during the spring spawn. It is a commonly used term in Wisconsin.
5. Note that some districts are Title VII but not AISAN because eligibility is defined differently. AISAN districts are those with a Native population at least twice that of the state average (1.5%), plus Milwaukee, whose numerically large AI/AN student population represents a small percentage of the total student body, for a total of 26 districts.

REFERENCES

Bauer, N. W. (1967). Guaranteeing the values component in elementary social studies. In J. Jarolimek (Ed.) *Social studies education: The elementary school* (p. 43). Washington, D.C.: National Council for the Social Studies.

Beaulieu, D. (2006). A survey and assessment of culturally based education programs for Native American students in the United States. *Journal of American Indian Education* 45(2): 50–61.

Brixley, E. (1990). Churches caught in treaty conflict. In F. Denton (Ed.) *Treaty crisis: Cultures in conflict*, Madison, WI: Wisconsin State Journal, 40. (Pamphlet 90–458 oversize) Retrieved from Wisconsin Historical Society web page: http://www.wisconsinhistory.org/turningpoints/search.asp?id=1115

Castagno, A.E. and B.M.J. Brayboy. (2008). Culturally responsive schooling for Indigenous youth: A review of the literature. *Review of Educational Research*, 78(4): 941–993.

Center on Education Policy. (December 2007). *Choices, changes, and challenges: Curriculum and instruction in the NCLB era*. Washington, D.C.: Center on Education Policy.

Christensen, R.A. (2006). Teaching within the circle: Methods for an American Indian teaching and learning style, a tribal paradigm. In V. Lea & J. Helfand (Eds.) *Identifying race and transforming whiteness in the classroom* (pp. 171–192). New York: Peter Lang International Academic Publishers.

Christensen, R.A. (2013). Connective pedagogy: Elder epistemology, oral tradition, and community. In R.A. Christensen & L.M. Poupart (Eds.) *Connective pedagogy: Elder epistemology, oral tradition, and community* (pp. 13–32). Winnipeg, MB, Canada: Aboriginal Issues Press.

DPI. (1996). *Classroom Activities on Wisconsin Indian Treaties and Tribal Sovereignty.* Madison, WI: State Department of Public Instruction.

Graham, P.A. Battleships and schools. *Daedalus*: 124 (Fall 1995): 43.

Heafner, T.L. & P.G. Fitchett. (Spring 2012). Tipping the scales: National trends of declining social studies instructional time in elementary schools. *Journal of Social Studies Research*, 36(2): 190–215.

Improving America's Schools Act (IASA) of 1994. P.L. 103–382. 108 Stat. 3518.

Leary, J P. (2012). The Tangled Roots of Act 31: American Indians and curriculum policy in Wisconsin. Dissertation. University of Wisconsin-Madison.

Leary, J P. (2013). Act 31: Issues and origins. *Mazina'igan*. (Spring/Summer 2013): 11–14.

Loew, P. & Thannum, J. (2011). After the storm. *American Indian Quarterly* 35(2): 161–191.

No Child Left Behind Act (NCLB) of 2001. PL107–110, 115 Stat.1452, 20 U.S.C. §§ 6301 *et seq.*

Nesper, L.N. (2002), *The walleye war: The struggle for Ojibwe spearfishing and treaty rights.* Lincoln: University of Nebraska Press.

Oberly, J. (1989). Race and class warfare: Spearing fish, playing 'chicken'. *The Nation* (June 19, 1989): 844–845.

Osawa, Sandra Sunrising (Director). *Lighting the seventh fire*, DVD. Seattle, WA: Upstream Productions, 1999.

Satz, R.N. (1991). *Chippewa treaty rights: The reserved rights of Wisconsin's Chippewa Indians in historical perspective.* Madison: Wisconsin Academy of Sciences, Arts, and Letters.

State of Wisconsin. (1991). Legislative Reference Bureau. *Chippewa off-reservation treaty rights.* Madison: State of Wisconsin. December 1991, 16.

State of Wisconsin. Department of Public Instruction. (1996). *Classroom activities on Wisconsin Indian treaties and tribal sovereignty.* Madison: Wisconsin Department of Public Instruction.

Terhune, C.P. (2006). "Can we talk?" Using critical self-reflection and dialogue to build diversity and change organizational culture in nursing schools. *Journal of Cultural Diversity*, 13(3): 141–145.

Tervalon, M. & J. Murray-Garcia. (1998). Cultural humility versus cultural competence: A critical distinction in defining physician training outcomes in multicultural education. *Journal of Health Care for the Poor and Underserved*, 9, 2.

Whaley, R. & Bressette, W. (1994). *Walleye warriors: An effective alliance against racism and for the earth.* Philadelphia: New Society Publishers.

Wisconsin Act 31 (1989). Senate Bill 31, 1989–1991 Biennial Budget Act. Sections 115.28(17)(d); s. 118.01(c)7–8; s. 118.19(8) 89–90; s. 121.02(1)(h) 89–90; s. 121.02(1)(L)4 89–90.

Part I Commentary
Literacy Instruction for Native Americans

Julie Ann Washington

The "achievement gap" in American education is longstanding and much discussed. Students from minority backgrounds and those who are impoverished are the subjects of these discussions, as it is these students who most often lag behind their peers educationally. In particular, the gap between the performances of Hispanic, African American, and American Indian students and their white and Asian peers has endured for decades and has been largely intractable. This is no surprise as these students not only enter the educational system with significant cultural and linguistic differences from mainstream expectations, but also are disproportionately poor. It is no secret that students who are culturally and linguistically different and those who are impoverished are least well served in our educational system. When a student is both poor and a cultural-linguistic minority, these educational failings are magnified.

Advances in literacy, mathematics, and science education and research seemingly have not "trickled down" to the groups most in need of the knowledge and the interventions that have been developed from that knowledge base. Given how much we do know, how did we get to this point at which we find ourselves in 21st-century education? Why aren't we making more progress in narrowing the education achievement gap? Why have we been chipping away at the same issues for decades with barely a measurable improvement? These are the questions being asked by many different cultural, ethnic, and education constituencies concerned with the performance of lower-performing, minority students. The six chapters in Part I offer insights and exciting solutions that have been developed for American Indian students, a group that performs consistently more poorly nationally than other students, including Latinos and African Americans.

The achievement gap is as much a social justice issue as it is an education one. Social justice implores us to fight inequality where it exists and to value diversity. At its most basic level social justice is concerned with the allocation of resources. When resources, whether economic or educational, are unevenly distributed the imbalanced outcomes should come as a surprise to no one!

Accordingly, Ladson-Billings (2006) encourages us to reframe the achievement gap as an "education debt" rather than simply as a gap in performance between key groups. She argues that focusing on the gap leads to short term solutions rather than a focus on the underlying, accumulated variables that created the problem. Education researchers typically talk about the gap as it relates to education data that has been available since the 1970s through the National Assessment of Education Progress (NAEP). Ladson-Billings argues that it is the historical decisions we have made as a nation that have led us to the generations-long education debt that we currently face in our schools: "In the case of education, each effort we make toward improving education is counterbalanced by the ongoing and mounting debt that we have accumulated" (2006, p. 9). In this volume, Beltran refers to it as the cumulative effects of historical trauma. Also in this volume, Craig encourages the telling and retelling of these stories to be used as "a call to action."

The consequences of decades of disenfranchisement and forced assimilation are evidenced in the consistently poor performance of Native children. The authors in Section 1 all acknowledge the impact of this education debt. Each of the five chapters focuses as much on history as on current educational performance, providing "insider" perspectives on the struggles and victories of American Indians in the Pacific Northwest and in Wisconsin. The authors overwhelmingly posit that it is impossible to effectively educate American Indian children and youth without first understanding the historical backdrop of American Indians in the history of the United States. In this vein, current performance represents an accumulation of social and educational injustice that must be acknowledged in order to move forward.

Historically, there has been high value placed on "sameness" and assimilation. For many students, in this case Native youth, the results have been catastrophic. The disaggregation of test results that initially highlighted the academic performance gap has unfortunately not led to disaggregation of approaches to educating students who need it. In Section I Hurtado and Brown describe development of a statewide curriculum, *Since Time Immemorial: Tribal Sovereignty in Washington State* (STI), designed to provide this differentiation of instruction in order to improve student achievement and increase relevancy to American Indian children. Similarly, Leary describes development of curriculum and policy in Wisconsin (Act 31) designed to improve understanding of the history, culture, and legal aspects of contemporary tribal nations of Wisconsin. Craig presents an approach to educating children that relies upon close collaboration between tribes, the community, and government. Beltran advocates the integration of oral traditions of the community into the educational environment and describes a program designed to accomplish that goal.

Taken together, these five authors present consistent characteristics of successful educational practices that are critical when educating Native children and youth:

- Collaboration between the school and community: inviting the culture into the classroom so that a bridge is built between the home and community and education is more inclusive.
- Differentiation of instruction with a culturally compatible focus: use of culturally-based education (CBE) practices such as oral narratives to enhance learning among students.
- Development of relationships and trust among key stakeholders: Hurtado describes relationships as the most important ingredient for making these educational efforts work.
- Ongoing professional development: the success of STI and Act 31 for improving student outcomes depends upon teachers understanding the curriculum and presenting it with integrity.

Overall, what these authors are describing is best practices for the education of all children with a special focus on practices that improve education of minority children. The Washington state model, in particular, provides an impressive blueprint for creating an inclusive and respectful educational environment for children from nonmainstream cultural and linguistic backgrounds. The architects of the STI curriculum considered all of the important stakeholders that they would need to impact in order to make a significant difference in educational practices in their state: state policymakers, schools, students, teachers, community leaders and, importantly, University teacher training programs. This comprehensive approach to addressing the educational needs of American Indian children if followed by other groups experiencing educational inequity could go a long way toward narrowing the achievement gap.

REFERENCES

Ladson-Billings, G. (2006). From the achievement gap to the education debt: Understanding achievement in U.S. Schools. *Educational Researcher, 35*(7), pp. 3–12.

Part II

A Developmental Approach to Merging Cultural Sensitivity and Evidence-Based Practice

8 A History of the Navajo Head Start Immersion Project 1995–2000

Completing the Circle of Knowledge

Louise Lockard and Jennie deGroat

This chapter describes the historical and social foundations of the Navajo Head Start Immersion program which operated from 1995 to 2000, from the perspectives of four Navajo Head Start teachers, based on the following research question: in what ways and to what extent was the project successful in increasing the collaboration of parents and teachers to support the teaching of Indigenous language in their schools and in their communities?

Schools are institutions that reflect the knowledge and assumptions held by educational authorities about the prior knowledge of students from the majority language group (McGroarty, 1986). Most education is systematically based on research on the development and experiences of these majority language speakers (Heath, 1986). For education to be appropriate to the experiences of Navajo students, we must focus our attention on significant background and learning factors particular to the development of these students (McGroarty, 1986). Teachers must actively seek to understand the backgrounds of these students in order to plan effective instruction for them. They must recognize the rich knowledge students bring to school with them (Moll, Amanti, Neff & Gonzalez, 1992). The contextual knowledge of language minority students, rather than being impoverished or deficient, is rich and multicultural (Pease-Alvarez & Vasquez, 1994).

LEGAL AND LINGUISTIC BACKGROUND

The Native American Language Act of 1990 (1990; PL 101–477) recognizes that "there is convincing evidence that student achievement and performance, community and school pride, and educational opportunity are clearly and directly tied to respect for, and support of, the first language of the child or student" (Native American Language Act, 1990). The Esther Martinez Native American Languages Preservation Act (2006) is an amendment of the Native American Language Act of 1990, and authorizes competitive grants to establish language nests and language immersion programs for children ages birth to seven years and their parents. The passage of this bill, following fourteen years of deliberation in the U.S. Congress, serves as an invitation to discuss the history and current situation of Indigenous languages in early childhood programs and to determine how systemic change in schools can support this model. The Navajo education policy states, "The Navajo language is an essential element of the life, culture and identity of the Navajo people" (Navajo Tribe Division of Diné Education, 1984). The Navajo Nation places great value on a Navajo-specific education that supports the self-identity of its teachers and students (Navajo Tribe Division of Diné Education, 1996, 2003a, 2003b, 2003c). A 1991 survey of 4,073 Navajo Head Start students found that 53.3% spoke only English, 17.7% spoke only Navajo, and 27.9% spoke both Navajo and English (Platero, 2001). These statistics indicate a severe immediate need and a growing alarm to include instruction in Navajo language in all schools serving Navajo students, an alarm that is echoed in the literature on Indigenous language loss (Appel & Muysken, 1987; Bauman, 1980; Crawford, 1994; McCarty, 1998; Nettle & Romaine, 2000; Slate, 1993).

Support for Navajo language programs in the schools is further documented in a survey of 242 schools on the Navajo Reservation in which 1,222 Navajo classroom aides and 2,474 aides of all types responded. The Navajo Tribe Diné Division of Education (2003) found that Navajo language and education are legitimate parts of the educational program. Research in Navajo communities demonstrates that place- and community-based curricula and instruction support students' academic success (Rosier & Holm 1980; McLaughlin, 1992; Goodluck, Lockard, & Yazzie, 2000; Zehr, 2007); this has also been shown to be true for students in non-Navajo communities (Pavel, Reyhner, Avison, Obester, & Sayer, 2003; Wilson, 2003).

Yazzie-Minz (2005) reviewed formal early childhood educational opportunities for American Indian and Alaska Native children. She questioned the relevance of these formal preschool programs for parents and children, quoting Diaz Soto and Swadener (2002) who call for a reconsideration of educators' total reliance on a scientific world view. Yazzie-Minz (2005) challenged Head Start programs serving reservation communities to infuse tribal values in the curriculum. This process is important if we are to effect systemic change to implement Navajo immersion in Head Start curricula (DeJong, 1999; Cahape & Slate, 1993; Slate, 1994).

Nissani (1993) found that for preschoolers who were speakers of other languages it was important to design preschool programs that support the identities of bilingual children and parents. With these cautionary notes and with a belief that teachers are agents of change in their institutions only when they understand these relations of power, we begin a discussion of the history of Navajo Head Start Immersion.

HISTORY OF NAVAJO HEAD START IMMERSION

This discussion began in a junior level writing course at Northern University—BME 331W: Structured English Immersion in Early Childhood

Settings. In class we discussed methods for teaching young English Learners. Two of the students, Eilene Joe and Caroline Wagoner, were Navajo Head Start teachers; another student, Judy de Hose, was a school board member who was interested in preparing bilingual teachers for a new immersion program in her community on the White Mountain Apache Reservation. In a class discussion I (first author Lockard) shared my own experiences of working as a teacher in Navajo Head Start and later as a Child Development Associate Advisor in Navajo Head Start Immersion classrooms. The Navajo Head Start Immersion program operated from 1995 to 2000. This discussion led to a review of current efforts to teach Navajo in the Head Start program.

To further understand the attitudes of the teachers, we examined transcripts of their interviews. To describe the attitudes of the teachers which supported the teaching of the Navajo language, we selected three themes: parents as first teachers, the bilingual classroom, and aspirations for the future.

Teachers of Navajo Language and culture work within the borders of state and federal language policies that have defined the opportunities of their students to learn. These borders have existed since the introduction of formal education with the signing of the treaty of 1868. (U.S. Congress, 1868). For teachers of Navajo language and culture today, these borders take the form of current legislation including Arizona Proposition 203 (2003), English Language Education for Children in Public Schools, legislation which imposes standards-based curricula on schools and limits the language of instruction for English Learners to English.

In this study, teachers of Navajo language and culture describe how their understanding of these borders, the social and historical roots of formal education, informs their classroom practice. They discuss how this understanding has been the impetus for new conversations with their current students about the dispositions of effort and resilience in learning Navajo as a heritage language and in studying Navajo culture as part of a broader investigation of the social and historical roots of schooling in their communities.

Caroline Wagner worked as a Navajo Head Start teacher in Rough Rock in the Chinle Agency in 1995. In personal communication to the authors, she shared the following reflections:

> *The Navajo Nation Department of Head Start has grown from serving 199 children in 1965. Dr. Robert Roessel was a part of getting Head Start started here on the Navajo Reservation. At the time Dr. Roessel proposed that teachers stay at the dorms at ASU through the summers to go through training. Dr. Roessel always stressed Navajo language and culture. He always asked, "How would you feel if you lost your language?"*
>
> *Former Navajo Nation President Mr. Albert Hale issued an executive order in July 1995 establishing the Navajo language as the primary means of instruction in all Head Start classrooms. This order decreed, "Navajo language shall be the medium of instruction for Navajo children, the*

Nation's future at all Head Start facilities. . . . the Department of Head Start, Division of Education, shall herewith implement, beginning with the Fall Semester 1995, the purpose and intent of this order in the curriculum, teacher education, facilities, extra curricular activities and all other relevant facets of the Navajo Head Start program." (She referenced the Navajo Tribe Division of Diné Language, 1995).

Later that year the Head Start Navajo language curriculum was developed and field tested. During the years 1995–1996 this special project was coordinated by Mrs. Afton Sells from the Office of Diné Culture with Chinle as the pilot site. This curriculum integrated the wisdom of traditional Navajo teaching with the day to day planning and activities in the current Head Start program. The children learned stories and songs. They learned about plants and animals by the seasons. They used concrete objects and their five senses to explore the world around them. Parents and elders understood the significance of early childhood and that all the knowledge and experience gained in the early years would stay with the child throughout their lives. The curriculum that was developed incorporated the wisdom of traditional teaching and learning for young children with the current head start program and learning environment.

Eilene Joe interviewed Dr. Wayne S. Holm in December 2006. Dr. Holm was part of the Navajo Nation Language Project funded by the Administration for Native Americans in partnership with the Navajo Nation Division of Diné Education which developed the curriculum for the Navajo Nation Head Start program. Holm described the curriculum that included Situational Navajo (Holm & Silentman, 1997; Holm, Silentman & Wallace, 2003). He described how Situational Navajo is supported by theories of second language acquisition and discussed how second language is more than just being exposed to the language; it is the ability to communicate in situations in which the child receives feedback.

Joe also interviewed Afton Sells in December, 2006, at Diné College in Tsaile, Arizona. Afton Sells was the Education Specialist for the Head Start Immersion Program. She supervised four full immersion classrooms in the Chinle Agency. Sells reported that in the Immersion each child was exposed to the Navajo language from the time the child got on the bus to the time the child got off the bus. The Navajo language was used in all communication with children and teachers in the classroom. Children were immersed in the Navajo language in every interest area and learning situation. Sells reported to Eilene Joe that when children are taught the Navajo language at an early age they have more confidence in themselves.

Caroline Wagner discussed the beginning of the immersion program in Rough Rock:

I worked with Head Start for a number of years. Our site was chosen to operate a full immersion program. That was an experience for all of us. The instruction was all in the Navajo language. The students would remind each other to speak in the Diné language. Diné ke ji. It was incredible to hear them say "diné keji". In the beginning it was a little difficult to constantly use Navajo while teaching throughout the day. Sometimes we would catch ourselves speaking English. The children that attended school during the years the full immersion program was being used learned a lot of Navajo. They would try to make sentences and could understand when someone spoke to them in Navajo. One day a parent came to the center and said, "Thank you for teaching my child Navajo. Yesterday my son wanted to feed the dogs some food that he didn't eat. He was actually calling to the dogs and telling them to come over and eat. He said it all in Navajo!" The mother said she was so amazed and almost started to cry. She was caught off guard and could not believe that he was making sentences. When she asked her son what it was that he said to the dogs, he replied with a smile, "I called the dogs to eat." As a teacher I was proud to learn that the children were learning the Navajo language. I then knew that the full immersion program was effective.

She described the curriculum which was infused with Navajo culture:

In a thematic unit on the four sacred mountains, students at Rough Rock learned the four sacred mountains, their colors, the directions and what the mountains represented. With the Head Start children, I had to do a lot of hands-on activities in order for them to understand the mountains and their colors. For example, we would go on a nature walk and collect different colored rocks. We would search for white, turquoise, yellow and black. The children would try to find rocks that were the same color as the four sacred mountains. If they couldn't find one by the time we got back to the center, the children would use paint to color the rocks that they found. After that the students would glue it onto a cardboard. They would use dirt to make models of the four sacred mountains. The children enjoyed putting their homes in the middle. With this activity the children learned that they lived within the four sacred mountains.

In Head Start the directors and teachers strive to achieve the goals of the program. The mission statement for Navajo Nation Head Start is "Life is a journey, not a destination". It is a journey that is not traveled alone. The development of the child is influenced by the world around him, mother earth, the air, water, and light as well as the family, the community and every individual around him. Even though this journey may lead the child beyond the boundaries of the four sacred mountains, the child will continue to be protected by the foundation provided by these elements and the child will work in beauty. Just as one will cross the path of the child in the future, we will strive to prepare the Navajo child, the family and the community for the challenges of the future using the foundation of our history and language.

The mission of the Navajo Department of Head Start is to strive to be a positive and integrating influence in this process. The curriculum was developed with this mission statement in mind. The Navajo basket was used to symbolically represent the curriculum with the seasons as a framework for the learning activities of young children. The basket incorporates the four directions and the blessings and teaching of the twelve Holy People as they relate to the four seasons. The basket also carries the symbol of the four seasons and the four original words of the Navajo Language and the four stages of life and the human cycle.

The curriculum consisted of Situational Navajo and the Diné Curriculum, a curriculum designed by Navajo Nation Head Start. Several years after this Diné Curriculum was implemented, the Department of Health and Human Services wanted all Head Start programs to have a research-based curriculum. The Ade'e'honiszin Curriculum was created. The Ade'e'honiszin curriculum is a curriculum made up of the Diné Curriculum and the Creative Curriculum (Navajo Tribe Division of Diné Education, n.d.; Dodge, 2002). The Ade'e'honiszin Curriculum infuses the Dine language and culture in the daily classroom experiences of the child. Eilene Joe, in a personal communication with the authors reflected: *Today in some Head Start classrooms English is the language of instruction while in other classrooms the Navajo language is used for enrichment. Since NCLB [No Child Left Behind Act of 2001] there has been a shift to the use of more English for literacy; this is where the Navajo Nation Head Start made the mistake in teaching more English.*

This history of the Navajo language curriculum and pedagogy reflects changes in the institution of the school which both supported and conflicted with traditional mainstream institutions. This history includes the stories of transformative teachers who acted to create this curriculum. This Navajo language curriculum must be seen not only as a technological development, as a literature which is criticized for its accuracy in portraying the Navajo experience, or as literature which is criticized for its aesthetic value. This Navajo language curriculum should also be seen as a medium used by teachers to share stories which were part of the oral tradition of their communities.

Teacher-educator Bernard Spolsky (2001) wrote of the influence of the institution of the school in disrupting intergenerational language transmission.

Seemingly protected by its isolated geographical position and by the formal recognition of its autonomy as a Nation, the Navajo people were denied any real control of the one institution, schooling, which can play a central role in a campaign to reverse language shift. With this lack of autonomy came a language shift which disrupted intergenerational language transmission. (Spolsky, 2001, p. 46)

By reflecting on this history, teachers may begin to reclaim their language for their profession and for future generations. They may use this transformative knowledge to ask themselves how they would feel if they lost their language. This question completes the circle of knowledge from parent to child and from teacher to student within the institution of the school.

REFERENCES

Appel, R., & Muysken, P. (1987). *Language contact and bilingualism*. London: E. Arnold.

Arizona Proposition 203. (2000). Section 3, Title 15, Chapter 7, Article 3.1, English Language Education for Children in Publish Schools. Retrieved from: http://www.azsos.gov/election/2000/info/PubPamphlet/english/prop203.htm.

Bauman, J. (1980). *A guide to issues in Indian language retention*. Washington, D.C.: Center for Applied Linguistics.

Cahape, P. & Demmert, W. (2003). *American Indian and Alaska Native early childhood health, development, and education research*. (EDO-RC-030012) Washington, D.C.: U.S. Department of Education.

Crawford, J. (1994). Endangered Native American languages: What is to be done and why? *Bilingual Research Journal, 19*(1) pp. 17–38.

DeJong, D. (1999). Is Immersion the key to language renewal? *Journal of American Indian Education. 37*(3), 31–46.

Diaz Soto, L. & Swadener, B. (2002). Toward a liberatory early childhood theory, research and praxis: Decolonizing a field. *Contemporary Issues in Early Childhood, 3*(2), 38–66.

Dodge, D. (2002). *The creative curriculum for preschool*. Washington, D.C.: Teaching Strategies.

Esther Martinez Native American Languages Preservation Act of 2006. Public Law 109–394. 120 Stat. 2705. December 14, 2006.

Goodluck, M., Lockard, L., & Yazzie, D. (2000). Language revitalization in Navajo/English dual language classrooms in Jon Reyner et al. (Eds.) *Learn in beauty: Indigenous education for a new century*. Flagstaff: Northern Arizona University.

Heath, S. (1986). Sociocultural contexts of language development. In C. Cortez (Ed.) *Beyond language: Social and cultural factors in schooling language minority students* (pp. 143–186). Los Angeles: Evaluation, Dissemination and Assessment Center. California State University.

Holm, W., & Silentman, I. (Eds.) (1997). *Situational Navajo: The specific language used in recurring situations by Navajo Head Start teachers and children*. Window Rock, AZ: Navajo Nation Language Project Navajo Tribe, Division of Diné Education.

Holm, W., Silentman, I., & Wallace, L. (2003). Situational Navajo: A school-based, verb-centered way of teaching Navajo. Paper presented at the Annual Stabilizing Indigenous Languages Symposium (8th, Flagstaff, AZ, June 14–16, 2001). In J. Reyner, O. Trujillo, R. Carrasco, & L. Lockard (Eds.) *Nurturing Native Languages*. (pp. 25–52). Flagstaff: Northern Arizona University.

McCarty, T. (1998). Schooling, resistance, and American Indian languages. *International Journal of the Sociology of Language 132*, 27–41.

McGroarty, M. (1986). Educator's response to sociocultural diversity: Implications for practice. In Bilingual Education Office, California State Department (Eds.) *Beyond language: Social and cultural factors in schooling language minority students* (pp. 299–343). Los Angeles: Evaluation, Dissemination and Assessment Center.

McLaughlin, D. (1992). *When literacy empowers: Navajo language in print.* Albuquerque: University of New Mexico Press.

Moll, L., Amanti, C., Neff, D., & Gonzalez, N. (1992). Funds of knowledge for teaching: Using a qualitative approach to connect homes and classrooms. *Theory into Practice, 31*, 132–141.

Native American Language Act of 1990. Public Law 101–477. 104 Stat. 1152. October 30, 1990.

Navajo Tribe Division of Diné Education (1984). *Navajo Nation education policies.* Window Rock, AZ: Division of Diné Education.

Navajo Tribe Division of Diné Education (1995). *Executive Order Title X.* July 19, 1995.

Navajo Tribe Division of Diné Education. (1996). *Diné culture and language curriculum framework.* Window Rock, AZ: Division of Diné Education.

Navajo Tribe Division of Diné Education. (2003a) *Diné language standards.* Window Rock, AZ: Division of Diné Education.

Navajo Tribe Division of Diné Education. (2003b). *Diné Culture-based curriculum.* Window Rock, AZ: Division of Diné Education.

Navajo Tribe Division of Diné Education. (2003c). *The Navajo Nation teacher education initiative and SITE.* Window Rock, AZ: Division of Diné Education.

Navajo Tribe Division of Diné Education (n.d.). *Ade'e'honiszin Doleel curriculum.* Window Rock, AZ: Division of Diné Education.

Nettle, D. & Romaine, S. (2000). *Vanishing voices.* London: Oxford University Press.

Nissani, H. (1993). Early childhood programs for language minority students (ED 355836) Washington, DC: ERIC Clearinghouse on Language and Linguistics.

No Child Left Behind Act of 2001, PL 107–110, 115 Stat. 1425, 20 U.S.C. §§ 6301 *et seq.*

Pavel, M., Reyhner, J., Avison, C., Obester, C., & Sayer, J. (2003). *American Indian & Alaska Native education research agenda literature review.* Rockville, MD: Westat. Commissioned paper prepared for American Indian & Alaska Native Education Federal Interagency Task Force.

Pease-Alvarez, C. & Vasquez, O. (1994). Language socialization in ethnic minority communities. In F. Genesee (Ed.) *Educating second language children* (pp. 82–102). New York: Cambridge University Press.

Platero, P. (2001). Navajo Head Start language study. In L. Hinton & K. Hale (Eds.) *The green book of language revitalization in practice:Toward a sustainable world* (pp. 87–100) San Diego: Academic Press.

Rosier, P. & Holm, W. (1980). *Bilingual education series: 8; The Rock Point experience: A longitudinal study of a Navajo school program (Saad Naaki Bee Na'nitin).* Washington D.C.: Center for Applied Linguistics.

Slate, C. (1993). On reversing Navajo language shift. *Journal of Navajo Education (X)3,* 30–35.

Spolsky, B. (2001). Prospects for the survival of the Navajo language: A reconsideration. Proceedings of the 2001 Athabaskan Language Conference, University of California Los Angeles, May 18–20, 2001.

U.S. Congress (1868). 57th Congress, 1st Session, Senate Document 452, Indian Affairs.

Wilson, S. (2003). Reclaiming Indian education through partnerships with engaged institutions. In The Rural School and Community Trust (Eds.) *Engaged institutions: Impacting the lives of vulnerable youth through place based learning.* Washington, D.C.: The Rural School and Community Trust.

Yazzie-Mintz, T. (2005). Early childhood educational opportunities for American Indian and Alaska Native children and families. Proceedings of the Rural Early Childhood Forum on American Indian and Alaska Native Children and Families Little Rock, AR Retrieved from http://www.createwisconsin.net/ecwebcast-documents/EC_Forum_Report.pdf

Zehr, M. (2007). A culture put to the test. For Navajo children, a rigorous program draws on traditions to spur achievement. *Education Week*, 26 (28), 25–28.

9 Supporting Early Oral Language and Written Literacy in Young Native American Children[1]

Angela Notari-Syverson and Jane Coolidge

At the end of a busy Spring week, Ms. Ramon and her assistant Ms. Pace sat down to debrief the series of lessons on fish conducted that week in their preschool classroom. The lessons had begun the first day by having Sofie, the program cook and a tribal member, show a salmon to the children. As she prepared it for lunch, Sofie talked about the important role salmon play in the lives of the S'Klallam tribe. She told of how the salmon return each Fall, and the gratitude of the people to the salmon for giving themselves to be caught to strengthen the people. The children observed as she skillfully prepared the fish, asking questions about where the salmon lived, and how it had managed to be caught.

Ms. Ramon and Ms. Pace had placed a large cardboard box in the dramatic play area which could serve as a fishing boat or canoe, along with fishing rods, play "spears", nets, baskets, buckets, miniature fish, crabs, and mussel and clam shells. In the science area they created a poster illustrating the different body parts of a fish and talked with the children about how fish move through water, explaining how fins help fish swim and how they breathe by moving water in through their mouths and out through their gills. Children talked about what they already knew about fish and where they had seen fish before. The art area had materials for children to draw and create their own fish and make fishing rods with wooden dowels and strings.

The book area showcased books about fish, including Native stories such as Little Silver Salmon *from* Stories of Our Ancestors *(Zahir, 2000), and* In the Land of the Salmon, *a Skokomish story from* The Indian Reading Series: Stories and Legends of the Northwest *(Everenden & Hart, 1982). Story time focused on one particular story—*Seya's Song *(Hirschi, 1992). In this story a young girl describes activities of the S'Klallam, a Pacific Coast tribe, through the year, including the life cycle of salmon, sharing stories and language passed on by her grandmother, Seya.*

The teachers were pleased to see how by the third reading of this book, children were answering questions about the story, contributing their own comments, and making connections between the story and their own daily lives. Some children talked about family outings to the beach and different fish and sea creatures they had seen. Some talked about their grandmothers and stories they had told. Together the children talked about different ways to name things in different languages and practiced pronouncing the words in S'Klallam from the book.

Reflecting on the week, Ms. Ramon and Ms. Pace were pleased that the children had learned new concepts and vocabulary about fish and had connected the lessons to experiences in their own lives. Given the children's interest in the topic, they decided to invite some elders to share stories and talk more with the class on the importance of fish in the traditions of the community.

In the fictional classroom described in this vignette, children were exposed to many and diverse experiences and opportunities to learn and develop language and literacy skills. The teachers played a critical role, intentionally planning activities that were meaningful to Native American children and culturally and linguistically responsive to their community. They knew that it was important to have continuity between family and school and to build on the children's prior language and literacy knowledge and on experiences first learned in children's homes. They made sure to incorporate multiple teaching strategies and adapt them so they were culturally responsive to the ways of learning characteristic of the children's community.

The teachers also constantly reflected on ways to build on children's interests and current knowledge to scaffold deeper understanding and learning. They integrated art and oral stories as tools to develop children's knowledge about fish and supported children's learning through modeling, questioning, and providing explicit explanations as needed. They fostered symbolic play using fishing-related materials and play scripts, and chose storybooks that reflected community traditions and values. They knew it was important for children to understand the purpose of activities and their relevance to the children's own lives.

EARLY LANGUAGE AND LITERACY LEARNING IN YOUNG NATIVE AMERICAN CHILDREN

Language and literacy are important tools we use to gain knowledge, express ideas, and make sense of our experiences (Bodrova & Leong, 1996; Vygotsky, 1978). They also play a primary role in transmitting beliefs and values of a culture from one generation to another (Romero-Little, 2010). Early in life, children learn to make sense of their world in the context of shared experiences with adults as they learn and develop foundational cultural and spiritual values (Rogoff, 1993).

Early language and literacy skills are key predictors of children's later success in school (Hart & Risley, 1995; Snow, Burns, & Griffin, 1998). Young children begin schooling with a wide variety of background knowledge and language and literacy experiences in terms of languages spoken in the home, and exposure to different types of print, technology, and other media. Children from cultural and linguistic minorities in communities with limited access to mainstream resources are especially at risk for learning difficulties (Heath, 1983; Snow et al., 1998).

Learning in an educational setting that fails to validate a child's social identity places Native children at risk for later academic difficulties (Demmert, McCardle, & Leos, 2006). It is widely acknowledged that Native American children experience challenges for their language and literacy development. In addition to a higher rate of poverty, reduced access to adequate health care, and other risk factors, a high number of Native American children experience reduced early exposure to language due to increased fluctuating early childhood hearing loss. The prevalence of chronic otitis media appears to be highest in the Inuit population, followed by Australian Aboriginals, Native Americans, and South Pacific Islanders, with prevalence rates ranging from 12–46% among the Inuit to 4–6% in South Pacific Islanders, compared with <1% for general populations in the United States and the United Kingdom (World Health Organization, 1996). Heredity is an important factor impacting the structure and function of the Eustachian tube in some ethnic groups (Bluestone, 2005). Persistent middle ear disease has been associated with delays in speech and language development impacting later academic performance and achievement in Native American children (Thielke & Shriberg, 1990).

A high prevalence of speech-language difficulties and learning disabilities makes it critical to address early language and literacy difficulties before children start school (Ball, 2007; Inglebret, Jones, & Pavel, 2008). However, educators are often from cultural and linguistic backgrounds that are different from the children and families they work with (Sanchez & Thorp, 2007). This results in a lack of knowledge and resources to provide effective support, especially in regard to Native American language and literacy acquisition. For example, teachers may not be aware of important cultural expectations for children's communication and responsiveness. In some Native American cultures, children may be expected to learn by listening, observing, and participating in authentic community activities. This "quiet reflective" holistic way of learning may not always be consistent with the more overt and explicit learning and communication style typical of many mainstream classrooms (Romero-Little, 2010). In addition, children with a home language other than English may use speech sounds from their home or tribal language while speaking English. If not familiar with the language, educators may erroneously assume the child has a speech disorder. Some tribal languages have a sound in the language that would be identified as a "lateral lisp" by a speech-language pathologist, when it really is dialectal variation (McCardle & Walton, 1987); sometimes these sounds may be present in a child's speech (the dialectal influence may persist), even if the tribal language is no longer the primary language spoken.

A major challenge for educators is the enormous diversity of children's language and cultural backgrounds. Some children enter preschool already speaking their native language, but most Native American children speak primarily English and may or may not have any exposure to the tribal language. Some may learn their Native tongue as a second language; others may speak a dialect of English influenced by the Native language, referred to as "Indian English" (Ball, 2007; Romero-Little, Duran, & Sanchez, 2012). In addition, children may come from a variety of cultural backgrounds and traditions. Some children may have a single tribal heritage, others a mixed heritage from multiple tribes as well as with other ethnic groups, including Caucasian and Hispanic (Cleary & Peacock, 1998).

Educators need to be aware of the importance of honoring local traditions and values and supporting Native language acquisition for promoting children's self-identity and optimal developmental and academic outcomes (Demmert & Towner, 2003; McCarty & Romero, 2005). In some preschools (e.g., programs on a reservation) where children share similar cultural and linguistic backgrounds, educators can plan instruction in collaboration with families and the community that supports both English and the Native language and traditions. When Native children are in classrooms where they are the minority group, as is often the case in urban areas, it is important to provide simple cultural support in the environment by including familiar and welcoming objects, such as a picture of an eagle or salmon, some native books on the shelf, a drum, or other Native instruments on display. Educators can also provide opportunities to focus on aspects of the child's culture, by recognizing a tribal event, inviting families to share tribal stories or activities, and giving even young children the opportunity to show leadership and to be the "expert" in some area of knowledge or skill from their culture. This is simply a reflection of best practice in ensuring that each child's culture and background is honored and respected, and that all children feel equally welcome and at home in their place of learning.

MULTIPLE ASPECTS OF LITERACY

A broader view of literacy provides educators with a conceptual foundation for early childhood education that promotes readiness skills for kindergarten while respecting cultural and linguistic diversity. In this chapter we adopt a broad comprehensive view of literacy that encompasses oral language, print, cognitive and social skills that are interrelated and mutually influence one another throughout development (Adams, 1990; Dickinson, McCabe, Anastasopoulos, Peisner-Feinberg, & Poe, 2003). Literacy is primarily about using symbols to communicate and to assign meaning to the world (Notari-Syverson, 2006). Literacy does not consist merely of reading and writing; rather it is a multifaceted and complex process that involves the use of multiple symbolic systems and is closely intertwined with knowledge of the world (Freire

& Macedo, 1987). The notion of "multiliteracies" (Cazden et al.,1996; New London Group, 1996) views literacy as multimodal, including not only oral language and traditional print but also nonverbal communication, and various symbols as well as visual, audio and digital media (e.g., television and the Internet). An approach that integrates visual and verbal learning may lend itself well as a framework for a better understanding of literacy in relation to Native American communities in which reading nonverbal social cues and learning to "read" the signs and symbols in nature and the physical environment play an important role (Ball, 2007).

Use of oral language and written literacy differs according to culture and context and may include experiences with books, signs and labels, drawing and writing, oral stories, songs, music, dances, as well as with the popular culture of television shows, cartoons, video games, computer icons, and movies (Knapp-Philo, Notari-Syverson, & Stice, 2007). This broad view of literacy offers programs a variety of ways to embed Native culture and language practices in daily classroom activities. Family-school-community engagement is key. Programs can offer a variety of opportunities for families and community partners to participate in curriculum planning (Dubosarsky et al., 2011; McWilliams et al., 2011). Teachers can invite families, elders, and other community members to share their ideas for books, videos, stories, dramatic play themes, science projects, music and art activities that reflect the local culture, and to participate in classroom activities and evening family programs.

HISTORICAL PERSPECTIVE

In 2007, the United Nations Declaration on the Rights of Indigenous Peoples (UN General Assembly, 2007) recognized the rights of Indigenous peoples to an education in their own culture and languages using methods of teaching and learning consistent with their traditions and values. A major challenge of early childhood education in Native American programs today is to provide culturally appropriate and evidence-based programming that supports language and cultural revitalization efforts of tribal communities. Before European contact, 300–500 Native languages were spoken by peoples Indigenous to what is now the United States and Canada, but currently only 34 are still being learned as a first language by children (McCarty & Romero, 2005). Unless the programs actively support the Native culture and language, there is danger that the younger generations will grow up with little knowledge of the culture and language of their ancestors (Romero-Little, 2010).

RESILIENCE

Resilience refers to factors and qualities that promote positive adaptation to less than ideal circumstances in a given group or community of people, usually groups with multiple stress and risk factors in areas such as mental or physical health, education, or economics. Evidence from the National Longitudinal Study of Adolescent Health indicated that Native American youth with high resilience factors tended to be those who felt good about their tribal culture, participated in cultural activities, and had strong positive responses to being part of a Native community (Strand & Peacock, 2003). By using culturally relevant teaching practices and supporting opportunities for Native American children to learn their Indigenous language, early childhood educators may be doing more than they know to build resilience in children who may encounter adversity.

Two highly successful models of Indigenous early education that have significantly impacted current efforts to resolve the conflict between families and Indigenous communities and schools are the Maori *TeKohanga Reo* programs in Aotearoa, New Zealand, and the *'Aha Pūnana Leo* program in Hawaii (Romero-Little, 2010). These programs began in the 1980s with a strong focus on Indigenous language renewal through language immersion and an emphasis on family and community participation in planning the curriculum and determining teaching practices (Hohepa & McNaughton, 2007).

In North America, some individual communities have developed their own approaches, adapting early childhood curricula and supplementing them with culturally based activities focused on traditional values, music and movement, storytelling, and dramatic play to support the cultural identity of Native American children and families.[2] One example is *Making a Difference*, a child-centered Head Start curriculum developed by tribal communities in the Northwest Territories in Canada (Chalmers, 2012). It is based on years of community-based research on child outcomes, includes a coaching component, and is one of few Native American programs that offer evaluation data (although results are difficult to interpret due to lack of a comparison group).

Another example is *the Storybook-Based Curriculum* (Fetherstone & England, 1998). Since 2000, early childhood programming at the Muckleshoot Tribe's Head Start and Birth-To-Three centers in Auburn, Washington, has used a curriculum with repeated, shared storybook reading based on the *Storybook-Based Curriculum*. This curriculum was selected and adapted to increase language, literacy, and school-readiness skills of Muckleshoot children, with the ultimate goal of increasing high school graduation rates in the tribe. Teachers carefully select both Native (Muckleshoot) and non-Native stories for daily presentation in three-week cycles. Daily planned extension activities address multiple areas of early childhood development and offer additional practice for learned skills. Whulshootseed language, customs, and arts are woven into the daily curriculum. Results of the use of the *Storybook-Based Curriculum*, as adapted and tailored to the specific needs of children at the Muckleshoot tribe, have been positively verified by Head Start federal review boards, quality monitoring using the Classroom Assessment Scoring System (CLASS) (Pianta, LaParo,

& Hamre, 2008), and subjective reports by Muckleshoot Kindergarten teachers, parents, and community members. The following is a description of the background and considerations leading to the implementation of *The Storybook-Based Curriculum* at the Muckleshoot Tribe.

THE IMPORTANCE OF STORIES

The Muckleshoot people reside in a strip of land along the Auburn-Enumclaw highway about ninety minutes southwest of Seattle, on the way to Mount Rainier. While the second author was working there as a speech-language pathologist a decade ago, a Muckleshoot friend tried to explain to her the importance of tribal stories as the friend was growing up. In the 1960s, there were still family and community events at which the old stories were told, usually by talented storytellers. She explained:

> *When I was little, there were these very entertaining stories about animals. As I heard the same stories a year or two later, they seemed different ... and the next time I would hear a story, I would think, "Wow, I didn't know that was in the story". At every step of my life those stories seemed richer and deeper, and it wasn't until much later that I figured out that the stories hadn't changed, but that I found different meanings at different stages of my life.*

She added that the stories she heard growing up, so different from the European fairytales and Disney stories of the outside culture, were instrumental in the development of her self-concept as a Muckleshoot.

Vi Hilbert, a revered Skagit tribal elder (now deceased), once said, "Our children don't need Goldilocks, they need to hear the stories of their people." Hilbert's own work involved passing down tribal history, language, and spiritual knowledge. A talented storyteller herself, she and Samish storyteller Johnny Moses produced a CD of traditional stories, told in Samish and Lushootseed (Hilbert & Moses, 2002). In 2003, she collaborated with linguist Zalmai (Zeke) Zahir to produce the *Grandmother Video Project*, a series of videos to promote and share tribal culture, language, and wisdom (Hilbert & Zahir, 2003). In one of the videos, Ms. Hilbert explains why Native stories in particular are important for young Native children:

> *Stories are treasured because they [contain] the important cultural teachings ... Stories tell us ... about geography, relatives, everything ... the earth and land. Stories are to teach and reinforce you. This is where the spirit is ... This is the spirit of stories, so that you will know the purposes of the ancestors. You are to listen to the stories so you will know how to conduct yourself ... The information comes from a long time ago. The beloved elders wanted everyone to understand*

and to walk tall as the First People . . . You will sit and listen, and your bank will become full. You will become enriched by your own heart-mind. This is how we learn to travel on a good road. (Transcribed from Hilbert & Zahir, 2003)

Vi Hilbert also collaborated with linguist Thom Hess to produce *Haboo*, a volume of traditional tribal stories from Northwest Washington State, transcribed from the original tribal language, Lushootseed (Hilbert & Hess, 1985). In *Haboo*, Hilbert outlined the values encompassed in many traditional stories of her culture: respect of all the earth; respect for each spirit; respect for the Creator; and honesty, generosity, compassion, cleanliness, and industry.

For many Native American cultures, rooted in oral storytelling traditions, stories have carried far more importance than mere entertainment. They have all along been a powerful tool for teaching. According to Native American storyteller Joseph Bruchac, "Lesson stories were used by every American Indian nation as a way of socializing the young and strengthening the values of their tribal nation for both young and old." (Bruchac, 2003, p. 37)

STORIES IN THE EARLY CHILDHOOD CURRICULUM

Stories may be appropriately used particularly in early childhood, as a basis for effective, culturally appropriate instruction. Reading stories with children that authentically reflect children's cultural values, topics, and worldviews can help educators better understand a child's experiences and help bridge home and classroom practices. The teacher becomes the raconteur, and repeated and extended storytelling activities may become a foundation for language, literacy, and concept development, extended thematic instruction, and tribal language revitalization. One evidence-based approach to promoting early language and literacy that appears consistent with Native cultural values is shared storybook reading (e.g., Dale, Crain-Thoreson, Notari-Syverson, & Cole, 1996; Ezell & Justice, 2005; Whitehurst et al., 1988). In this dialogic reading approach, rather than simply reading the text to a child, the adult engages in a meaningful conversation with the child about the story using various language facilitation and scaffolding strategies such as open-ended questioning, modeling, repeating, and expanding to scaffold and promote children's language (Inglebret et al., 2008; Notari-Syverson, O'Connor &Vadasy, 2007). These interactive, dialogic strategies can also be easily implemented by family members and caregivers across a variety of contexts. *Language Is the Key* (Cole & Lim, 2006), for example, is a video-based program that fosters the use of language facilitation strategies by parents and early childhood providers. This technique can be used not only in reading books but also with dramatic play, block building, art, and outdoor play, and is an ideal strategy for story-telling activities, dance, or the dramatic enactment of stories (Ball, 2007).

Inglebret et al. (2008) describe a successful implementation of a shared storybook intervention using select stories to provide speech and language intervention to a young Native American child. Stories were selected from the *Northwest Native American Reading Curriculum* (NWNARC) (Costantino & Hurtado, 2006), a series of stories by native authors, in a curriculum developed through the Washington State Office of the Superintendent of Public Instruction in collaboration with tribal culture and curriculum specialists. Preparation for the intervention involved clinicians meeting with the child's family and a tribal education specialist who provided background information on the values and ways of life of the Salish peoples of the Northwest coastal area. Educators should be cautious when selecting culturally appropriate stories (Mendoza & Reese, 2001). Some books may be "Native American" only in appearance, and authored and/or illustrated by non-Natives. Teachers should not overlook using the traditional local stories; those stories often are rooted in the local culture, lend themselves to community involvement and extension activities, and are more likely to be aligned with community values and language. The stories told by local elders may be told and written down, perhaps for the first time, and illustrated by children in book-making activities.

As in many other aspects of educational practice, there are differences in the social-cultural aspects of storytelling and listening in many Native communities. Some stories are told only at certain times of the year. Some stories may be perceived to belong to a certain family or group, requiring verbal acknowledgement of the source or even permission to tell the story. An old Northwest tradition required that the listeners of a story respond during a story by saying "Haboo", a kind of ongoing encouragement to the storyteller. Finally, children are expected to listen and draw their own conclusions. "My elders never said to me, 'This story carries such and such a meaning'", says Vi Hilbert in *Haboo*. "I was expected to listen carefully and learn why the story was being told. Though guided, I was allowed the dignity of finding my own interpretation." (Hilbert & Hess, 1985, p. ix).

FUTURE DIRECTIONS

There is a need for evidence-based curricula and teaching practices that are culturally and linguistically responsive to the values and traditions of Native American communities. These curricula and teaching practices need to prepare children for success in mainstream schooling, teach children the Native culture and language, and respect the sovereignty of tribes and their right to be involved in cultural and linguistic programming (Spicer, 2012).

A major challenge to developing a strong base of evidence on the effectiveness of Native American early education programs is that teaching and assessment practices developed in research and practice with European-heritage families do not seem to fit with the more ecological, holistic learning approach typical of many Native American communities (Romero-Little, 2010). There is a need for innovative, authentic, multimethod assessment and evaluation approaches that integrate participatory action research methodologies designed to involve families and community members, the use of multimedia such as photographs, audio and video recordings that capture holistic behaviors, and quantitative assessments that reflect the standards of controlled research studies (Ball, 2007; Romero-Little, 2010).

Successful early childhood programs for Native American children involve multi-generational family interactions that promote and enrich children's language and literacy development through interaction with elders, storytelling circles, family play and drama, and singing groups. The adoption of a broad comprehensive approach to early language and literacy provides programs with a framework that enables an integration of visual and verbal learning and the incorporation of multimodal texts and community-developed, culturally-specific language and literacy resources for teaching Native American languages (e.g., digital video and audio recordings of local stories and songs, books, and posters). It is critical that early childhood professionals work together with families and communities to adapt classroom practices to match community practices and to support communities in promoting skills and behaviors children need for school success (Hohepa & McNaughton, 2007). Professional development programs also need to work in partnership with families and communities to ensure that early childhood professionals gain the knowledge, skills, and attitudes that enable them to work successfully in diverse communities.

NOTES

1. Because of diverse and conflicting regional and tribal preferences regarding terminology, we have chosen to use the term "Native American" for consistency and inclusiveness. We apologize to those who prefer other terms, such as American Indian, Alaska Native, First People, or Indigenous people.
2. For more information on programs and evidence based practices to support programs working to preserve or revitalize Native American and other heritage cultures and languages, see the *Head Start Cultural and Linguistic Responsiveness Resource Catalogue, Volume Two* (National Center on Cultural and Linguistic Responsiveness, 2012).

REFERENCES

Adams, M.J. (1990). *Beginning to read: Thinking and learning about print*. Cambridge, MA: MIT Press.

Ball, J. (2007). *Aboriginal young children's language and literacy development: Research evaluating progress, promising practices, and needs.* Canadian Language and Literacy Networked Centre of Excellence. Retrieved from http://www.ecdip.org/docs/pdf/CLLRNet%20Feb%20 2008.pdf

Bluestone, C.D. (2005). Role in management of otitis media. In M. Bluestone (Ed.) *The eustachian tube: Structure, function, role in otitis media* (pp. 145–176). Hamilton, ON: BC Decker, Inc.

Bodrova, E., & Leong, D.(1996). *Tools of the mind. The Vygotskian approach to early childhood education.* Englewood Cliffs, NJ: Prentice Hall.

Bruchac, J. (2003). *Our stories remember: American Indian history, culture, and values through storytelling.* Golden, CO: Fulcrum Publishing.

Cazden, C., Cope, B., Fairclough, N., Gee, J., Cress, G., Luke, A., Luke, C., Michaels, S., & Nakata, M. (1996). A pedagogy of multiliteracies: designing social futures. *Harvard Educational Review,* 66(1), 60–92.

Chalmers, J.H. (2012). *Making a difference. Research and practice with a child-centered curriculum for Head Start children in indigenous and tribal communities.* Presented at the 11th National Head Start Research Conference, Washington, D.C., June 2012.

Cleary, L.M. & Peacock, T.D. (1998). *Collected wisdom: American Indian education.* Needham Heights, MA: Allyn and Bacon.

Cole, K.N. & Lim, Y.S. (2006). Language is the key: A proven approach to early language and literacy. In S. Rosenkoetter & J. Knapp-Philo (Eds.) *Learning to read the world. Language and literacy in the first three years* (pp. 537–551). Washington, D.C.: ZERO TO THREE Press.

Costantino, M., & Hurtado, D.S. (2006). Northwest Native American reading curriculum. *Journal of American Indian Education,* 45, 45–49.

Dale, P., Crain-Thoreson, C., Notari-Syverson, A., & Cole, K. (1996). Parent-child storybook reading as an intervention technique for young children with language delays. *Topics in Early Childhood Special Education,* 16, 213–235.

Demmert, W.G., & Towner, J.C. (2003). *A review of the research literature on the influences of culturally based education on the academic performance of Native American students.* Portland, OR: Northwest Regional Educational Laboratory. Retrieved from: http://educationnorthwest.org/webfm_send/196

Demmert, W.G., McCardle, P., & Leos, K. (2006). Conclusions and commentary. *Journal of American Indian Education,* 45(2), 77–88.

Dickinson, D., McCabe, A., Anastasopoulos, L., Peisner-Feinberg, E., & Poe, M. (2003). The comprehensive language approach to early literacy: The interrelationships among vocabulary, phonological sensitivity, and print knowledge among preschool-aged children. *Journal of Educational Psychology,* 95(3), 465–481.

Dubosarsky, M., Murphy, B., Roehrig, G., Frost, L.C., Jones, J., & Carlson, S.P. (2011). Animosh tracks on the playground, minnows in the sensory table: Incorporating cultural themes to promote preschoolers' critical thinking in American Indian Head Start classrooms. *Young Children,* 66(5), 20–29.

Everenden, J., & Hart, W. (1982). *In the land of the salmon.* Pacific Northwest Indian and Language Development Program, Northwest Regional Education Laboratory, Portland, OR.

Ezell, H.K., & Justice, L.M. (2005). *Shared storybook reading: Building young children's language and emergent literacy skills.* Baltimore: Paul H. Brookes Publishing.

Fetherstone, K., & England, K. (1998). *Storybook-based curriculum.* Portland, OR: Hearing & Speech Institute.

Freire, P., & Macedo, D. (1987). *Literacy: Reading the word and reading the world.* Westport, CT: Bergin & Garvey.

Hart, B., & Risley, T. (1995). *Meaningful differences in the everyday experiences of young American children.* Baltimore: Paul H. Brookes Publishing.

Heath, S.B. (1983). *Ways with words: Language, life and work in communities and classrooms.* Cambridge: Cambridge University Press.

Hilbert, V., & Hess, T. (1985). *Haboo: Native American stories from Puget Sound.* Seattle: University of Washington Press.

Hilbert, V., & Moses, J. (2002). *When the humans thought they were people* [audio CD]. Ten wolves. Retrieved from: www.10wolves.com.

Hilbert, V. & Zahir, Z. (2003). *The grandmother video project* [video series]. King County, WA: King County Landmarks & Heritage Commission.

Hirschi, R. (1992). *Seya's song.* Seattle: Sasquatch Books.

Hohepa, M., & McNaughton, S. (2007). Doing it 'proper': The case of Maori literacy. In L. Makin, C.J. Diaz, & C. McLachlan (Eds.) *Literacies in early childhood: Changing views, challenging practices* (2nd ed.) (pp. 217–229). Marrickville, NSW, Australia: Elsevier.

Inglebret, E., Jones, C., & Pavel, M. (2008). Integrating American Indian/Alaska Native culture into shared storybook intervention. *Language, Speech and Hearing Services in Schools, 39,* 521–527.

Knapp-Philo, J., Notari-Syverson, A., & Stice, K. (2005). Tools of literacy for infants and toddlers. In E. Horn & H. Jones (Eds.) Young Exceptional Children Monograph Series No. 7 *Supporting early literacy development in young children,* 43–58.

McCardle, P. & Walton, J. 1987. A preliminary analysis of English phonological trends in MS Choctaw children. In Cole & Deal (Eds.) *Communication disorders in multicultural populations.* Rockville, MD: American Speech and Hearing Association.

McCarty, T.L., & Romero, M.E. (2005). What does it mean to lose a language? Investigating heritage language loss and revitalization among American Indians. *Show & Tell: A Magazine from ASU's College of Education.* Fall 2005: 13–17. Retrieved from: http://www.u.arizona.edu/~aildi/Useful_Links/McCarty_Romero_article.pdf

McWilliams, M.S., Maldonado-Mancebo, T., Szczepaniak, P.S., & Jones, J. (2011). Supporting Native Indian preschoolers and their families: Family-preschool-community partnerships. *Young Children, 66*(6), 34–41.

Mendoza, J., & Reese, D. (2001). Examining multicultural picture books for the early childhood classroom: Possibilities and pitfalls. *Early childhood research and practice, 3*(2). Retrieved from http:// ecrp. uiuc.edu/v3n2/ mendoza.html

National Center on Cultural and Linguistic Responsiveness (2012). *Head Start cultural and linguistic responsiveness resource catalogue, volume two: Native and Heritage language preservation, revitalization, and Maintenance* (2nd ed.). Washington, D.C: Office of Head Start. Retrieved from: http://eclkc.ohs.acf.hhs.gov/hslc/tta-system/cultural-linguistic/docs/resource-catalogue-main-book-4.pdf

New London Group (1996). A pedagogy of multiliteracies: Designing social futures. *Harvard Educational Review, 66*(1), 60–92.

Notari-Syverson, A. (2006). Everyday tools of literacy. In S. Rosenkoetter & J. Knapp-Philo (Eds.) *Learning to read the world. Language and literacy in the first three years* (pp. 61–78). Washington, D.C.: ZERO TO THREE Press.

Notari-Syverson, A., O'Connor, R.E., &Vadasy, P. (2007). *Ladders to literacy: A preschool activity book.* Baltimore: Paul H. Brookes Publishing.

Pianta, R.C., LaParo, K.M., & Hamre, B.K (2008). *Classroom assessment scoring system pre-K.* Baltimore: Paul H. Brookes Publishing.

Rogoff, B. (1993). Children's guided participation and participatory appropriation in socio-cultural activity. In R.H. Wozniak & K.W. Fischer (Eds.) *Development in context: Acting and thinking in specific environments* (pp. 121–153). Hillsdale, NJ: Lawrence Erlbaum Associates.

Romero-Little, M.E. (2010). How should young indigenous children be prepared for learning? A vision of early childhood education for indigenous children. *Journal of American Indian Education, 49*, 7–27.

Romero-Little, M.E., Duran, L.K., & Santos, R.M. (2012). Supporting the maintenance and revitalization of indigenous languages and cultures through early childhood practice. In R.M. Santos, G.A. Cheatham, & L. Duran (Eds.) Young Exceptional Children Monograph Series No. 14 *Supporting young children who are dual language learners with or at risk for disabilities,* 148–163.

Sanchez, S.Y., & Thorp, E.K. (2007). Teaching to transform: Infusing cultural and linguistic diversity. In P.J. Winton, J.A. McCollum, & C. Catlett (Eds.) *Practical approaches to early childhood professional development: Evidence, strategies, and resources* (pp. 81–97). Washington, D.C.: ZERO TO THREE Press.

Snow, C.E., Burns, M.S., Griffin, P. (1998). *Preventing reading difficulties in young children.* Washington, D.C.: National Academy Press.

Spicer, P. (2012). *Language and culture in American Indian Head Start.* Paper presented at the 11th National Head Start Research Conference, Washington, D.C., June 2012.

Strand, J., & Peacock, R. (2003). Nurturing resilience and school success in American Indian and Alaska Native students. *The International Child and Youth Care Network, Issue 59.* Retrieved from: http://www.cyc-net.org/cyc-online/cycol-1203-resilience.html

Thielke, H., & Shriberg, L. (1990). Effects of recurrent otitis media on language, speech, and educational achievement in Menominee Indian children. *Journal of American Indian Education, 29*, 1–10. Retrieved from http://jaie.asu.edu/v29/V2952eff.htm

UN General Assembly, United Nations declaration on the rights of Indigenous Peoples: resolution/adopted by the General Assembly, 2 October 2007, A/RES/61/295. Retrieved from: http://www.refworld.org/docid/471355a82.html [accessed 22 July 2013

Vygotsky, L.S. (1978). *Mind in society: The development of higher psychological processes.* Cambridge, MA: Harvard University Press.

Whitehurst, G.J., Falco, F.L., Lonigan, C.J., Fischel, J.E., DeBaryshe, B.D., Valdez-Menchaca, M.C. et al. (1988). Accelerating language development through picture book reading. *Developmental Psychology, 24*, 552–558.

World Health Organization (1996). Prevention of hearing impairment from chronic otitis media: Report of a WH/CIBA Foundation workshop. London: 19–21. Retrieved from http://www.who.int/pbd/publications/en/

Zahir, Z. (2000). *Stories of our ancestors.* Des Moines, WA: Zahir Consulting Services.

10 Supporting Native Hawaiian Children and Families through Traditional Native Hawaiian Values
Three Partners in Development Foundation Education Programs

Toni Porter, Jan Dill, Alison Masutani, Danny Goya, and Lora Perry

Native Hawaiians[1] (NH) account for the largest Pacific Islander group in the United States (Hixson, Hepler, & Kim, 2013). They also represent a significant proportion of Indigenous groups: approximately 540,000 individuals self-identified as NH in the 2010 census, accounting for 16% of those who self- identified as Native Americans and Alaskan Natives (Humes, Jones, & Ramirez, 2011). More than half of NH individuals live in the state of Hawai'i; they represent approximately 25% of the state's population of 1.4 million (Hixson et al., 2013).

NH families in Hawai'i struggle with many of the same challenges that other Indigenous communities face. Poverty levels are high, having exceeded the national rate in 2011 (Macartney, Bishaw, & Fontenot, 2103); approximately 22% of children under age five and 17% of school-age children were living in poverty (Office of Hawaiian Affairs, 2011). Unemployment in 2011 was higher than the national average (Bureau of Labor Statistics, 2011), and homelessness has reached epidemic proportions (Lee, Geminiani, & Su, 2012).

Compared to other major ethnic groups in the state, NH have lower levels of education: 7% had completed an associate's degree and 9%, a bachelor's degree in 2000 (Malone & Shoda- Sutherland, 2005). NH children lag behind in math and reading scores (Kamehameha Schools, 2009), and have the lowest timely graduation rates of any ethnic group in the state (Kamehameha Schools, 2009). Health outcomes are poor: NH have the highest death rate for cardiovascular disease and high rates of diabetes, far exceeding those of other ethnic groups in the state, in large part due to the prevalence of obesity (Department of Native Hawaiian Health, 2013); nearly one third of NH middle schoolers were overweight or at risk of becoming overweight compared to approximately one quarter of non-Hawaiians (Kamehameha Schools, 2009). NH also have the highest arrest rate for violent crimes of all the major ethnic groups in the state (Kamehameha

Schools, 2009); in 2006, they accounted for 40% of all inmates in Hawai'i's prison system (Kamehameha Schools, 2009).

PARTNERS IN DEVELOPMENT FOUNDATION

These are the stark and negative realities that the Partners in Development Foundation (PIDF)[2] has sought to address for more than a decade. Over the years, it has developed and implemented programs to improve educational outcomes for NH children and their families; to strengthen stewardship and management of the environment, including sustainable agriculture for its island community; and to support families through social services. In 2012, PIDF operated 10 primary programs, which served approximately 3,700 children from birth to age 18, 4,100 caregivers, and 3,000 families. These programs, which extend throughout the Hawaiian islands, are offered at no-cost to families and children (Table 10.1).

Table 10.1   Partners in Development Foundation Programs, 2013

	Type of Program	Population Served	Location (# of sites)	# Served in 2012
Tūtū and Me Traveling Preschool	Family–child interactive learning program to promote school readiness, caregiver skills, and healthy families	Children birth to age 5 and their caregiver	O'ahu (6) Hawai'i (10) Kaua'i (4) Maui (4) Moloka'i (2)	452 children, 712 caregivers 493 children, 755 caregivers 276 children, 369 caregivers 295 children, 798 caregivers 150 children, 306 caregivers
Nā Pono No Nā 'Ohana	Family education program for Native Hawaiians and others in Waimānalo area	Birth to adult	O'ahu *Windward*	157 families (476 individuals) - 44 adult students working towards GED
Ka Pa'alana Homeless Family Education Program	Tūtū and Me/ Nā Pono model to homeless families on beaches and in shelters	Birth to adult	O'ahu *Leeward Coast*	452 children, 959 caregivers
'Ike No'eau	Mobile computer lab with culturally appropriate science/math curriculum	Children birth to age 5 and their caregiver	O'ahu *Leeward Coast* (2) *Windward* (1)	148 children, 129 caregivers

(continued)

Table 10.1   (continued)

	Type of Program	Population Served	Location (# of sites)	# Served in 2012
Ka Hana No'eau	Intergenerational youth mentoring	Middle and High School students	Hawai'i (4)	188 teens, 243 tutored 9 mentor groups
Tech Together	STEM workshops	6th grade students	O'ahu (8) Hawai'i (2) Moloka'i (3)	798 students 359 students 66 students
Ke Kama Pono	Safe house for adjudicated youth, working with families to ensure successful re-entry	13- to 17-year-old males	O'ahu (1)	34 youth, 83 parents
Hui Ho'omalu	Recruit, train, assess, and support (foster) resource families in HI	All ages	All major islands	66 families licensed
Pili A Pa'a	Teacher professional development	Middle and High School teachers	Hawai'i *Kohala, Honoka'a*	N/A (training for first cohort began Jan. 2013)
Baibala Hemolele	Preserves/ marks the Hawaiian Bible	All ages	Sold worldwide and accessible online at www. baibala.org	Over 3,700 sold 7000 hits/month on website

PIDF's work is grounded in, and guided by, traditional NH values and perspectives, which include the following: *aloha* (showing respect to elders, families, peers, and the environment); *lōkahi* (bringing everyone together in a balanced, cohesive way without being one-sided or single-minded); *mālama* (nurturing to ensure that all efforts provide for the betterment of the whole; *pono* (showing by example through thinking and acting holistically and doing what is right for all as opposed to the individual); and *po'okela* (practicing all of these values with excellence, and purposefully creating a climate of caring, knowledge, and support that will reach far into the future of Hawai'i). Hawaiian culture, language, and traditions are embedded in all of the programs. Other values that inform PIDF's efforts include *pa'ahana* (righteousness), *kela* (excellence), *alaka'i* (leadership), and *ku i ka ni'o* (achievement), which are practiced by striving for achievement and excellence through working hard for the benefit of the whole rather than the individual.

PIDF'S EDUCATIONAL PROGRAMS

This chapter highlights three of PIDF's educational programs: *Tūtū and Me Traveling Preschool*, *Ka Pa'alana Homeless Family Education Program*, and *Nā Pono No Nā 'Ohana*, the family education program in Waimānalo. Each is based on research and evidence-based practice as well as community involvement and interaction. All three include an early childhood education (ECE) component to improve positive outcomes for children's school readiness and school success, and one or more components to improve adult positive outcomes such as caregiving skills, literacy, and well-being. Consistent with PIDF's philosophy, the ECE curriculum is sensitive to NH culture, incorporating values and Hawaiian language in songs and activities, an approach that research indicates is an effective strategy for improving educational outcomes among Indigenous peoples (Regional Educational Laboratory, 2011). Teaching strategies integrate approaches such as avoiding placing blame for children's failure on families, actively engaging families in their children's education, and individualizing instruction, all of which evidence also suggests are effective with NH or Indigenous peoples (McBay, 2003). Each program collects a variety of data to track implementation and outcomes, and each serves specific target populations based on identified needs. *Tūtū and Me* aims to reach NH caregivers, particularly *tūtū* (grandparents) and parents, with preschool children in low-income/high risk communities throughout the state. *Ka Pa'alana* works with homeless families and their young children who live on the beaches and in shelters on the Leeward Coast of O'ahu. *Nā Pono*'s target population is families with children from birth to age eight in an elementary school on O'ahu, which has the largest population of NH in the state.

Service delivery dosage and intensity also vary among the programs. *Tūtū and Me* offers two hours of family interaction in which children and caregivers engage in activities together twice a week. *Ka Pa'alana* provides four hours of services—two hours of ECE alone for children, while their parents participate in adult educational activities, and two hours of family interaction—four days a week. Of the three programs, *Nā Pono* is the most intensive, providing a comprehensive five-day-a-week, 20-hour family education program that consists of a combination of parents and children together time (PACT), ECE, and tutoring, in all of the classes of the elementary school (K-6), and parent and adult education.

TŪTŪ AND ME

Initiated in 2001, *Tūtū and Me* is the oldest of PIDF's education programs. It was created in response to the perceived ECE crisis for NH families.

Research indicated that four in ten children, most of them NH, who entered kindergarten were not ready to learn and that some of them were two years behind, unable to identify colors or count to five (Kana'iaupuni, Malone, & Ishibashi, 2005a). More than half of NH children entered school without any preschool experience (Kana'iaupuni et al., 2005a). In addition, many NH grandparents had primary responsibility for raising the youngest members of their extended families (U.S. Census, 2011). Research on NH families indicated that a strong supportive relationship with someone like a *tūtū* was a significant factor in children's resiliency (Werner & Smith, 1982). These data were supported by additional research that pointed to the relationship between parental or grandparental involvement in children's early learning and young children's positive outcomes (Bredekamp & Copple, 1997; Marcon, 1999; Shoda-Sutherland, 2005; Thornburg, 2002).

Early in its development, *Tūtū and Me* created a logic model that identifies the long-term and intermediate outcomes it aims to achieve. For caregivers, the long-term goals are to "provide optimal learning experiences at home" so that the children "enter school ready to learn and succeed at high standards" (Porter et al., 2010, p. 256) and to increase caregivers' understanding of the role they play in children's school success. The other major goals are strengthening families and nurturing caregiver-child bonds.

Tūtū and Me's approach is to provide high quality ECE through a traveling preschool. Caregivers must participate along with their children, not only to enhance caregivers' support for their children's learning and development, but also to strengthen the connection between school and home.

Tūtū and Me sends a four-member teaching team (a teacher, two assistant teachers and an assessment specialist) to communities in vans equipped with teaching materials and resources. At a community center, church, or public school cafeteria, the teams transform the space into a rich learning environment with at least 20 different learning centers ranging from a library and block play to outdoor art and a math center, all carefully planned to provide the experiences children need in order to gain a good foundation for future learning. The curriculum is organized around monthly learning themes and Hawaiian values. Informational signs in English and Hawaiian at each learning center provide information on the key developmental domains that it supports, directions for how to use the materials, and suggested vocabulary words related to the activity.

Caregivers learn strategies to promote school success as they join their children in their learning activities, explain what may be happening, and gain skills that they can use at home. Staff members model interactions with children and are available for consultations on a variety of issues. Additional caregiver support is provided through several means: daily two-minute *Tūtū* Talks on a variety of topics including child development, parenting, and health; a Caregiver Resource Center with books and materials related to child-rearing and adult interests; parenting workshops; and newsletters. To encourage caregivers to create a stimulating home learning environment and continued involvement, *Tūtū and Me* provides numerous take-home activities, including the *Keiki* (child) Book Bag for borrowing materials, a book lending program, and a Monthly Activity calendar.

Tūtū and Me has consistently used data for continuous improvement and assessment of its effectiveness. To document the program's implementation, it tracks caregiver and child attendance, books borrowed by individual children and the number of times caregivers read these books to children each week, the number of resources borrowed from the Caregiver Resource Center, and fidelity to the model through a Site Checklist. In addition, *Tūtū and Me* collects a variety of data to assess child and adult outcomes.

Findings from these assessments consistently point to the program's effectiveness in enhancing children's school readiness. In the three years between 2010 and 2013, for example, there were statistically significant increases in raw scores on the Peabody Picture Vocabulary Test IV™ (PPVT-IV: Dunn & Dunn, 1997), which measures receptive language, as well as increases in Work Sampling System® (WSS: Meisels, Liaw, Dorman, & Nelson, 1995) mean scores on proficient ratings for personal-social, language and literacy, gross and fine physical development, health and safety, and math domains among three- and four-year-olds (Scott Ray & Associates, 2013). In addition, an average of 93% of students over the three-year period scored at the highest level of the Hawai'i State School Readiness Assessment (HSSRA: State of Hawai'i Department of Education, 2013) in the five domains for kindergarten entry skills, and there were significant improvements from fall to spring in Get Ready To Read! (GRTR: Whitehurst & Lonigan, 2001) early literacy scores for four- and five-year-old children (Scott Ray & Associates, 2013).

A longitudinal study of a cohort of children enrolled in *Tūtū and Me* at age three in 2008 points to similarly positive effects (Porter, unpublished). Preliminary findings indicate that participation in *Tūtū and Me* had a positive effect on children's school readiness, particularly in social-emotional development, language development, and cognitive development, domains that are most salient for school readiness. Between the fall of 2008, when the children were first assessed, and fall of 2011, when the children entered kindergarten, there were statistically significant decreases in behavioral concerns as measured by the Devereux Early Childhood Assessment (DECA: LeBuffe & Naglieri, 1999) and in the Child Behavior Checklist (CBCL: Achenbach & Rescorla, 2000) development factors such as fear of trying new things and inability to get along with others. In addition, there were statistically significant increases in age equivalent scores on the Woodcock Johnson-Revised (WJ-R: Woodcock, McGrew, & Mather, 2001) tests for listening ability, comprehension, and language development as well as significant gains in age equivalent and grade equivalent scores on the WJ-R test for quantitative achievement, math reasoning, and math knowledge.

Findings also indicate that *Tūtū and Me* has a positive effect on caregiver skills. A 2008 pre/post study with the Child Care Assessment Tool for Relatives (CCAT-R: Porter, Rice, & Rivera, 2006), an observation instrument designed to assess quality in care provided by relatives, showed improvements in the quality of interactions that support children's cognitive and language development, and significant improvements in these factors for parents of children under three (Porter & Vuong, 2008). The 2010–2013 evaluation found similar results: There were significant increases on the on-site Caregiver Skills Assessment observations, which measure caregiver-child interactions such as the use of language, understanding of children's development, and encouragement in supporting children's problem-solving skills (Scott Ray and Associates, 2013). Caregiver self-reports on the Annual Caregiver Survey also pointed to positive changes in caregiver knowledge about how children learn, new activities to do at home, and new ideas about parenting and discipline. Over the past 12 years, *Tūtū and Me* has served more than 19,000 children and caregivers.

KA PAʻALANA

As the *Tūtū and Me* program expanded, PIDF sought to address the ECE needs of the most fragile members of its community—the children and families facing the challenges of homelessness on the beaches and in the bushes of the leeward coast of the island of Oʻahu. This community—living in an area which houses the largest population of NH in the state—struggles with generational poverty and is plagued by many negative social indicators: family dysfunction, inadequate preparation for kindergarten, high dropout and low graduation rates, high juvenile pregnancy rates, and incarceration. In addition, preschool enrollment is low: between 55% and 78% of kindergartners at the two local elementary schools had not attended preschool in 2011 (State of Hawaiʻi Department of Education, 2011).

In 2007, PIDF created *Ka Paʻalana*, which addresses these issues by providing comprehensive family education services. Consistent with the federal Department of Housing and Urban Development's Continuum of Care and Opening Doors initiatives, *Ka Paʻalana* aims to support families throughout each step of the housing process from the beaches to permanent housing. Its family education program draws from the *Tūtū and Me* traveling preschool approach to ECE and the National Center for Family Literacy (NCFL)'s family literacy model, which research shows produces positive outcomes for children and parents (National Center for Family Literacy, 2012).

Many government agencies and non-profit groups have been largely unsuccessful in working with the NH homeless population. This particular at-risk group is apprehensive of rules and regulations, and education for their children is viewed as "something schools do, not me." *Ka Paʻalana* initially approaches families to gain their trust through Mālama Mobile—vans loaded with basic necessities such as canned goods, food, diapers, and tarps—which are staffed predominantly by NH personnel from the Leeward Coast. Once trust is gained, ECE staff conduct *Ka Paʻalana*'s traveling preschool, often called, "Preschools under the Blue Tarps," right on the beach. They also offer adult educational opportunities directly or through vocational programs.

With *Ka Pa'alana*'s encouragement, families move from the beaches into shelters, where *Ka Pa'alana* offers its family education program. Each of the four components—ECE for children alone, adult education services, parenting education, and PACT—meets national standards and is culturally responsive. The program's success is evidenced by the fact that *Ka Pa'alana* is in seven shelters and three public housing complexes on the Leeward Coast. The program also employs seven former program participants who have been mentored to positively transform their lives and the lives of their children, and now mentor other participants and serve as strong ambassadors of hope for them. Since 2007, *Ka Pa'alana* has served more than 7,900 homeless children and caregivers.

NĀ PONO NO NĀ 'OHANA

PIDF believes that the family is the most important factor in growing successful communities. PIDF's *Nā Pono* is a model of the ways in which a comprehensive family education program can serve and partner with a community, so that the families, schools, and community are inspired and equipped for success. Over the last 10 years, this program has served more than 1,600 families and has become an integral partner in the Waimānalo community. The program seems to have had an effect: one school, which had been rated as needing corrective action under the No Child Left Behind Act (2001) standards, was named as a National Blue Ribbon school by the federal Department of Education in 2013.

CONCLUSION

PIDF's work with NH families and children has received significant national recognition. *Tūtū and Me* has been highlighted as an innovative strategy for NH education, because it draws from the strength of NH families and builds on multi-generational influences on child development (Kana'iaupuni et al., 2005b). In 2010, it was profiled as one of 23 initiatives in a compendium of efforts to improve child-care quality provided by home-based caregivers for low-income families (Porter et al., 2010). In the spring of 2013, *Ka Pa'alana*'s homeless preschool at Kalaeloa became one of the first National Association for the Education of Young Children accredited preschool programs to serve the homeless in the United States under the category of "Unique Program Structure." In May 2013, PIDF was also selected as a recipient of the Generations United 2013 Intergenerational Innovation Award, in recognition of its innovative contributions to the intergenerational field.

Since its inception, PIDF has committed its efforts to inspiring families and children in its communities to improve their lives. It has held steadfast to the integration of Native Hawaiian culture, honoring values, language, and tradition in all of its programs. This strong culturally-responsive approach, combined with research-based program models and practices, has produced positive results and offers viable options for other Indigenous communities who seek to address similar issues.

NOTES

1. In the U.S. Census, Native Hawaiian or Other Pacific Islander" refers to a person having origins in any of the original peoples of Hawai'i, Guam, Samoa, or other Pacific Islands. It includes people who indicated their race(s) as "Pacific Islander" or reported entries such as "Native Hawaiian," "Guamanian or Chamorro," "Samoan," and "Other Pacific Islander" or provided other detailed Pacific Islander responses (U.S. Census, 2010).
2. Founded in 1997, Partners in Development Foundation (PIDF) is a public, not-for-profit organization dedicated to creating and nurturing healthy, resilient communities. Its mission is to inspire and equip families and communities for success and service, using timeless Native Hawaiian values and traditions.

REFERENCES

Achenbach, T.M., & Rescorla, L.A. *(2000)*. *Manual for the ASEBA preschool forms & profiles.* Burlington: University of Vermont, Research Center for Children, Youth, and Families.

Bredekamp, S. & Copple, C. (1997). *Developmentally appropriate practice in early childhood programs.* Washington, D.C.: NAEYC.

Bureau of Labor Statistics. (2011). *Racial and ethnic characteristics of the U.S. labor force, 2011: The editor's desk.* Washington, D.C.: Bureau of Labor Statistics, U.S. Department of Labor. Retrieved from: http://www.bls.gov/opub/ted/2012/ted_20120905.htm

Department of Native Hawaiian Health. (2012). *Assessment and priorities for health and well-being in Native Hawaiians & other Pacific peoples.* Honolulu, HI: Center for Native and Pacific Health Disparities Research, John A. Burns School of Medicine, University of Hawai'i at Mānoa.

Dunn, L.M., & Dunn, L. (1997). *Peabody Picture Vocabulary Test (3rd ed.).* Circle Pines, MS: American Guidance Services.

Hixson, L., Hepler, B.B., & Kim, M.O. (2012). *The Native Hawaiian and other Pacific Islander population: 2010. 2010 Census Briefs.* C2010BR-12 Washington, D.C.: U.S. Census Bureau. Retrieved from: http://www.census.gov/prod/cen2010/briefs/c2010br-12.pdf

Humes, K.R., Jones, N.A., & Ramirez, R.R. (2011). *Overview of race and Hispanic origin: 2010. 2010 Census Briefs.* C2010BR-02. Washington, DC: U.S. Census.

Kamehameha Schools. (2009). *Native Hawaiian educational assessment update 2009: A supplement to Ka Huaka'i 2005.* Honolulu, HI: Research & Evaluation Division, Kamehameha Schools.

Kanaʻiaupuni, S., Malone, N., & Ishibashi, K. (2005a). *Native Hawaiian educational assessment 2005. Kamehameha Schools–PASE 04–05:29.* Honolulu, HI: Research & Evaluation Division, Kamehameha Schools.

Kanaʻiaupuni, S.M., Malone, N.J., & Ishibashi, K. (2005b). *Income and poverty among Native Hawaiians: Summary of Ka Huakaʻi findings.* Honolulu: Policy Analysis and System Evaluation, Kamehameha Schools.

LeBuffe, P.A., & Naglieri, J.A. (1999). *Devereux early childhood assessment technical manual.* Lewisville, NC: Kaplan Early Learning Company Publishing.

Lee, J.L., Geminiani,V., & Su, J. (2012). *The state of poverty in Hawaii & how to restore our legacy of fairness: How the great recession disproportionately impacted Hawaiʻi's disadvantaged and policy recommendations to achieve fairness.* Honolulu: Hawaiʻi Appleseed Center for Law and Economic Justice. Retrieved from: http://hiappleseed.org/sites/default/files/State%20of%20 Poverty%20FINAL.pdf

Macartney, S., Bishaw, A., & Fontenot, K. (2103). *Poverty rates for selected detailed race and Hispanic groups by state and place: 2007–2011* (American Community Survey Briefs ACSBR/11–1). Washington, D.C.: U.S. Census Bureau.

Malone, N.J., & Shoda-Sutherland,C. (2005). *Kau liʻiliʻi: Characteristics of Native Hawaiians in Hawaiʻi and the continental United States.* Kamehameha Schools–PASE, 04–05:21. Honolulu: Policy Analysis and System Evaluation, Kamehameha Schools.

Marcon, R. (1999). Positive relationships between parent-school involvement and public school inner-city preschoolers' development and academic performance. *School Psychology Review, 28*(3), 395–412.

McBay, S.M. (2003). Improving education for minorities. *Issues in Science and Technology,* Summer, 36–42. Retrieved from: http://www.issues.org/19.4/ updated/

Meisels, S.J., Liaw, F.R., Dorman, A., & Nelson, R. (1995). The work sampling system: Reliability and validity of a performance assessment for young children. *Early Childhood Research Quarterly, 10*(3), 277–296.

National Center for Family Literacy. (2012). *Sustain & gain: Blueprint for a long-term, thriving family literacy/parent engagement program.* Louisville, KY: author. Retrieved from: http://www.famlit.org/wp-content/uploads/2012/04/ NCFL-Sustainability-Guide_F.pdf

No Child Left Behind Act of 2001. PL.107–110, 115 Stat.1452, 20 U.S.C. §§ 6301 et seq.

Office of Hawaiian Affairs. (2011). *Native Hawaiian data book.* Honolulu: author. Retrieved from: http://www.ohadatabook.com/T02-POVERTY01-new.pdf

Porter, T. (2011). Preliminary results from the Tūtū and Me longitudinal survey. Prepared for Partners in Development Foundation.

Porter, T., Paulsell, D., Nichols, T., Begnoche, C., & Del Grosso, P. (2010). *Supporting quality in home-based child care: A compendium of 23 initiatives.* Princeton, NJ: Mathematica Policy Research.

Porter, T., Rice, R., & Rivera, E. (2006). *Assessing quality in family, friend, and neighbor care: The child care assessment tool for relatives.* New York: Bank Street College of Education.

Porter, T., & Vuong, L. (2008). *Tūtū and me: Assessing the effects of a family interaction program on parents and grandparents.* New York: Bank Street College of Education.

Regional Educational Laboratory for the Central Region. (2011). *Compilation of abstracts: Effective teaching of American Indian students: A preliminary response.* Prepared the Regional Educational Laboratory for the Central Region for The National Indian Education Association and including ADDENDUM: Additional Native Hawaiian Resources Prepared by Kauhale Kipaipai,

Kamehameha Schools. Retrieved from: http://www.niea.org/data/files/rel%20central%20american%20indian%20abstract%20compilation%202011.06.01. pdf

Scott Ray, & Associates. (2013). *Unpublished analysis: Three-year outcomes for Tūtū and Me Traveling Preschool, 2010–2013.* New Orleans: author.

Shoda-Sutherland, C. (2005). *Preschool and beyond: Two-year report to parents.* Honolulu: Policy Analysis and System Evaluation, Kamehameha Schools.

State of Hawai'i Department of Education. (2011). *Hawai'i state school readiness assessment: School results.* Honolulu: Systems Accountability Office, System Evaluation and Reporting Section, Office of Superintendent, Hawai'i State Department of Education and the Good Beginnings Alliance: Retrieved from http://arch.k12.hi.us/PDFs/hssra/2012/Leeward/School-270-Waianae%20El. pdf

State of Hawai'i Department of Education. (2103). Hawai'i state school readiness assessments. Honolulu: Systems Accountability Office, System Evaluation & Reporting Section, State of Hawai'i Department of Education. Retrieved from: http://arch.k12.hi.us/PDFs/hssra/Q&A_HSSRA20100719.pdf

Thornburg, K.R. (2002). Perspectives on school readiness: The roles of families, programs, professionals, and communities. *International Journal of Early Childhood Education, 8*(1), 7–36.

U.S. Census Bureau. (2010). The Native Hawaiian and Other Pacific Islander Population: 2010. *2010 Census Briefs.* U.S. Department of Commerce, Econimics and Statistics Administration. Retrieved from http://www.census.gov/prod/cen2010/briefs/c2010br-12.pdf

U.S. Census Bureau. (2011). 2011 American community survey. Retrieved from: http://factfinder2.census.gov/faces/tableservices/jsf/pages/productview. xhtml?src=bkmk

Werner, E.E., & Smith, R.S. (1982). *Vulnerable but invincible: A study of resilient children.* New York: McGraw-Hill.

Whitehurst, G.J., & Lonigan, C.J. (2001). *Get ready to read! Screening tool.* New York: National Center for Learning Disabilities.

Woodcock, R.W., McGrew, K.S., & Mather, N. (2001). *Woodcock-Johnson III Tests of Achievement.* Itasca, IL: Riverside Publishing.

11 Model for Narrowing the Achievement Gap for Native Students from Middle and High School to College Graduation

Iisaaksiichaa Ross A. Braine and Glaadai Tommy Segundo[1]

The purpose of this chapter is to build upon prior chapters in Section II of this volume on a developmental approach to merging cultural sensitivity and evidence-based practice. The earlier chapters deal with preschool and early childhood models, which are desirable and necessary, but not sufficient. Ongoing efforts during middle school, high school, and higher education are also needed to narrow the achievement gap.

This "hybrid" chapter combines written text in this volume with websites to model innovative use of technology in the information age with the oral tradition of Native Peoples. The conversation between the first author, who grew up on a reservation, and the second author, who was raised as an urban Indian, was recorded on October 4, 2013 at the University of Washington (UW).[2]

The oral tradition of Native culture is a medium for transmitting the wisdom of past generations with the challenges of the present and the dreams and visions for the future. As Little Tree explained in *The Education of Little Tree* (Carter, 2004), "If ye don't know the past, then ye will not have a future. If ye don't know where your people have been, then ye won't know where your people are going" (p. 40).

Part of the past for Native students is cultural trauma due to treatment by those who invaded and took away their land, removed their children from their homes and sent them to boarding schools, and govern them as a foreign government on the land that once belonged to them. Part of the present is persisting cultural stereotypes.

However, our recorded conversation provides a vision of a more hopeful future in which mentoring Native students from middle childhood to adolescence to young adulthood, and recruiting them for and sustaining them in higher education can narrow the current achievement gap. We are actively involved in implementing the vision and collecting the evidence that shows this model can work and help Native students succeed across the life span.

Some readers may wish to view and listen to our recorded conversation on one of the posted websites before reading this overview of that conversation. Other readers may first wish to read this written overview before accessing our recorded conversation. One of us, the first co-author of this story told in oral tradition, grew up on the Crow and Cheyenne reservations in Montana, while the other, the second co-author, whose family is Haida from Alaska, was raised as an urban Indian in Seattle. From these contrasting perspectives, we both observed how often Native students wear "masks" hiding who they are, do not participate in class, are misunderstood, and are all too often referred to special education, where they are overrepresented. Each of us was fortunate to have a mentor who showed us there was another path, which we have followed; in turn, we have dedicated our lives to showing others the paths they might follow and supporting their journey to successful completion.

This conversation begins with each author's story ("My Story"), continues with our collaborations ("Our Story") as the Tribal Liaison between Tribes and the University of Washington Administration (Ross Braine) and the Tribal Recruiter for the University of Washington (Tommy Segundo), and sets the scene for "Their Stories", the Native students who successfully complete higher education. Please see the posted website for the complete conversation. What follows is just the introduction to or summary overview of the stories.

MY STORY

First co-author. My name is *Iisaaksiichaa,* which roughly translates to "Good Ladd"; my English name is Ross Braine. I am an enrolled member of the Apsaalooke Nation in Montana, a Big Lodge Clan member, and a part of the Nighthawk Society. At the school I attended off the reservation, I never raised my hand or actively participated and was referred to special education. Later it was decided that I was bored and needed gifted programming, where I flourished and became a more involved student. I attended the University of Washington where I became a student leader but I never found my talents until I was hired as an office assistant for the Federal TRiO Educational Opportunity Program in the UW Office of Minority Affairs & Diversity headed by Julian Argel, who mentored and encouraged me to finish my UW degree. While I did so, I volunteered in after school/out of school programs in local schools such as Clear Sky Youth Council. These programs provided food, tutoring in STEM (science, technology, engineering and math), foreign language, and other school subjects, and cultural activities (e.g., bead work, singing, storytelling, making drum sticks, hunting, visits from elders, and even summer basketball camp). That participating middle school and high school Native students achieved 100% high school graduation and access to higher education was as gratifying to me as earning my own college degree and recently being admitted to graduate studies in the information school.

Second co-author. My name is Tommy Segundo and I'm Kaigani Haida from the Prince of Whales Island located in Southeast Alaska. I'm a Double Finned Killer Whale of the Raven Clan. My Haida name is *Glaadai,* which best translates to "endures much within." I was born and raised in the greater Seattle area and attended urban public schools in which I was one of very few, if not the only Native student attending the school. Because of this, one challenge I faced was lack of cultural identity while at school and with that, the lack of a sense that I could be a high achieving student. That changed when my Indian Education advisor, who knew I had potential, advised me to apply to and attend a community college as a stepping stone to a 4-year university. I followed her advice, eventually completed my undergraduate degree at the UW, and devoted much time along the way to helping other Native students achieve the same goal of obtaining a college education. I've worked for various Native organizations within the Seattle area such as the Seattle Indian Health Board, Huchoosedah Indian Education Program, and United Indians of All Tribes Foundation, which all revolved around education. I plan to pursue graduate studies in education while continuing to advocate and build programs that will successfully recruit, retain, and graduate Native students from kindergarten all the way through college.

OUR STORY

Both of us work closely together in our jobs in the UW Office of Diversity. Both our cultural descriptions and job descriptions inform the work we do. Although many Native youth get off to a good start in reading now that more schools are using evidence-based early literacy instruction, they tend to shut down in 4th grade and thereafter. Overcoming that shutdown requires both addressing cultural identity and providing academic support. For access to higher education, programs are needed that will (a) ensure academic success in middle and high school through culturally sensitive, evidenced-based instruction, (b) recruit for higher education, and (c) support retention and completion of degree(s). The after school/out of school programs are proving effective in achieving high school graduation. Recruitment benefits from visiting the reservation and urban schools to talk in person to prospective Native youth. Sustaining enrollment until graduation is achieved through student support groups like the UW First Nations support groups for matriculated students and the Raven's Feast graduation for Native students.

THEIR STORIES

Of the 40, 000 UW students, about 450 to 500 are Native students. It is their stories and those of other students in higher education that are the future of Native Americans, as they gain access to higher education in the 21st century. Recently we witnessed a long awaited dream come true. Over a hundred years ago, the UW was built on Duwamish land. Multiple tribes resided on this land, which included not only Duwamish, but also Snoqualmish, Snohomish, Tulalip, and Muckleshoot; but there is no federal recognition of the Duwamish tribe, to which Chief Seath for whom Seattle is named, belonged. For 42 years a Long House was promised to give recognition to the Native roots for the university. Finally on October 25, 2013, ground was broken to build this "Intellectual House",[3] which will sustain the Native students through their university studies and also visibly demonstrate the Native roots, presence, and visions for intellectual development and contributions of First Peoples. Ultimately, their stories are the future in this unfolding plot, which is "To Be Continued." The audience is also invited to become part of the story to help Native students from preschool to early to middle childhood to adolescence to young adulthood gain their cultural identities and succeed educationally in the 21st century.

NOTES

1. The co-authors of this chapter and the co-editors of this volume thank Ryan Stewart, Director of Technology Services University of Washington (UW) College of Education, for recording the conversation; Peter Wallis, Instructional Technologist Learning Technologies, UW-IT for editing it; and Paul Keys, Web Manager, UW College of Education for creating the link and posting the video on line.
2. To view the video recording of the co-author's conversation, please access UW OMAD/College of Education Discussion: Native American Outreach at: https://www.youtube.com/watch?v=g_2jU9AwtQg. The UW College of Education Technology Services grants permission for this link to be published in this volume, but retains rights for the UW Office of Diversity to use it in recruitment and other activities on behalf of Native Americans and the College of Education to use it in preparing educators to meet the educational needs of Native American students.
3. Information about the Intellectual House can be found at http://www.washington.edu/diversity/tribal-relations/intellectual-house/ on the University of Washington web site.

REFERENCES

Carter, F. (2001). *The Education of Little Tree.* Albuquerque: University of New Mexico Press.

Part II Commentary
Building Successful Identities with Evidence-Based Practice— A Commentary Across the Pacific

David Rose

The chapters in this section cover a lot of ground in Indigenous education in North America, from Indigenous language programs, to literacy learning in the early years of school, to family support programs, to college recruitment and student support programs. In a concluding commentary for this section, I relate these North American experiences to my own, as an educator in Indigenous Australia, which are fortunately relevant to the themes of these papers. Over thirty years ago I started working for Indigenous communities in central Australia, was adopted into the kinship system though my ancestors were not Indigenous, and learned to speak the Pitjantjatjara language. Since then I have been involved in teaching language and literacy in schools in both Indigenous languages and English, in Indigenous family support programs, and in tertiary education for Indigenous students. But my primary focus for the past two decades has been on changing the practices of schools and teachers, to better meet the needs of Indigenous students to succeed in the school. This goal was given to me by the Indigenous Elders who taught me and directed my work, particularly my adoptive parents Nganyinytja and Charlie Ilyatjari, who devoted their lives to teaching their community's children about the world, and teaching the world about their culture,[1] and has been sharpened by experience over the years. To achieve the twin goals of enabling Indigenous children to succeed in school, while strengthening their Indigenous identities and community languages, we cannot simply focus on the children themselves, or their home and cultural backgrounds; we have to focus on what schools do that currently fails to meet the learning needs of so many Indigenous children, and fails to give them coherent, secure identities as both Indigenous community members and successful learners in school. Armed with this knowledge, we can re-design what schools and teachers do. This has been my mission and that of my colleagues, resulting in a teacher education program, *Reading to Learn*, that has now trained many thousands of teachers around Australia and the world in the strategies needed to make every student successful, particularly Indigenous students. The following commentary is offered from this experience.

A significant common theme in each of the chapters in this section is an historical and political perspective on the problems for Indigenous children in school. Lockard and deGroat's description of Navajo language programs explicitly recounts the historical struggle to have instruction in Navajo language instituted in Navajo community schools. They survey the borders of state and federal language policies which have defined the opportunities of their students to learn for a century, from the introduction of formal education with the signing of the treaty of 1868 to the Esther Martinez Native American Languages Preservation Act (2006). Syverson and Coolidge's major focus is on the value of story telling and reading for Indigenous children's language and literacy development, but this is against the historical background that 300–500 Native languages that were spoken by peoples Indigenous in what is now the United States and Canada; currently only 34 are still being learned as a first language by children. Porter, Dill, Masutani, Goya, and Perry frame their description of family support programs in Hawaii against the same challenges faced by other Indigenous communities, including poverty, extremely low education levels, poor health and homelessness. Braine and Segundo's brief introduction to their oral conversation personalizes this historical struggle, which for Native students is cultural trauma due to treatment by invaders who took away their land, removed their children from their homes and sent them to boarding schools, and govern them as a foreign government on land that once belonged to them.

History for these authors and their communities is not just an abstract set of facts and dates in a school curriculum, but a lived reality that continues to have dramatic effects on Indigenous children's education. The national histories of Canada and the US may have been glorious for some, but for Indigenous peoples they are ongoing traumas, echoing down the generations. Yet these authors and their communities are deeply concerned to conserve the past, in the form of their languages and cultural traditions, and all see a potential role of schools to support this. This is not an easy role to negotiate, as schools have been deliberately used in the past to suppress traditional languages and cultures, and as Lockard and deGroat point out, schools "reflect the knowledge and assumptions held by educational authorities about the prior knowledge of students from the majority language group".

Another common theme is the apparent mismatch between the teaching practices of the school and of Indigenous families and communities. Lockard and deGroat call for "reconsideration of educators' total reliance on a scientific world view". Syverson and Coolidge characterize the learning expectations of children in Native American cultures as a "'quiet reflective' holistic way of learning" in contrast to "the more overt and explicit learning and communication style typical of many mainstream classrooms". Porter, Dill, Masutani, Goya, and Perry foreground Native Hawaiian values and perspectives, in sum "working hard for the benefit of the whole rather than the individual", implicitly contrasting with the competitive individualism of modern western culture and the school. Braine and Segundo personalize this mismatch: "I never raised my hand or actively participated and was referred to special education", an experience that many Indigenous children have shared.

In this commentary, I draw together these themes of historical contexts and mismatched teaching practices, to consider the history of the teaching practices of the school and its impacts on many Indigenous children. Such an analysis will form a sound basis for re-designing the school's teaching practices to better serve the needs of Indigenous students, helping students build secure cultural identities while gaining the skills they need for further education.

While schools were deliberately used in the past to suppress traditional languages and cultures, they were also once deliberately designed to reproduce class inequalities in the wider society, which may have a more insidious effect on the education of Indigenous children. As the chapters in this volume make clear, the injustices of the past did not simply disappear in the last generation, but continue to cast a shadow on the culture of schooling today. Mass schooling was designed early in the last century to provide no more than an elementary education for working-class children, who were then expected to go into manual trades; a much smaller number of middle-class children were expected to complete secondary and further education in professions. This system continued in modified forms until quite recently. Even today, secondary school curricula are deliberately stratified for students with higher 'ability', tracked towards further education; those with lower 'ability' are not. This has recently gone out of fashion in the primary school, but children are even now often put into groups within each class, according to 'ability levels'.

Despite changes in teacher education, curricula, organization, and resourcing of schools, inequalities in outcomes remain little changed. In developed nations (e.g., the U.S., Canada, Australia), a minority of students attain university qualifications, a larger proportion gain vocational training, while a significant number receive no further education. Indigenous students are massively over-represented in the latter group, as Porter and colleagues report for Native Hawaiians: only "7% had completed an associate's degree and 9% a bachelor's degree in 2000". Education outcomes for Indigenous Australian students are even lower: children may be three to seven years behind national averages (Rose, Gray & Cowey, 1999). Within schools, inequalities in outcomes are almost universally understood as differences in students' 'ability', despite widely reported correlations between outcomes and levels of socio-economic advantage. Educational sociologist Basil Bernstein (2000) sees this as a maneuver to distract attention from ineffective teaching, that "failure is attributed to inborn facilities (cognitive, affective) or to the cultural deficits relayed by the family which come to have the force of inborn facilities" (p. 5). In other words, class inequalities are masked as individual 'ability', but when applied to Indigenous children, the implications are unacceptably racist. Still, the focus of legitimation remains steadily on the child rather than the teaching, so that inequalities in outcomes are attributed to differences in children's cultures and languages. The solution often prescribed is to incorporate elements of the child's culture into the classroom, or at least value the child's culture rather than ignoring it. This is a critical factor in fostering a secure identity for Indigenous children in school, as all the chapters in this volume attest. Unfortunately it does little to improve the effectiveness of teaching for these children, as education outcomes show.

Why is classroom teaching so ineffective for many Indigenous children? Lockard and deGroat's claim, that education is systematically based on research on majority language speakers, idealizes what actually happens in school. In fact, much of teachers' classroom practice is based on their own experience, strategies they have picked up after they have started teaching. Teachers regularly report that their preservice training (including the research they may have studied) has relatively little impact on their practices. In short, most of what happens in the classroom is not scientifically designed from research, but is inherited from past practices (Nuthall, 2005).

HOW CHILDREN BECOME LITERATE IN MIDDLE-CLASS FAMILIES: PARENT–CHILD READING

One such inherited practice, known as 'shared book reading', is strongly advocated by Syverson and Coolidge, and I agree is a crucial component of early years teaching, particularly for Indigenous children. Shared book reading has been researched in the academy, and is advocated in teacher training, yet it does not originate from research, but from the middle-class cultural practice of parent-child reading in the home (Adams, 1990; Williams, 1995). Its evolution is intimately entwined in the development of mass schooling and the growth of the western middle class in the past century, with origins related to the traditions of governesses educating upper-class children in the 18th and 19th centuries (Bernstein, 1975). It has also created the market in children's picture books, which today form the content for shared book reading in the primary school.

The middle-class practice of parent-child reading is not simply to read a book, but to thoroughly discuss the meanings in the pictures and the text. Children's picture books are designed to encourage such parent-child interaction, with stories generally far outside children's experience and pictures with complex relations to the written text. At its best, shared book reading in school reproduces this type of discussion, so that children experience the same learning and pleasure as they would reading with their caregivers. Syverson and Coolidge characterize shared book reading with "language facilitation and scaffolding strategies such as open-ended questioning, modeling, repeating, and expanding to scaffold and promote children's language". These are very broad categories that could be interpreted in all kinds of ways.

When we investigate in detail, we find that middle-class caregivers tend to negotiate the meanings in picture books, through cycles of interaction, each with four types of moves (Rose 2004, 2011, Rose & Martin 2013). The caregiver first *prepares* the child to recognize a feature of the text, the child *identifies* a text feature, the caregiver *affirms* the response, and may then *elaborate* with more information. Success and affirmation enhance the child's potential for learning more, and caregivers typically capitalize on this potential by elaborating with more information. The text feature may be an element of a picture, which the caregiver points to and names. The child may respond by identifying another feature, and the caregiver will affirm and elaborate the response with more information about the feature. In each cycle, the child thus receives a series of micro-lessons in features of written texts, from articulation of words, to grammatical sentences, to engaging with characters, predicting what's to come in the story, sharing the characters' emotional reactions, and judging their behavior. Through these cycles of success and affirmation, these micro-lessons are delivered at the moments when the child is emotionally and cognitively most ready to learn. According to Adams (1990), children in literate middle-class families will experience approximately 1,000 hours of this highly specialized type of talk-around-text unique to middle-class culture before they start school. In a large scale study, Williams (1995) showed that it is not so of less highly educated parents, who may read with their children but are less likely to have this kind of discussion about the meanings in a text. It also contrasts strongly with storytelling practices often reported for Indigenous families. For example, Syverson and Coolidge quote Vi Hilbert in *Haboo:*

> My Elders never said to me, 'This story carries such and such a meaning' . . . I was expected to listen carefully and learn why the story was being told. Though guided, I was allowed the dignity of finding my own interpretation. (Chapter 9, this volume)

RECONTEXTUALIZING MIDDLE-CLASS CULTURE IN THE SCHOOL: CLASSROOM INTERACTION

The talk-around-text of parent-child reading is mirrored in many ways in the discussion that early years teachers have with their students in shared book reading. However, crucial differences are that (1) the relation is no longer one-on-one, but one-to-many, (2) the goal is not simply sharing a pleasurable activity between parent and child, but teaching supposed cognitive skills such as 'inferencing', and (3) the teacher's initiating move is less often to prepare, but more often to ask questions of the class.

Teachers typically ask interpretive questions of their class, for which the answer must come from students' own knowledge and experience. Only a few students in any class can usually give the answer the teacher is after. These few students are regularly able to understand the teacher's questions, and infer the needed answers, and so regularly receive the teacher's affirmation. The point of teachers' questions is not simply to test students' knowledge, but to engage them in an exchange of knowledge. Teachers universally use students' responses to elaborate with further information, just as caregivers do in parent-child reading, but only a few students in any class are ideally prepared, through success and affirmation, to receive the maximum benefit from the elaboration.

This is a normal pattern of classroom interaction at every level of school: teachers question, one or more students respond, providing stepping-stones in the lesson. If we don't get the right responses, we take a step back and prepare for the response we want. As with shared book reading, this pattern of interaction does not come from research and is not explicitly taught in preservice training, but is inherited by teachers from their own experience, and applied intuitively in practice. The teacher's conscious focus is on the knowledge being learned, but the children are learning something far more personal and powerful, that there is a hierarchy in every classroom, in which some students are more likely to be successful and affirmed than others. Over time, this experience relentlessly shapes children's identities as more or less successful learners. Indigenous children are widely reported to find it alienating, as Braine and Segundo report: "I never raised my hand or actively participated" (see Malin, 1994; Malcolm, 1979, 1991, for Indigenous Australian children's experiences). Indeed, Braine and Segundo emphasize this point in their videoed oral discussion (https://www.youtube.com/watch?v=g_2jU9AwtQg[2]). Indigenous children are routinely alienated by the competitive practice of responding to teachers' classroom questions, as are many other students. Rather than risk continual rejection, they remain silent. Appallingly, as Braine and Segundo discuss, Indigenous children's silence in classroom discussions is often interpreted as evidence of a learning disability, for which they may be referred to special education classes.

It must be emphasized, however, that teachers rarely set out to deliberately alienate children. On the contrary, teachers often ask questions of less vocal children because they would like to engage them in the discussion. Most teachers are concerned to engage all their students as much as possible, but they are often hamstrung by the school's cultural practice of asking interpretive questions that weaker students cannot confidently or successfully answer. Unfortunately, this too often includes Indigenous students.

REDESIGNING TEACHER-CLASS INTERACTIONS TO ENGAGE ALL STUDENTS

One response to this problem has been to denounce explicit teaching activities as 'teacher-centered' practice, and advocate individuated activities that are supposed to be 'learner-centered'. This false dichotomy has little real benefit for understanding and designing classroom practices. The term 'teacher-centered' is designed to resonate with 'self-centered' and imply an uncaring attitude; in fact teaching and learning in all cultures is a relationship that unfolds over time, in the kinds of cycles we see in parent-child reading. This is most apparent in manual activities in which teachers prepare learners for a learning task, by demonstrating how to do it, handing control to the learner to do the task, and guiding them to do it successfully. This kind of practice is just as familiar in Indigenous cultures. The central phase of the cycle is the learning task, which only the learners can do for themselves; the teacher can prepare the learner to do the task successfully, if the teacher understands the nature of the task. Once a task is done successfully, it can be elaborated with a higher level of understanding.

This pattern of explicit teaching seems to contrast with Syverson and Coolidge's description of Native learning by "listening, observing, and participating in authentic community activities". Similar statements about so-called 'learning styles' in Indigenous Australian cultures (Harris, 1982) seem to explain the pattern of Indigenous children's silence in the classroom, but there are many situations in all cultures in which children are expected to participate silently, particularly in formal activities such as religious ceremonies. The learning task may indeed involve listening, observing, and participating, but these tasks have typically been prepared by children's cultural experience over time, and will eventually be elaborated by explanation of the meanings involved. As Braine and Segundo point out, "oral tradition of Native culture is a medium for transmitting the wisdom of past generations with the challenges of the present and the dreams and visions for the future". Such wisdom cannot just be acquired passively; it must at some point be transmitted explicitly by teachers, elaborating on learners' experience.

In school interactions, the universal teaching/learning cycle of Prepare-Task-Elaborate is distorted by the hierarchical social structure of the classroom. Teachers ask interpretive questions that require students to interpret from their own knowledge, so that only a few students can answer successfully. Teachers are taught that this will encourage inferencing or critical thinking in students, just as Syverson and Coolidge advocate open-ended questioning in shared book reading to scaffold and promote children's language. This widespread notion is not based on evidence of value for the weaker students in a class, but does resonate with teacher educators' practice of asking interpretive questions.

The solution to this problem is actually relatively simple. Instead of asking interpretive questions of the whole class, which only a few students can answer, teachers can carefully prepare their questions so that any student can answer. The interpretive level of understanding can then be left to the elaboration. If all students can answer successfully and be affirmed, then all can benefit equally from the elaboration, instead of just the top few. A simple way to ensure that all students can answer is if the answer comes from a text that the whole class is reading, rather than from students' individual knowledge. If the preparation guides students to successfully identify words or images in the text, as the mother does in parent-child reading above, then any student can be asked and affirmed. The ideal practice is thus to prepare the whole class, and then ask individual students to identify the feature so that all can be affirmed in turn. The meaning can then be elaborated, either by the teacher explaining, or by asking the children's own experience. At this point, it doesn't matter if only a few students respond, because all students have successfully identified the text feature and can benefit from the elaboration of its meaning.

SHARED BOOK READING: A WHOLE CLASS TEACHER-GUIDED ACTIVITY

This is in fact the ideal practice of shared book reading: the teacher prepares children to understand by talking them through the illustrations in a big book, guiding them to identify elements in the pictures, as the mother does in the earlier description. Shared book reading can thus be classified as a whole class teacher guided activity, not simply 'teacher-centered'; the children are all doing the learning tasks with the teacher carefully guiding them to success. A shared reading book will typically be read aloud again and again, until all children thoroughly understand the story, and can say many of its sentences along with the teacher. This resonates with Indigenous storytelling practices, in which children may hear the same story many times until they can repeat it from memory.

I have seen many early years teachers do this successfully with classes of Indigenous Australian children, who have no books in the home, and little or no English. After a few days of repeated preparation, reading, and elaborating, every child understands the story (which is usually far outside their experience and often quite bizarre), and can say the English words perfectly along with the teacher. This is why I consider shared book reading to be the most important single literacy activity for Indigenous children in the early years of school, which should form a basis for them to become successful readers, but at this point disaster often strikes. In the remote Indigenous community schools I have studied, not one child was reading independently before the end of Year 3, and no child could read more than basal picture books by the end of primary school (Rose, Gray & Cowey, 1999).

The cause of this disaster is not that shared book reading is insufficient, but that the other 'literacy activities' in the early years fail to build on the meaningful engagement with written texts that parent-child reading and shared book reading provide. These literacy activities universally include drills memorizing the alphabet and letter formation, letter-sound correspondences, and sight-words, 'phonemic awareness' for children who speak other languages at home, and English grammar structures, and individuated or group reading of basal picture books, leveled to children's assessed 'ability levels'. I refer to this assortment of activities as 'dis-integrating' the tasks of reading and writing, fragmenting them in disconnected activities, using disconnected texts, words, letters, and sounds (Rose, 2011).

For children from literate middle-class backgrounds, with 1,000 hours of parent-child reading before school, these activities make sense. In almost every sense, these children already know how to read; their vocabulary of written English is large, they understand how written stories unfold, and they know how to relate them to their own experience. All they need to learn is how to decode the written words in texts they already understand. This is what the alphabet, phonics and sight-word activities give them, and individual or group reading gives them practice with reading for meaning. But for children from oral cultural backgrounds, without this experience of parent-child reading, these literacy activities are literally meaningless.

RE-INTEGRATING LITERACY LEARNING: READING TO LEARN

As with teacher-class interactions, the solution to this problem can be relatively simple. It does not mean abandoning explicit teaching of foundation skills in literacy, but rather re-integrating them into a carefully planned sequence, starting with meaning. Instead of treating literacy as something separate from the pleasure of reading, the shared reading book, with which children are thoroughly familiar, can be used for all literacy activities. Once all children thoroughly understand the book, after repeated readings, and can say many of its sentences along with the teacher, one sentence at a time can be used to teach foundation skills in reading and writing, including word recognition, sentence structure, letter-sound correspondences, spelling, letter formation, and sentence writing.

As part of the Reading to Learn program, many Indigenous teachers, teaching assistants, and student teachers have been trained in these strategies in Australia, and have taught children to read and write within an hour, when they have been failing to read for three or more years with standard methods. Briefly, the teacher writes out a sentence from the shared reading book, that the children can already say and understand thoroughly. She first guides the children to recognize each word, then to cut up and manipulate groups of words, then to cut up and manipulate individual words, creating new sentences by moving and recombining the words. She then guides the children to cut words into their letter patterns, and practice writing them on small whiteboards, and finally to write the whole sentences they have been reading. Once children have built up sufficient language resources, they practice innovating on the texts they have been reading, until they are ready to write texts of their own. These activities are explained in detail, and demonstrated on video, in the *Reading to Learn* teacher resource materials (Rose, 2014, and www.readingtolearn.com.au).

This carefully sequenced, explicit teaching of literacy skills contrasts with the common early years practice of getting children to try writing stories from their own experience, whether or not they have the skills to do so. This is another well-worn inherited practice in the primary school, which was appropriated by academics in the 1960s and re-badged as 'process writing' or 'whole language' (Graves, 1983). In Australia it has been disastrous for Indigenous students, as it fails to take into account the variations in literacy skills that children bring to school (Gray, 1990; Rose, 2011; Rose & Martin, 2012).

IMPLICATIONS FOR TEACHER EDUCATION AND FAMILY SUPPORT PROGRAMS

The complexity of teacher-class interactions and shared book reading, and the simplicity of the *Reading to Learn* strategies described above, have implications for both teacher education and family support programs for Indigenous children in school. Indigenous families cannot be expected to compensate for ineffective literacy teaching in the early years of school. It is crucial to give the kinds of support and connection between Indigenous families and school provided by the programs described by Porter et al. in Hawaii, but it is equally important to provide teachers with the skills they need to make all their children successful, no matter what their cultural and language backgrounds.

The strategies above are very easy to learn and apply, require few materials, and are appropriate for Indigenous families with limited resources (Rose, 2014). They can be very easily taught as part of teacher preservice and inservice training, and as part of support programs for Indigenous families. This would certainly give most cultural minority children's foundation literacy skills a valuable boost, as it has for many Indigenous families in Australia.

On the other hand, the parent-child reading practices described above involve a more complex orientation to written ways of meaning. To reiterate, these practices have evolved within literate middle-class culture; parents' orientation to the practice is typically acquired in the course of a long formal education, including university, often built on their own experience of growing up in literate families. Careful, large scale research has consistently shown that caregivers from less highly educated backgrounds tend not to engage in the same kinds of talk-around-text, even when they spend as much time reading with their children (Williams 1995). In my experience, it is not easy for caregivers from oral cultural backgrounds, including Indigenous caregivers, to acquire these kinds of skills through short-term training programs. This does not mean that Indigenous caregivers cannot do this for their children; as Braine describes in his videoed account, his parents thoroughly prepared him for school. But as Braine and Segundo make clear in their discussion, this is exceptional for Indigenous families.

These practices give children from middle-class families an enormous advantage in the early years of school. It is unrealistic, and I believe unreasonable, to expect Indigenous families to provide the same preparation for school learning that middle-class families do. Rather it is the responsibility of teachers, and their academic trainers, to learn how to provide Indigenous children with the higher level orientations to written meanings, and the engagement in talk-around-text, that will make them successful in school. On one hand, this implies that teachers must be trained to do shared book reading effectively, so that it supports all students to gain the inferential and interpretive comprehension of texts that the most literate students currently enjoy. On the other, it requires teachers to understand the structures of their own discourse in the classroom, so that they can engage all children successfully in the conversation. Teachers need to know how to analyze the patterns of meaning in the reading books they are using, and how to draw each child's attention to these patterns, in terms that all can easily understand, and that engage them all in the meaningful, pleasurable activity of reading. In my experience, this is more than most teachers currently receive in preservice training, and it requires detailed knowledge about classroom discourse. The business of teachers is language, and to do the job well for the benefit of all their students, teachers must have a strong, practical grasp of how language works.

INDIGENOUS CULTURES AND LANGUAGES IN THE SCHOOL

With these kinds of analysis and planning by teachers, there need be no conflict between the home cultures of Indigenous children and the culture of the classroom; and no need for Indigenous children to be left out, left behind, or alienated from classroom learning. All children can build secure, confident identities as successful learners, in harmony with their identities as Indigenous community members. Schools can provide Indigenous children with the skills they need to succeed in mainstream schooling and further education, at the same time fostering their Indigenous cultural identities and languages.

However, it is critical to recognize that the school is a different cultural context from the contexts of Indigenous children's homes and communities. When a practice or knowledge is taken from the community context into the school, it is no longer the same but is transformed into another kind of practice or knowledge; it is recontextualized, in Bernstein's terms (2000). For example, Syverson and Coolidge discuss both Native (Muckleshoot) and non-Native stories being used in shared book reading. There is now a wealth of Indigenous stories published as picture books that can be used in this way, but this is a very different context from the original context of oral storytelling. In Indigenous cultures, the relationships between storyteller and listeners is often as important as the story itself, alongside all the cultural experience they share. In shared book reading, the teacher becomes the storyteller, and the story is abstracted from the personal relations of family and community. Furthermore, shared book reading involves elaborate discussion of the meanings in the text, as described above. Its purposes are for children to develop generalized skills in inferential and interpretive comprehension of written texts. This contrasts with the purposes and modes of Indigenous storytelling, as Syverson and Coolidge illustrate with their quote of Vi Hilbert, "My elders never said to me, 'This story carries such and such a meaning'".

Indigenous oral stories are not originally designed to be discussed and have their layers of meaning unpacked by children. Although they often have layers of meaning, they may be revealed gradually through repeated tellings, as children mature and become aware of their deeper implications. Because these Indigenous storybooks are often transcribed oral stories, they may not have the elaborate patterns of written language characteristic of children's books created for parent-child reading. On the other hand, Indigenous children's books may be rewritten, often by non-Indigenous authors, and their meanings significantly changed. It is common to see such stories that have been adapted to the pattern of Rudyard Kipling's 'just-so stories', whose main message seems to explain why animals have certain features (Martin & Rose, 2012). Finally, a common activity with shared book reading in the school is to use their stories as models for children to write stories of their own. Yet many Indigenous oral stories actually have deep religious significance, and have been handed down from the community's ancestors. How appropriate is it to encourage children, Indigenous or not, to make up their own creation stories using these sacred stories as models? For all these reasons, careful thought needs to be given to the place and use of Indigenous stories in activities like shared book reading and rewriting.

Another alternative is to bring Indigenous storytellers into the school, a growing practice in Australia and noted as a feature of family/community involvement in the Washington State curricula implementation (Hurtado, Chapter 6). In this way, children hear the stories from the elders who are their custodians and can explain their cultural significance. With the elders' permission these can also be used for literacy activities in both Indigenous languages and English. Teachers can record and transcribe these stories, and print them so that children can illustrate and practice reading them. Older children can also learn to record and transcribe them themselves. This activity can also be used for studying Indigenous languages, as a powerful method for students to learn about the grammars and semantics of both languages, by actively comparing how each language expresses similar meanings in different wordings (Rose, 2005).

This raises the wider issue of teaching Indigenous languages in the school, the topic of Lockard and deGroat's chapter. Here again a key issue to grapple with is recontextualization of Indigenous knowledge as school curriculum. The question is what functions the language serves in the culture of the school, which cannot be identical with its traditional functions in the home culture. As with all languages, Indigenous children have traditionally learned their mother tongues largely unconsciously, through interacting with caregivers and peers. In this regard, the work on language learning in the home, by Halliday (1975, 1993) and Painter (1991, 1996), is invaluable for understanding how caregivers guide children in learning their mother tongue. This research is an essential corrective to notions that children passively absorb language from their environments, rather than actively interact with it.

However, the Navajo language 'immersion' programs described by Lockard and deGroat appear to have been carefully based on context-specific language learning, in which children are explicitly guided to study selected aspects of traditional Navajo culture through the medium of Navajo language. These might be compared with some programs for Indigenous Australian children, such as the Yipirinya School in Alice Springs, in central Australia. In this community-controlled school, children spend some weeks each year in excursions to their families' homelands, accompanied by community elders. What they learn in these excursions, including stories and knowledge about the country and kinship systems, forms the basis for language and literacy work back at the school. Children are guided to write these stories and topics, extending their command of the oral language at the same time.

In these kinds of activities, children are learning to become ethnographers of their own communities (Martin, 1990). These are different functions for culture and language learning than traditional (pre-colonial) contexts, in which children were participants in, but not recorders of their cultures. The ethnographic activities of recording community language and culture do not exclude participation, but add another layer of analysis and reflection, that are central components of school learning. Learning to speak one's mother tongue is a largely unconscious process, even though guided by one's caregivers; learning to read and write in school are conscious processes, involving reflection on meanings and how they are expressed as wordings (Halliday, 1993). These differences in contexts and processes of learning have implications for how teachers plan and guide students in Indigenous language learning programs.

Lockard and deGroat quote Eilene Joe's lamenting "a shift to the use of more English for literacy; this is where the Navajo Nation Head Start made the mistake in teaching more English". My own view is that such conflicts between learning Indigenous languages and English are unnecessary and potentially counterproductive. As with the activity of transcribing and translating traditional stories outlined above, each language can be used to reflect on and enhance the learning of the other; this is a powerful way to build strong, coherent identities that comprehend and control the very different cultures in which Indigenous children must learn to live, but demands explicit, effective teaching of both languages.

For Indigenous languages to survive and revive they must fulfill social functions that are significant and meaningful enough for children and young people to want to speak them, and these functions must be distinct enough that English cannot be more easily used. Some common functions for language revival are in formal contexts such as ceremonies, songs, and 'welcome to country' speeches in Australia, but these contexts and the language used are very restricted. Another promising context for expanding language learning and use is in ethnographic activities that involve recording, transcribing, translating and discussing, as outlined earlier. Through these active processes, students expand their language knowledge, and this expanded knowledge can be applied in other contexts in the school and beyond, in storytelling, in speeches, in dialogue, and in writing.

It is essential that schools and communities are crystal clear about their goals in language teaching and the functions that Indigenous languages and English serve in the school and in students' future lives. These functions may include qualifying for further education, for which a high level of English literacy is essential, or conserving a community language which young people may have stopped using, for which targeted, explicit language teaching programs are essential. Or the goal may be to give students strong, coherent identities as both Indigenous community members and citizens of the modern world. For this goal, language programs that integrate explicit teaching of Indigenous languages and English, building oral and written skills in both languages, and critical skills for reflecting on the meanings in both cultures, are what is needed.

SUPPORTING INDIGENOUS STUDENTS THROUGH PRIMARY, SECONDARY AND TERTIARY EDUCATION

Braine and Segundo's oral discussion about recruiting and supporting Indigenous students through college echoes many of the same issues faced by Indigenous students in Australia: the struggles of Indigenous children in the competitive environment of the classroom; the shame associated with being referred to special education; and Indigenous secondary students' lack of preparation and motivation for college education and their struggles once they get to college in coping with both the social environment and the academic work required. The program run by Braine and Segundo is inspirational and essential, and is mirrored by comparable programs in many Australian universities and technical colleges, to attract Indigenous students and keep them to graduation.

Nevertheless, the numbers of Indigenous students making it to further education and staying there is still well below what it should be, as Porter et al. cite for Hawaii. I consider that the fault for this lies squarely in the hands of schools and their ineffective teaching practices. I have outlined above what schools can do in the early years, to give all their students the foundation skills they need to succeed. The same principles can be applied in the upper primary, secondary, and tertiary classroom.

It is neither acceptable nor necessary for universities to blame secondary schools for students' lack of preparation, or for secondary teachers to blame primary schools, any more than primary schools should attribute failure to children's 'abilities' or home cultures. To take responsibility for teaching all their students effectively, schools must first acknowledge that reading is one of the fundamental modes of language learning in the school, and that all teachers should know how to teach all their students how to learn from reading. Reading must be placed at the center of classroom practice. Evidence-based practices such as those outlined above can enable teachers to accomplish such success. For example, *Reading to Learn* strategies have consistently been shown to accelerate the learning of the weakest students at an average four times above standard growth rates, while top students accelerate at 1.5 times standard rates (Culican, 2006; McRae et al., 2000; Rose, 2011; Rose & Martin, 2012, 2013). This rate of growth for the bottom students is essential if the achievement gap in each classroom is to be narrowed and more Indigenous students are to succeed.[3] The support such programs provide Indigenous students is an essential complement to the social support provided by the programs that Braine and Segundo describe; they demonstrate that the meshing of evidence-based practice with respect for and accommodation of cultural traditions is entirely possible.

NOTES

1. Information and videos about Nganyinytja and Charlie can be accessed on the web at, e.g., http://www.youtube.com/watch?v=eUCSc57t0d0
2. The University of Washington College of Education Technology Services grants permission for this link to be published in this volume, but retains rights for the University of Washington Office of Diversity to use it in recruitment and other activities on behalf of Native Americans and the College of Education to use it in preparing educators to meet the educational needs of Native American students.
3. The detailed strategies of this program are available in various publications, particularly in Rose (2005, 2014); at the tertiary level, their application with Indigenous academic students is discussed in Rose (2008), Rose, Lui-Chivizhe, McKnight & Smith (2003), and Rose, Rose, Farrington & Page (2008).

REFERENCES

Adams, M.J. (1990). *Beginning to read. Thinking and learning about print: A summary.* Urbana-Champaign: University of Illinois Press.

Bernstein, B. (1975). Class and pedagogies: Visible and invisible. *Educational Studies,* 1(1), 23–41.

Bernstein, B. (2000). *Pedagogy, symbolic control and identity: Theory, research, critique.* London: Taylor & Francis.

Culican, S. (2006). Learning to read, Reading to learn: A middle years literacy intervention research project. Final Report 2003–2004. Melbourne: Catholic Education Office: Melbourne. Retrieved from: http://www.readingto learn.com.au

Graves, D. (1983). *Writing: Teachers and children at work.* London: Heinemann.

Gray, B. (1990). Natural language learning in Aboriginal classrooms: Reflections on teaching and learning (pp. 105–139). In C. Walton & W. Eggington (Eds.) *Language: Maintenance, power and education in Australian Aboriginal contexts.* Darwin, N.T.: Northern Territory University Press.

Halliday, M.A.K. (1975). *Learning how to Mean: Explorations in the development of language.* London: Edward Arnold.

Halliday, M.A.K. (1993). Towards a language-based theory of learning. *Linguistics and Education,* 5(2), 93–116.

Harrris, S. (1082). Aboriginal learning styles and the teaching of reading. In J. Sherwood (Ed.). *Aboriginal Education: Issues and Innovations.* Perth: Creative Research.

Koop, C. & Rose, D. (2008). Reading to learn in Murdi Paaki: Changing outcomes for Indigenous students. *Literacy Learning: The Middle Years* 16(1), 41–46. Retrieved from: http://www.alea.edu.au/

Malcolm, I. (1991). "All right then, if you don't want to do that . . .": Strategy and counter-strategy in classroom discourse management. *Guidelines,* 13(2), 11–17.

Malcolm, I. (1979). The Western Australian Aboriginal child and classroom interaction: A sociolinguistic approach. *Journal of Pragmatics,* 3, 305–320.

Malin, M. (1994). Why is life so hard for Aboriginal students in urban classrooms? *The Aboriginal Child at School,* 22(2), 141–154.

Martin, J.R. (1990). Language and control: Fighting with words (pp. 12–43). In C. Walton & W Eggington (Eds.) *Language: Maintenance, power and education in Australian Aboriginal contexts.* Darwin, N.T.: Northern Territory University Press.

Martin, J.R. & D. Rose (2012). Recontextualising Indigenous culture: Genres, interests and multimodal affordances in children's picture books (pp. 377–391). In Wang Zhenhua (Ed.) *CDA/PDA Vol. 6: Collected Works of J R Martin.* Shanghai: Shanghai Jiao Tong University Press.

McGee, L.M. (1998). How do we teach literature to young children? (pp. 162–179). In S.B. Neuman & K.A. Roskos (Eds.) *Children achieving: Best practices in early literacy.* Newark, DE: International Reading Association.

McRae, D., Ainsworth, G., Cumming, J., Hughes, P., Mackay, T. Price, K., Rowland, M., Warhurst, J., Woods, D. & Zbar, V. (2000). *What has worked, and will again: The IESIP strategic results projects* (pp. 24–26). Canberra: Australian Curriculum Studies Association. Retrieved from: http://www.acsa.edu.au/pages/images/What%20works_.pdf

Nuthall, G.A. (2005). The cultural myths and realities of classroom teaching and learning: A personal journey. *Teachers College Record,* 107(5), 895–934.

Painter, C. (1991). *Learning the mother tongue* (Second Edition). Geelong, Vic.: Deakin University Press.

Painter, C. (1999). *Learning through language in early childhood*. London: Cassell.

Rose, D. (1999). Culture, competence and schooling: Approaches to literacy teaching in Indigenous school education (pp. 217–245). In F. Christie (Ed.) *Pedagogy and the shaping of consciousness: Linguistic and social processes* London: Cassell.

Rose, D. (2004). Sequencing and pacing of the hidden curriculum: How Indigenous children are left out of the chain (pp. 91–107). In J. Muller, A. Morais, & B. Davies (Eds.) *Reading Bernstein, researching Bernstein*. London: Routledge Falmer.

Rose, D. (2005). Democratising the classroom: A literacy pedagogy for the new generation. *Journal of Education*, 37, 127–164. Retrieved from: http://dbnweb2. ukzn.ac.za/joe/joe_issues.htm

Rose, D. (2008). Redesigning foundations: Integrating academic skills with academic learning. Keynote for Conversations about Foundations Conference, Cape Peninsula University of Technology, Cape Town, October 2007. Retrieved from: http://associated.sun.ac.za/heltasa/foundationprogram.html

Rose, D. (2010). Meaning beyond the margins: Learning to interact with books (pp. 177–208). In S. Dreyfus, S. Hood and M. Stenglin (Eds.) *Semiotic margins: Reclaiming meaning*. London: Continuum.

Rose, D. (2011). Beating educational inequality with an integrated reading pedagogy (pp. 101–115). In F. Christie and A. Simpson (Eds.) *Literacy and social responsibility: Multiple perspectives*. London: Equinox.

Rose, D. (2014). *Reading to learn: Accelerating learning and closing the gap.* Teacher training books and DVDs. Sydney: Reading to Learn. Retrieved from: http://www.readingtolearn.com.au

Rose, D., Gray, B., & Cowey, W. (1999). Scaffolding reading and writing for Indigenous children in school (pp. 23 http://www.readingtolearn.com.au60). In P. Wignell (Ed.) *Double Power: English literacy and Indigenous education*. Melbourne: National Language & Literacy Institute of Australia (NLLIA).

Rose, D., Lui-Chivizhe, L., McKnight, A., & Smith, A. (2003) Scaffolding academic reading and writing at the Koori Centre. *Australian Journal of Indigenous Education*, 33/30th Anniversary Edition, 41–49. Retrieved from: http://www.atsis.uq.edu.au/ajie/index.html?page=33821

Rose, D. & J.R. Martin 2012. *Learning to write, reading to learn: Genre, knowledge and pedagogy in the Sydney School*. London: Equinox.

Rose, D. & J.R. Martin 2013. Intervening in contexts of schooling (pp. 447–475). In J. Flowerdew (Ed.) *Discourse in context: Contemporary applied linguistics Volume 3*. London: Continuum.

Rose, D., Rose, M., Farrington, S., & Page, S. (2008) Scaffolding literacy for Indigenous health sciences students. *Journal of English for Academic Purposes* 7(3), 166–180.

Williams, G. 1995. *Joint book-reading and literacy pedagogy: A socio-semantic examination*. Volume 1. CORE. 19(3). Fiche 2 B01- Fiche 6 B01.

Part III

Diversity of Native American Student Populations, Instructional Approaches, and Research Applications

12 *Ho'opili ka Mana'o i ke Kūkākūkā*

Instructional Conversation as an Effective Strategy for Indigenous Students' Engagement and Learning

Lois A. Yamauchi, Rebecca J. 'Ilima Luning, and Kristin Kawena Begay[1]

The first part of our title, *Ho'opili ka mana'o i ke kūkākūkā*, is based on a Hawaiian proverb (Pukui, 1983) and translates as "Discussion brings ideas together." This refers to the classroom strategy, Instructional Conversation (IC), which can promote learning and engagement among students from Indigenous backgrounds. Drawing on our experiences as classroom teachers and teacher educators for Native Hawaiians, we describe the strategy, provide an example, discuss research and theoretical background, and outline how IC aligns with Native Hawaiian values and cultural practices. IC is one of the strategies of the Center for Research on Education, Diversity, and Excellence (CREDE) Standards for Effective Pedagogy, which provides research-based strategies for teaching students from culturally and linguistically diverse backgrounds (Tharp, Estrada, Dalton, & Yamauchi, 2000).

We write this chapter in honor of William Demmert, who was a friend, colleague, and member of CREDE, where much of the work on IC developed. An Alaska Native from the Tlingit Eagle clan, Bill promoted IC in classrooms for Indigenous students, introducing many educators to these ideas and connecting those of us who worked in different Native communities to each other in order to promote collaboration across our settings. Bill brought together Indigenous education leaders from Greenland and the Circumpolar North, American Indian tribes, Alaska, Canada, New Zealand, and Hawai'i. He used IC in his own practice, by creating settings in which diverse groups of people shared their perspectives, developed common understandings, and worked toward mutual goals.

HAWAIIANS AND FORMAL EDUCATION

In this section, we situate our chapter in the historical context of formal education in Hawai'i. Prior to the overthrow of the Hawaiian Kingdom in 1893, the Hawaiian language was the official language used throughout Hawai'i in all government activities and classrooms (Kawakami & Dudoit, 2000). By the 1850s, it was reported that Hawaiians had the highest literacy rates in the world, being able to read and write in their native language (Kamakau,

1868; Silva & Basham, 2004). After the overthrow of the Hawaiian monarchy, the Hawaiian language was banned in public schools (Kawakami & Dudoit, 2000). Corporal punishment was used to enforce this ban on children who spoke Hawaiian in school, creating a hostile environment. Use of the Hawaiian language and educational success for Native Hawaiians declined significantly, and current statistics indicate that educational success has been depressed but is slowly rising. Compared to peers from other ethnic backgrounds, Hawaiian students typically score lower on standardized measures of achievement, have higher drop-out rates, are over-represented in special education, and are under-represented in post-secondary education (Kanaʻiaupuni & Ishibashi, 2003; Office of Hawaiian Affairs, 2011; University of Hawaiʻi Institutional Research Office, 2013).

The Hawaiian Language Immersion program began in 1987 as a grass-roots effort to revitalize the Hawaiian language and bring it back from the brink of extinction (Kameʻeleihiwa, 1992; Wilson, 1998). Before 1987, there were about 2,000 native speakers of Hawaiian, with the majority over age 50 and only about 30 under 18 (Heckathorn, 1987). This movement faced many challenges (Jacobson, 1998; Warner, 2001). Hawaiian language advocates started a private preschool called *Pūnana Leo*, which translates to "Language Nest," creating the first Hawaiian immersion school. Later, through political lobbying, *Papahana Kaiapuni*, a K-12 public school program that uses the Hawaiian language as the medium of instruction, was founded. In 2012, there were 19 Kaiapuni sites located on five of the eight major Hawaiian islands, namely Hawaiʻi Island (Big Island), Oʻahu, Kauaʻi, Maui, and Molokaʻi. In 1999, the first class of students in the Kaiapuni program graduated from high school. That year, there were approximately 1,700 children and youths involved in the program, dramatically increasing the number of Hawaiian language speakers under age 18 (Yamauchi & Wilhelm, 2001).

THEORETICAL FOUNDATIONS

Instructional Conversation (IC) is one the CREDE Standards for Effective Pedagogy, strategies of instructional practice for use among learners from culturally and linguistically diverse backgrounds (Tharp et al., 2000). (See Table 12.1 for a summary of all of the CREDE Standards.) IC is based on Vygotsky's (1978) theory of cognitive development and over 40 years of research on what works for students from diverse backgrounds. Vygotsky (1978) emphasized the importance of social interaction, particularly via language, in the development of conceptual understandings. His theory places importance on the social and cultural context for teaching and learning, as well as the assistance that teachers provide to students in the learning process. As Tharp and Gallimore (1988) suggested, from this perspective, teaching can be conceived as assisted performance. The best teaching occurs as educators provide just the right assistance to learners,

Table 12.1 The Center for Research on Education, Diversity, and Excellence (CREDE) Standards for Effective Pedagogy (adapted from CREDE Standards, publicly available on the CREDE web site: http://manoa.hawaii.edu/coe/ credenational/the-crede-five-standards-for-effective-pedagogy-and-learning/)

CREDE Standard	Description
1[a] Joint Productive Activity	Teachers and students working together to create shared understandings and tangible products.
2[a] Language and Literacy Development	Promoting language goals throughout the school day.
3[a] Contextualization	Connecting new information to what students already know from their previous home, community, and school experiences.
4[a] Complex Thinking	Developing students' high-level thinking and problem solving skills.
5[a] Instructional Conversation	Using small group discussions to develop conceptual understandings.
6[b] Modeling	Providing examples of what students are required to do and providing feedback when they practice.
7[b] Student Directed Activity	Providing opportunities for students to be involved in classroom decision-making about what and how they learn.

Note. [a] Universal best practices for all students (Tharp et al., 2000).
    [b] Indigenous Standards based on observations of teaching and learning in traditional Indigenous contexts (Tharp, 2006).

within their "zones of proximal development" (Vygotsky, 1978), that is, the level that is just beyond a learner's current level of proficiency.

INSTRUCTIONAL CONVERSATION

Coined by Tharp and Gallimore (1988), IC involves a teacher facilitating a discussion with a small group of learners to promote conceptual development related to a specific learning goal. As its name implies, IC is both conversational and instructional. It is conversational in that IC provides a setting in which students are comfortable sharing their ideas and views, and what they say shapes where the discussion will go. Ideally, ICs incorporate the cultural norms students bring to conversations. For example, conversations among Hawaiians and others who speak Hawai'i Creole English often involve patterns of co-narration and overlapping speech, such that a speaker starts talking before the previous speaker is finished, and in doing so, participants take cues and co-construct the conversation with one another (Watson, 1975). When teachers incorporated this speech pattern into their ICs and allowed children to speak in their first language (Hawai'i Creole English), student participation increased (Au & Mason, 1981). The teachers themselves modeled Standard English, the language of instruction. The idea was to maximize participation by allowing children to engage in ways that were most comfortable.

In addition to being conversational, an IC also includes an instructional element in that teachers come to the discussion with a specific conceptual goal (Tharp et al., 2000). They may plan an IC around something students need assistance in understanding, and use the discussion to help relate previous experiences to build new, shared knowledge (Wells & Haneda, 2005). In other words, teachers have ideas of what they want the IC to be about, but are responsive to students, as the educators listen carefully to assess what students know and question them on their views, judgments, and rationales. This can be tricky, and many teachers find ICs to be difficult to conduct (Goh, Yamauchi & Ratliffe, 2012; Yamauchi, Taum, & Wyatt, 2006). There is an inherent conflict between maintaining one's instructional goals whilst being responsive and flexible to allow a "true" conversation to flow (Wells & Haneda, 2005).

Ideally, ICs occur with small groups that include the teacher and about 5–7 students (Tharp et al., 2000). With very young children (ages 2–5), the group could be as small as two children and a teacher (Yamauchi, Im, & Schonleber, 2012; Yamauchi, Im, & Mark, 2013). This group size is necessary for the teachers to assess what individual students know and to create opportunities for all students to participate. Participation may be non-verbal, especially when students are very young or are still learning the language of instruction, and the ideal ratio of teacher to student communication turns is 1 to 1 (Yamauchi et al., 2013). For example, the teacher may say something and a child may nod. Next, the teacher may say something else, and another child may say one word and point to what they are talking about, and so on. With older students and those who already speak the language of instruction, one of the goals is for the students to speak more than the teacher (Luning, Wyatt, & Im, 2011), as it is important that teachers not dominate the conversation.

CREDE researchers recommend that ICs with older students (elementary and higher levels) involve homogenous groups (Tharp et al., 2000). This allows the teacher to use the IC to differentiate instruction. Applying Vygotsky's (1978) notion of the zone of proximal development, teachers can then direct the conversation about a concept that is just a little more difficult than what the learners can understand on their own. For the most advanced learners, this is an opportunity for the teacher to have a conversation about a topic that might be beyond what others in the class can understand. Likewise, for those who are struggling, the teacher can use the IC to slow down and assist them in understanding more basic ideas. Because the groups rotate, everyone has an opportunity for a sustained conversation with the teacher.

One of the challenges is that in order for the teacher to hold sustained ICs with small groups of students, those in the class not currently engaged in IC need to be able to work independently from the teacher. The CREDE model involves students rotating through a series of activity centers, one of which is the IC Center with the teacher (Tharp et al., 2000). The model incorporates a "phasing in" process that allows for a gradual transition from whole group to small group instruction, as students acquire the skills they need to work independently from their teacher. Although researchers advocate homogenous groupings for the IC groups, they suggest that when students work in small peer-directed centers, those peer groups are heterogeneous, maximizing the kinds of assistance peers can give to one another.

RESEARCH ON THE EFFECTS OF INSTRUCTIONAL CONVERSATION

Research on IC has been conducted with students in a variety of contexts. Researchers at the Kamehameha Early Education Program developed the strategy for Grades K–3 Native Hawaiians learners (Tharp et al., 2007; Tharp & Gallimore, 1988). They found that IC was effective in promoting both children's understanding of complex ideas and their learning to read, and its use was related to children's scores on language achievement tests (Tharp et al., 2007). Later, Saunders and Goldenberg (2007) compared use of IC to more traditional didactic reading instruction among Latino elementary students. In follow up assessments, the researchers found that children in both groups had equal factual recall of story details, but that children in the IC group had a greater conceptual understanding of the book's theme. Based on these investigations and their review of 73 studies of English language learning, the U.S. Department of Education What Works Clearinghouse deemed IC as the most effective method for reading achievement and the second most effective for English language learning in promoting literacy development among second language learners (Institute of Educational Sciences, 2006).

Other studies indicated that teachers' use of IC was related to learners' achievement, as assessed by various classroom assessments in elementary and secondary schools (e.g., Estrada, 2005; Hilberg, Tharp & DeGeest, 2000). Researchers also found IC to be successful in increasing the engagement and learning of adults (Kim, 2013; Wells & Haneda, 2005; Yamauchi, Trevorrow, & Taira, 2013).

INSTRUCTIONAL CONVERSATION IN A HAWAIIAN LANGUAGE IMMERSION CLASSROOM

In the next section, we provide an example of an IC conducted by third author Kawena Begay, when she was a teacher in a Hawaiian language immersion classroom. In 1st grade at *Ke Kula 'o 'Ehunuikaimalino*, a Hawaiian immersion school on the Kona coast of the island of Hawai'i, the challenge for Kawena, the teacher, was to get students to speak at a higher rate than she did. During a previous lesson, Kawena taught students strategies to avoid spreading or catching illnesses. This led to the current lesson, a discussion about how germs spread and a science experiment. The experiment involved four cut pieces of potatoes left to sit in separate, sealed plastic bags for a week. The students had handled the first potato with unwashed hands, and rubbed the second over their desks. They each blew on the third potato, while Kawena, with freshly washed hands, was the only one to handle the fourth. The students wrote and illustrated predictions about each potato slice, and would later add their actual observations.

During the lesson, Kawena guided small groups of 4–5 students through an IC to discuss the results of this experiment and its practical implications. The students first described each potato in its bag and determined whether their predictions from the previous week were correct. From there, Kawena asked them about the differences they noticed between the appearance of the four potato slices, and the possible reasons for those variations. Through this discussion, Kawena was able to clarify and expand vocabulary, encourage deeper thinking, and question students' thoughts. For example, one student explained how one potato slice had more black spots *no ka mea ua hoʻopā nui* (because it was touched a lot). During the ensuing conversation, Kawena was able to clarify and expand some basic vocabulary after realizing that the student had mistaken the Hawaiian word *hoʻopā* (touch) with the word *ānai* (rub), as that was the potato that had been rubbed on the table, not the one that had been touched by students. Another student commented that one potato looked *pupuka, ʻeleʻele*, and was encouraged to explain his thoughts and describe what *pupuka* (ugly) and *ʻeleʻele* (black) meant in this context, requiring him to expand his thinking. By listening to each student's contribution, Kawena was able to assess individual levels of understanding, as well as identify areas of needed language instruction.

The students noticed that the potato that had been rubbed on the table had the most black spots, while the slice that had been handled only briefly by the teacher's washed hands looked untouched. From this observation, Kawena was able to guide the students into a conversation about why the four slices looked so different. During this part of the discussion, one student commented *ua hoʻopā a me ʻānai kākou kēia mea* (suggesting that one particular potato had been both rubbed and touched). When the comment was restated, using proper grammar, and the student questioned, the student expanded, *no ka mea hoʻopā nā keiki i ke pākaukau i nā lā āpau!* (further explaining that the kids touch the table every day). Kawena then guided students into talking about what that might imply for healthy hygiene practices, which included a discussion of how germs are spread. By the end of the small-group conversation, students had brainstormed ways to prevent the spread of germs.

In this example, IC was used to help clarify students' understanding of the academic topic, and further their thinking. The lesson was planned to be instructional in that it was designed to teach a specific concept; in this case, to help students build a joint understanding of how germs are spread and how to prevent such spreading. Each child had something to contribute, providing a building block for additional information. Kawena questioned the students on their contributions, helping them to clarify their own thoughts, increase vocabulary, and state and defend their rationales. Although Kawena had a plan for the direction of the conversation, the input of the students was essential for helping her promote student understanding.

The IC was also conversational in that students were able to freely share their ideas, often interrupting one another as they excitedly described what they saw on the potato slices. Although one goal was to increase Hawaiian language expression, all attempts at conversation were accepted, including those that were nonverbal in nature, and comments made in English. As the students in this example had limited experience speaking Hawaiian, with most having only a year or less of experience in the immersion program, formulating thoughts and commenting in Hawaiian was difficult for many. Allowing for the conversation to flow naturally, regardless of language of contribution, encouraged students who were not proficient in Hawaiian to benefit from participating, thereby promoting conceptual understanding for all students.

For this age level, having a conversation in the context of an actual experiment with real potato slices to manipulate and observe helped students focus on the conversation and provided a tangible context in which to understand the academic topic. Saunders and Goldberg (2007) maintain that ICs are of higher quality when the instruction has a thematic focus that includes a plan to allow for the introduction of new information, along with the use of relevant materials within the context of the theme. This lesson was part of a health theme. All children participated in the IC at some point in time. At other times, they were working in small peer-led activity centers that also incorporated the theme. At a follow-up center, students recorded observations discussed during the IC and noted whether their previous hypotheses regarding the potato slices were accurate. All students wrote observations and made comparisons, and those who were able added comments on the implications of their results. At another center, students worked collaboratively to create a joint product of their choice that illustrated for others the need for good hygiene. Most groups chose to create a poster, although one group created a rap song, and these products were shared with the whole class at the end of the lesson. The final center involved students working on a class book that described community health workers.

ALIGNMENT OF THE CREDE STANDARDS AND HAWAIIAN VALUES AND CULTURAL PRACTICES

Pūpūkahi i holomua: by working together we make progress (Pukui, 1983). This *'ōlelo no'eau* (Hawaiian proverb) is one of many that demonstrate the importance on working together and sharing *kuleana* (responsibility) in Hawaiian culture. However, in school settings, the collectivistic values of the Hawaiian culture often conflict with the individualistic environment of formal Western education. Hawaiian teaching practices typically emphasize holistic, experience-based learning and place value on the social context of the learning environment (Chun, 2006; Pukui, Haertig, & Lee, 1972). Compared to more didactic instruction, IC and the CREDE model offer a more natural environment for Hawaiian children, focusing on the socio-cultural aspects of learning and emphasizing peer-assisted, cooperative learning.

At home, Hawaiian children more often engage in child-child interactions than adult-child interactions (Tharp et al, 2007). Children as a group often carry out common home activities such as household chores and sibling caretaking, with older siblings having responsibility over the younger ones. Thus, children typically work together with siblings, cousins, and peers. The IC's focus on small group, peer-directed discussions and interactions allows Hawaiian students to converse freely and comfortably with peers, while the teacher's role is as a facilitator.

The Native Hawaiian process of learning, called *Tēnā*, uses a multistep method of assessing and assisting learners as they work toward a common goal (Beniamina, 2010). Similar to an IC, this process adjusts the learning based on the learner's ability and skill level, allowing for the more knowledgeable learners to assist. This practice places the responsibility on the learners to be attentive and to contribute to the group. In this setting, the teacher is able to function mainly as a guide and to assess the student's readiness to take on more advanced work. The value of *kuleana* is at the heart of this learning process. Each individual is expected to contribute to the larger group and to fulfill responsibilities towards the completion of the task at hand.

APPLICATION TO OTHER INDIGENOUS CULTURES

In this chapter, we have described IC and presented an example from a Hawaiian language immersion classroom. We hope that educators in other Indigenous communities will be inspired to use IC as a means of promoting student engagement and achievement, as use of this strategy in other Native communities has resulted in positive student outcomes (Tharp, 2006). After IC was developed for Hawaiian learners, KEEP[2] researchers attempted to apply the strategy with students in the Navajo Nation in Rough Rock, Arizona. Similar to Hawaiian children, Navajo students responded well to questions posed to the whole group, rather than to individual children, especially when the teacher did not express too much enthusiasm after an individual's contributions (Vogt, Jordan, & Tharp, 1987). However, the researchers found that, unlike the Hawaiian children with whom they had developed strategies for using IC to promote reading comprehension, the Navajo did not like to dissect a story into segments and discuss each piece separately. Instead, these students found it much more comfortable and meaningful if they could hear the whole story and discuss it as one unit, reflecting a cultural preference for more holistic approaches to learning and understanding.

In the 1990s, IC was further developed and applied at the Zuni Middle School in the Pueblo of Zuni, New Mexico. Zuni educator Georgia Epaloose helped to develop the first instrument to measure IC and the other CREDE Standards (Hilberg, Doherty, Epaloose, & Tharp, 2004). Epaloose collaborated with other educators and researchers to develop a guide for teachers who wished to transform their classrooms from being whole group teacher-dominated to enacting the more collaborative activities that included IC (Hilberg, Chang, & Epaloose, 2003). Zuni educators found that use of IC was related to greater student achievement (Tharp et al., 1999). For example, Hilberg, Tharp and DeGeest (2000) compared use of IC with more traditional middle school mathematics instruction that included review of the previous day's assignment, lecture-based instruction of new material, followed by individual practice. An experimental group received instruction of the same content that incorporated IC with the teacher. Results indicated that the experimental group scored higher in retention of concepts and reported more enjoyment, value, and self-efficacy in mathematics.

More recently, IC has been used in the country of Greenland, where the Ministry of Education adopted the model for a nation-wide reform of education from preschool to higher education in their process to decolonize their country from a Danish-dominated school system and way of life (Olsen & Tharp, 2012; Wyatt, 2011). Bill Demmert, to whom this chapter is dedicated, introduced IC and the broader CREDE model to Greenlandic educational leaders, suggesting that it could be relevant to their context. It was surprising to many of us who work with IC in Hawai'i that educators in a country so different from our setting would find it applicable to their context; however, their adoption and adaptation of IC (Wyatt, 2011; Wyatt, Yamauchi & Chapman, 2012) speaks to its utility for many Indigenous groups. The success of IC for many native groups also reflects Bill Demmert's wisdom and vision as an Indigenous leader and educator.

NOTES

1. The authors wish to thank the teachers and students who are described in this chapter. We are grateful for funding provided by federal grants from the U.S. Department of Education (#S362A060022 and #S362A110016) and support from Kamehameha Schools. We wish to thank Ernestine Enomoto, Seongah Im, Kathy Ratliffe, and Tracy Trevorrow for helpful comments on earlier drafts of this chapter.
2. KEEP is the Kamehamela Early Education Program, a language arts program designed for underachieving Hawaiian children. See http://www.ncrel.org/sdrs/areas/issues/educatrs/presrvce/pe3lk43.htm for additional information.

REFERENCES

Au, K.H., & Mason, J.M. (1981). Social organizational factors in learning to read: The balance of rights hypothesis. *Reading Research Quarterly, 17,* 115–152.

Beniamina, J. (2010). *Tēnā:* A learning lifestyle. *Hūlili: Multidisciplinary Research on Hawaiian Well-Being, 6,* 9–23.

Chun, M. N. (2006). *A'o: Educational traditions.* Honolulu: University of Hawai'i Curriculum Research & Development Group.

Estrada, P. (2005). The courage to grow: A researcher and teacher linking professional development with small-group reading instruction and student achievement. *Research in the Teaching of English, 39,* 320–364.

Goh, S.S., Yamauchi, L.A., & Ratliffe, K.T. (2012). Educators' perspectives on instructional conversations in preschool settings. *Early Childhood Education Journal, 40,* 305–314.

Heckathorn, J. (1987). Can Hawaiian survive? *Honolulu Magazine,* April, 48–49.

Hilberg, R.S., Chang, J.M, & Epaloose, G. (2003). *Designing effective activity centers for diverse learners.* Santa Cruz: University of California Center for Research on Education, Diversity, and Excellence.: Author.

Hilberg, R.S., Doherty, R.W., Epaloose, G., & Tharp, R.G. (2004). The Standards Performance Continuum: A performance-based measure of the Standards for Effective Pedagogy. In H. Waxman, R. Tharp, & R. Hilberg (Eds.), *Observational research in U.S. classrooms: New approaches for understanding cultural and linguistic diversity* (pp. 48–71). New York: Cambridge University Press.

Hilberg, R.S., Tharp, R.G., & DeGeest, L. (2000). The efficacy of CREDE's Standards-based instruction for American Indian mathematics classes. *Equity and Excellence, 33*(2), 32–40.

Institute of Educational Sciences. (2006). What Works Clearinghouse: Instructional conversation and literature logs. Retrieved from: http://ies.ed.gov/ncee/wwc/pdf/intervention_reports/WWC_ICLL_102606.pdf

Jacobson, L. (1998). Turning the tide. *Education Week, 18*(6), 28.

Kamakau, S.M. (1868, January 18). *Ka Nupepa Kuokoa.* Ka mo'olelo o nā Kamehameha. *Ka Nupepa Kuokoa,* 7(3), 1.

Kame'eleihiwa, L. (1992). *Kula Kaiapuni*: Hawaiian immersion schools. *The Kamehameha Journal of Education, 3*(2), 109–118.

Kana'iaupuni, S.M., & Ishibashi, K. (2003). *Left behind? The status of Hawaiian students in Hawai'i public schools.* (PASE Report No. 02.03.13). Honolulu: Kamehameha Schools.

Kawakami, A.J., & Dudoit, W. (2000). *Ua Ao Hawai'i*/Hawai'i is enlightened: Ownership in a Hawaiian language immersion classroom. *Language Arts,* 77(5), 384–390.

Kim, H. (2013). *The perceptions of students with different learning preferences regarding their learning experiences in a university classroom that incorporates instructional strategies for diverse learners.* (Unpublished master's thesis.) Honolulu: University of Hawai'i.

Luning, R.I., Wyatt, T. & Im, S. (2011). *Classroom observation rubric: Development and validation of a measure of effective pedagogy.* Honolulu: CREDE Hawai'i Project, University of Hawai'i.

Office of Hawaiian Affairs (2011). *The Native Hawaiian data book.* Honolulu: Author.

Olsen, K.K. & Tharp, R.G. (2012). Indigenous education in Greenland: Effective pedagogy and the struggles of decolonization. In Craven, R.G., Bodkin-Andrews, G., & Mooney, J. (Eds) *International advances in education: Global initiatives for equity and social justice* (pp. 95–118). Charlotte, NC: Information Age.

Pukui, M.K. (1983). *'Ōlelo no'eau: Hawaiian proverbs and poetical sayings.* Honolulu: Bishop Museum Press.

Pukui, M.K., Haertig, E.W., & Lee, C.A. (1972). *Nānā i ke kumu (Look to the source).* Honolulu: Hui Hānai.

Saunders, W.M. & Goldenberg, C. (2007). The effects of an instructional conversation on English language learners' concepts of friendships and story comprehension. In R. Horowitz (Ed.) *Talking texts: How speech and writing interact in school learning* (pp. 221–252). Mahwah, NJ: Erlbaum.

Silva, N.K., & Basham, J.L. (2004). *I ka 'olelo no ke ola*: Understanding indigenous Hawaiian history and politics through Hawaiian language sources. Retrieved from http://citeseerx.ist.psu.edu/viewdoc/download?doi=10.1.1.164.6154&rep=rep1&type=pdf

Tharp, R.G. (2006). Four hundred years of evidence: Culture, pedagogy, and Native America. *Journal of American Indian Education, 45*(6), 6–25.

Tharp, R.G., Estrada, P., Dalton, S.S., & Yamauchi, L.A. (2000). *Teaching transformed: Achieving excellence, fairness, inclusion, and harmony.* Boulder, CO: Westview.

Tharp, R.G., & Gallimore, R. (1988). *Rousing minds to life: Teaching, learning, and schooling in social context.* New York: Cambridge University Press.

Tharp, R.G., Jordan, C., Speidel, G.E., Au, K.H., Klein, T.W., Calkins, R., Sloat, K.C., & Gallimore, R. (2007). Education and Native Hawaiian children: Revisiting KEEP. *Multidisciplinary Research on Hawaiian Well-Being, 4,* 1–49.

Tharp, R.G., Lewis, H., Hilberg, R.S., Bird, C., Epaloose, G., Dalton, S.S., Youpa, D.G., Rivera, H., Riding In-Feathers, M., & Eriacho, W. (1999). Seven more mountains and a map: Overcoming obstacles to reform in Native American schools. *Journal of Education for Students Placed At-Risk, 4,* 5–25.

University of Hawai'i Institutional Research Office (2013). *Enrollment of Hawaiian students, University of Hawai'i at Mānoa,* Spring. Honolulu: Author.

Vogt, L.A., Jordan, C., & Tharp, R.G. (1987). Explaining school failure, producing school success: Two cases. *Anthropology and Education Quarterly, 18,* 276–286.

Vygotsky, L.S. (1978). *Mind in society: The development of higher psychological processes.* Cambridge: Harvard University Press.

Warner, S.N. (2001). The movement to revitalize Hawaiian language and culture. In L. Hinton & K. Hale (Eds.) *The green book of language revitalization in practice* (pp. 133–144). San Diego: Academic Press.

Watson, K.A. (1975). Transferable communicative routines: Strategies and group identity in two speech events. *Language in Society, 4,* 53–72.

Wells, G., & Haneda, M. (2005). Extending instructional conversation. In C.R. O'Donnell & L. A. Yamauchi (Eds.) *Culture and context in human behavior change: Theory, research, and practical application* (pp. 151–178). New York: Peter Lang.

Wilson, W.H. (1998). The sociopolitical context of establishing Hawaiian-medium education. *Language, Culture and Curriculum, 11*(3), 325–338.

Wyatt, T.R. (2011). *Atuarfitsialak:* Greenland's culturally compatible reform. *International Journal of Qualitative Studies in Education, 25,* 1–18.

Wyatt, T.R., Yamauchi, L.A., & Chapman De Sousa, E.B. (2012). Using the CREDE Standards for Effective Pedagogy in a Greenland settlement school. *Multicultural Perspectives, 14,* 65–72.

Yamauchi, L.A., Im, S., & Mark, L. (2013). The influence of professional development on educators' Instructional Conversations in preschool classrooms. *Journal of Early Childhood Teacher Education, 34,* 140–153.

Yamauchi, L.A., Im, S., & Schonleber, N. (2012). Adapting strategies of effective instruction for culturally diverse preschoolers. *Journal of Early Childhood Teacher Education, 33,* 54–72.

Yamauchi, L.A., Taum, A.H., & Wyatt, T.R. (2006, April). The effects of professional development to promote instructional conversations in high school classrooms. Paper presented at the annual meeting of the American Educational Research Association, San Francisco.

Yamauchi, L.A., Trevorrow, T., & Taira, K. (2013, April). Invitational instructional strategies for engaging culturally diverse students in higher education. Paper presented at annual meeting of the American Educational Research Association, San Francisco.

Yamauchi, L.A., & Wilhelm, P. (2001). E ola ka Hawai'i i kona 'ōlelo: Hawaiians live in their language. In D. Christian & F. Genesee (Eds.) *Case studies in bilingual education* (pp. 83–94). Alexandria, VA: TESOL.

13 Ka Mālama Na'auao Ohana a Keiki 'Ōiwi Ma o Ka 'Ike Ku'una a Nohona Hawai'i

Nurturing Native Hawaiian Families with Children with Disabilities through Hawaiian Traditional Values and Practices

Patricia Sheehey and Brinda Jegatheesan

To families of Hawaiian descent: May they continue to reclaim their culture that was suppressed so many years ago. May their voices be heard as they share their stories teaching us *'aloha, 'ohana, laulima,* and *kokua.*

This chapter builds on our earlier work with best practices in special education with Asian Americans, Pacific Islanders (Jegatheesan, Sheehey, & Ornelles, 2010) and other Indigenous families. In this chapter we discuss the discrepant views of mainstream special education and Native Hawaiian culture; then as an example we focus specifically on the special education experiences of one Native Hawaiian mother with a child with Down syndrome (drawn from a study reported in Sheehey, 2001).

First we briefly describe the problems that the standard approach to special education services creates for minority families, particularly for Native Hawaiians. We then provide an overview of the Hawaiian people: their values and beliefs on disability. Next we provide an in-depth portrait of the Native Hawaiian mother's experiences with health care and special education professionals, and outline key Native Hawaiian values that professionals need to be knowledgeable about, using this family's experiences as examples. We showcase how professionals can use specific Native Hawaiian practices with families that have relevance to their everyday socio-cultural and familial realities in order to facilitate active and meaningful participation in developing educational plans for their children with disabilities.

BACKGROUND ON SPECIAL EDUCATION AND NATIVE HAWAIIAN CULTURE

The Individuals with Disabilities Education Act (IDEA) of 2004 ensures procedural and substantive rights to students with disabilities and their families. Students with disabilities are entitled to receive a free and appropriate public education in the least restrictive environment; that is, they must be educated in settings as close to the general education classroom as possible, in which the student can make satisfactory progress. The nature of the disability should not influence placement decisions. Rather, the first setting option to be considered should be the general education classroom with supplemental supports and services. If the team determines that the students could not make adequate progress on specific goals and objectives (e.g., reading or math) under these conditions, other placement options (e.g., special education resource room, separate special education classroom [fully self-contained classroom]) should be considered. The placement decision is made by the interdisciplinary team with the parent as an equal member of the team.

A cornerstone of IDEA is the right of parents of children with disabilities to be meaningfully involved in the special education process. Nearly three and a half decades have passed since parent involvement was stated as a vital element in the original Education for All Handicapped Children Act of 1975. Since then, with each reauthorization of IDEA, parents' involvement in the development of their children's education plan has been strengthened (Heward, 2009).

Despite this legal emphasis to include parents in the development of children's special education programs, professionals have often resisted the attempts made by parents to be meaningfully involved. Negative experiences with professionals have been increasingly common among minority parents, particularly those who are from immigrant, refugee and Indigenous backgrounds (Jegatheesan, 2009; Jegatheesan, Fowler & Miller, 2010; Park & Turnbull, 2001; Sheehey, 2006). Minority parents are often ill-equipped with knowledge of their rights and entitlements and hence are not able to be powerful advocates for their children. These parents are often sidelined by professionals, forced to remain passively involved in educational processes (e.g., development of their child's IEP) or to rely on the recommendations of their child's teachers (Jung, 2011; Vaughn, Bos, Harrell, & Lasky, 1988). Even parents who are knowledgeable about their rights may not advocate for their children out of fear of people in power and negative consequences for their children (Jung, 2011).

PARENT–PROFESSIONAL COLLABORATION: A LEGAL REQUIREMENT IN THE INDIVIDUALIZED EDUCATION PLAN PROCESS

The Individualized Education Plan (IEP) is a legal document that specifies the individual's strengths and needs as well as identifies appropriate goals and objectives for a student with disabilities. It serves as a guide and a means to monitor student progress. The IEP, intended to reflect a collaborative process across all individuals involved in the education of a student with disabilities, falls short of its intent if team members simply sign off as part of protocol. Professionals adhering to best practices collaboratively develop an IEP through use of structures that establish parity, ensuring that the IEP genuinely reflects the unique needs and perspectives of students and their families. The development of a legally valid IEP is a collaborative process between parents and professionals (Heward, 2009). It is unfortunately also a process during which parents commonly have negative experiences with professionals.

NATIVE HAWAIIANS AND SPECIAL EDUCATION

In the state of Hawaii'i, there continues to be a dominance of non-Hawaiian educational professionals in the public education system (Matayoshi, 2013). Native Hawaiians have historically experienced challenges in their educational experiences (Ogata, Sheehey, & Noonan, 2006). The emphasis on high stakes testing and independent academic achievement does not support many of the Hawaiian values which emphasize collective learning. Native Hawaiian students continue to be overrepresented in special education for high incidence disabilities (e.g., emotional disturbance, learning disability). Although 28% of the school population is Native Hawaiian (Matayoshi, 2013), 46% of students receiving special education services are Native Hawaiian or Other Pacific Islanders (Data Accountability Center, 2012).

Native Hawaiians' learning and communication are informed by their traditions. Curricula and pedagogical practices may significantly differ from the cultural traditions and values of Hawaiian students, thereby contributing to inaccurate assessments and referrals to special education (Ogata et al., 2006). Professionals' lack of knowledge of home practices and values, interaction and communication styles, and cultural views of disability result in cross cultural conflicts and have created hardships for parents and families. Native Hawaiians were integrated into the American society by means of occupation, colonization, or slavery, and typically continue to hold a subordinate position of power. Their history of denigration and unequal economic and educational opportunities often inhibits the development of trusting relationships. Therefore, some Native Hawaiian families may be reluctant to develop a trusting relationship with professionals whose values are similar to those who hold political, social, and economic power (Sheehey, 2006).

OVERVIEW OF THE HAWAIIAN PEOPLE

Kanaka Maoli (the Hawaiian people) are natives to the islands of Hawai'i. Their history of subjugation and denigration began when Captain Cook arrived in 1778. New England missionaries arrived in the 1800s and began the process of acquiring land and power while demolishing the Hawaiian culture. With the assistance of the U.S. military, American businessmen overthrew the Hawaiian monarchy in 1893 and established a provisional government. Despite the opposition of Native Hawaiians, Hawaii was annexed to the United States in 1898 and all available royal lands became property of the United States. Hawaii became the 50th state in 1959. Recently, Hawaiians have initiated a movement to reclaim their lands and their culture (Mokuau & Tauili'ili, 2006). After much legal and political advocacy, the Native Hawaiian population has been defined as a distinct ethnicity (U.S. Census, 2000).

HAWAIIAN VALUES

The world view of Native Hawaiians is different from the mainstream U.S. culture. In general it is based on the assumptions of a collectivist society where the group's goals hold more importance than those of the individual. Relationships are the core to Hawaiian values (Mokuau & Tauli'ili, 1998). In particular, the relationship of the individual to the family, the community, the land, and the spiritual world is emphasized. The *'ohana* (family), defined as relatives by blood, marriage, and adoption (Handy & Pukui, 1977), is the fundamental unit in Hawaiian culture. The needs of the family override the needs of individual family members.

This strong emphasis on relationships guides how one behaves within families and communities. The key values underlying this are *laulima* (cooperation), *kōkua* (helpfulness), *hilina'i* (trust, be able to rely on), and *lōkahi* (unity) (Kanahele, 1986; Mokuau, 1990). The Hawaiian emphasis on family, cooperation, helpfulness, and unity may seem to contradict the assumptions of special education that is grounded in mainstream values, given that in Hawaiian culture family is extended to include those beyond blood ties and these individuals may be children's primary caregivers. The child-centered nature of the IEP process is incongruent in a culture that centers on the good of the entire family.

HAWAIIAN PERCEPTIONS ON DISABILITY

Little is written on Native Hawaiian children with disabilities and their families. It is not known whether this is a result of a lack of historical information on children with disabilities or because of a preference to emphasize healthy children. According to Kale'a, a Native Hawaiian linguist, there is no common usage or terminology for "disabilities" or "special needs" in the Hawaiian language and Hawaiian worldview. Kale'a confirmed her findings with a few other *kumu 'olelo hawai'i* (Hawaiian language teachers). She explained that these terms might be an emerging perspective (as opposed to a cultural and traditional lens) in terms of viewing children as having a disability, hence the difficulty in finding a Hawaiian word (Kale'a Silva, personal communication, June 26, 2013).

Native Hawaiians believe in the interrelatedness of all lives. They believe that *mana* (engery) permeates and connects all aspects of life, and concepts such as *lokahi* (harmony/unity) and *pono* (balance/proper order) are vital. In traditional Native Hawaiian culture it is believed that illness and misfortunes are caused by a lack of *mana* or a loss of *pono*. To rectify this problem Native Hawaiians strive to maintain *lokahi* (harmony) between biocentric living things (humans and environmental life) and the spiritual realms (Blaisdell & Mokuau, 1991). The use of herbs, massage, chants and prayers are used to reestablish balance.

PORTRAIT OF THE KAUAHI FAMILY

Palapala and Toni Kauahi lived in Hawaii in a rural area of an outer island where agriculture was the primary industry. They had two sons, one was Jessi, who was developing typically, and Makana, who was diagnosed with Down syndrome. Jessi was a doting big brother, and Makana was a good-natured happy boy who loved to please everyone. The Kauahi family was a Native Hawaiian family who exemplified the Hawaiian values of *'aloha*, (love), *'ohana* (family), *laulima* (cooperation), and *kokua* (helpfulness). Hawaiian culture was an integral part of this family's lifestyle. Hawaiian was spoken fluently at home. Jessi attended a Hawaiian immersion school where all courses were taught in the Hawaiian language. Makana, however, has a very different educational story.

THE PREBORN CHILD: WHEN MAKANA WAS IN THE WOMB

The Kauahi *'ohana's* story began when Palapala and Toni received a diagnosis of Down syndrome for their child Makana while he was still in the womb. As part of Palapala's prenatal care she underwent amniocentesis, which indicated that the baby had a chromosomal abnormality identified as Down syndrome. Palapala and Toni were told that their preborn son had a large sized *puka* (hole) in his heart and that he would require open-heart surgery to repair it when he grew older and stronger, hopefully before his first birthday. Palapala and Toni had heard of Down syndrome and thought that raising a child with Down syndrome would be difficult, but they believed that their having this child in their family was meant to be. Their doctor sent them to genetic experts for more information on Down syndrome. Palapala described her visit: *One geneticist recommended an abortion. These genetic guys gave us the worst possible literature, the worst . . . they just leave out loving the child. We were horrified that medical professionals think our child's life has so little value. I told my unborn child, 'I won't hurt you bra, no worry.'*

THE BIRTH OF MAKANA

Makana was listless at birth and struggled to thrive after birth. Palapala said, *I learned that he was not able to sit or crawl because his muscles don't develop, yeah, when they have the big puka (hole) because all that energy goes to try to pump the heart. So Makana was having a hard time adjusting to life outside of the womb.*

When Makana was found not to be thriving, the doctors assessed Palapala and reported that the baby was "suffering from failure to thrive because of Palapala's inadequate mothering techniques." The nurses at the hospital then taught Palapala how to force-feed Makana. Palapala explained that she had been following her pediatrician's orders regarding medications and that she had not received additional instructions regarding feeding Makana; as a result she had fed him the same way she did her older child, Jessi. She said, *I saw in his chart where the nurses had written "inadequate mothering techniques." They taught me to open his mouth and force the food in until he swallowed. We also listened to the advice of the professionals and force-fed Makana even though we did not like it. Forcing a baby to eat was not natural. But we followed their orders. What saddened me was that the doctors didn't see my commitment to my child.*

For the next 17 months, Palapala and Toni, for the sake of their child's well-being, relentlessly adhered to a strict 24-hour-a-day schedule for dispensing the exact amounts of medication required to assist his heart. At 17 months, Makana had open heart surgery and the *puka* in his heart was repaired. Makana made a remarkable recovery and as he became stronger his parents began to help him meet his physical developmental milestones with great and earnest dedication.

BIRTH TO AGE THREE: EARLY
INTERVENTION (EI) EXPERIENCES

The doctors had made a referral to the early intervention program as soon as the diagnosis was made. The early intervention program director had called Palapala prior to Makana's birth and offered to provide services for Makana to assist his language and fine and gross motor development. At just a few weeks of age, Makana began receiving physical therapy, occupational therapy, and speech therapy at his home, and

Palapala reported that the professionals behaved like they were part of her *ohana* (family).

TRANSITIONING FROM EARLY INTERVENTION TO SPECIAL EDUCATION SERVICES

A few months prior to Makana's third birthday the early intervention professionals prepared Palapala and Toni for his transition to the Department of Education (DOE) special education preschool. They were informed that Makana would attend the local public school for his special education preschool experience. When Makana turned three years of age, the preschool special education teacher called her and scheduled a meeting for Makana's first school-based IEP. When Palapala arrived at the school she found that there were no representatives from Makana's early intervention team to help with the transition; there was a Japanese American principal, a Caucasian teacher who had recently moved from the mainland U.S., a part-Hawaiian speech pathologist, an occupational therapist, and a physical therapist. Palapala knew none of them. She had anticipated that during this IEP meeting she would help develop Makana's educational program, but to her surprise she found that the IEP was already prepared by the special education teacher prior to the meeting. Copies were provided. Professionals in the IEP team did not seek Palapala's views or approval. She felt she was not included in the decision making for her son's learning and she also did not agree with everything in that IEP. Nevertheless Palapala went with the flow because she did not want to speak against teachers and administrators. When asked *what else* she wanted for Makana, Palapala did not know what to say, other than that she wanted her child to be happy, safe, and healthy as well as to continue living and earning to his potential.

UNTIL SOMEONE HEARS ME I WILL ENDEAVOR: PALAPALA EMPOWERS SELF, BECOMES AN ADVOCATE

After that first IEP meeting, Palapala realized she needed information on the federal law governing special education, the IEP process, and Makana's legal rights. She began reading and attending conferences and workshops on topics that she thought would benefit Makana. She watched for notices regarding training on special education, IDEA, IEPs, and interventions. Palapala received a copy of the law at one the workshops. She said, *Yeah, that's where I got the book of laws. "Give it to me. I'll read it." I learned that Makana had rights similar to other children his age without disabilities and that he had the right to be educated in the least restrictive environment. He has the right to be educated with his peers that are not disabled.*

I learned all this by reading and studying the law. First, you have to know the law. There is no way around it because they [administrators and educational professionals] throw any kind at you and it's all false . . . . And you've got to be able to say, I even used to know the numbers, I forget them now but I used to know all the numbers of the laws. He has to be around normal children . . . . Well, you have to go from a socialization thing. That's the only way you're gonna get anywhere with them.

Studying the law gave Palapala knowledge of timelines regarding eligibility, re-evaluations, and IEP meetings. Experience taught her to request an IEP at the end of the year to ensure Makana's supports would be in place prior to the beginning of the next school year.

As his mother, Palapala knew what behavioral techniques worked with Makana. She said, *Punishing him when he won't do it . . . I hate that because it doesn't work for him. It doesn't work at all. I don't know who it does work with but it sure doesn't work with him. He just gets more stubborn and more resistant to it.*

From 3rd grade through several years of high school Palapala attended IEP meetings for Makana. She continued bringing suggestions for goals and objectives for Makana to be in an inclusive setting. *They would accept it and appear to be listening but did not follow up; they did nothing about it. And Makana continued receiving special education services in a self-contained classroom and not with his same aged peers without disabilities.*

With every IEP meeting Palapala attended, she fortified her presence and involvement with her knowledge and understanding of special education law. According to her, at times the IEP team was an obstacle. But knowledge of the law was a tool she used. *They are so intimidating, especially if they bring everybody, the physical therapist and the higher guys and all the teachers. . . . The minute you say that [P.L. 94–142] they think, oh my gosh, here comes a lawsuit. They'll [administrators] give you what you want. And if you're unprepared it's horrible. They don't scare me. I figure, if you do this to me you're gonna do paperwork, yeah.*

PALAPALA SHUTS DOWN A CLOSET-CONVERTED PRESCHOOL CLASSROOM

Palapala grew stronger as an advocate and prepared herself mentally and physically for each IEP meeting. Soon after the first IEP had ended when Makana was entering preschool, Palapala had decided to visit her son's classroom. She was horrified to discover that the special education classroom for children from preschool through 6th grade was actually an old custodian's closet, approximately 12x6 feet in size. Her 3-year-old child with Down syndrome would be in the same class as a 10-year-old with a behavioral disorder. Palapala knew that the school included grades K–8 but she thought her Makana would be educated with peers of the same age. The day she visited she saw older children yelling curse words through the windows of the special education classroom that Makana was scheduled to attend. She knew that Makana would soon begin to imitate these words and was determined to do something. She said, *"Oh, oh, you showed me the wrong thing there."* I made such a stink they [early intervention professionals] investigated it, they closed it down; they sent all the kids to an elementary school that has a preschool on campus. There they placed the children in age-appropriate classes. Makana's new school had acres of classes and beautiful equipment . . . I was grateful that I had the support of the early intervention staff and had researched Makana's legal rights. If I had not, then Makana would have been subjected to a classroom and classmates that could have hurt him and his progress.

NOT WITHOUT SPEECH SERVICES FOR MY SON: PALAPALA STANDS FIRM FOR MAKANA

At one IEP meeting Palapala had wanted Makana to continue to receive speech services, as he had at the early intervention program. The school administrator recommended that Makana not receive speech, saying he did not need it because he was not talking! Palapala said, *I felt angry. Makana did speak, but only a few words and those were only under-standable to those who knew him well. I wanted him to talk better and to also learn to speak Hawaiian, so I said "he needs speech because he doesn't talk . . . "*

At the following IEP meeting requested by Palapala, she was supported by a resource teacher from the DOE district office. Palapala described the situation, *And I had to fight so I read the laws and I found out that they had to do a hundred pieces of paperwork; they had to re-evaluate him. I made her [administrator] do all that so it would be plenty work for her. Go ahead, do this to me, okay. And I got him speech and she's balking every inch of the way and she tried to give him as little as possible. I said, "No he needs as much as possible."* Her son began to receive speech services the day after the IEP meeting.

FULL INCLUSION FOR MAKANA: TRIUMPHS, TRIBULATIONS, AND TRIALS

Makana remained at the preschool located on the elementary school campus for nearly two years, until he returned to his local school for kindergarten. The local school was the one where the special education class that Palapala had ensured closed down had been located. In its place were two new portable buildings for special education.

Kindergarten through 3rd Grade: Full Inclusion in General Education Classroom

When Makana was 5 years old, Palapala faced yet another challenge. She wanted him to be fully included in a general education kindergarten classroom. Palapala believed that general education would best support Makana's social and communication needs. She also knew that Makana had the right to be educated in the least restrictive environment with his peers without disabilities. The general education teachers were skeptical. They had received no training on including a child with a disability in their classrooms.

The administrator was not willing to allocate an educational assistant (EA) for Makana even in the event a teacher volunteered to include Manaka in his or her classroom. Palapala had requested the IEP meeting at the end of his preschool year to give the school time to plan for Makana's inclusion. She wanted Makana to begin the year in the inclusive classroom. When the first IEP did not result in inclusion, Palapala asked for another meeting to be held ten days later. *I called an IEP every ten days. I'd sign them and then I'd call another one and I'd sign them, and then I'd call another one, and I think I had about nine meetings before I got what I wanted, because that's your right. You can call one every ten days, so I did.*

The general education teacher was doubtful, but she and the special education teacher worked with the EA to ensure Makana's inclusion. Palapala said it was a "difficult but successful year."

Before the end of Makana's Kindergarten year Palapala called an IEP meeting and brought goals and objectives that she had written that required inclusion. She knew that Makana needed social and communication goals, and that socializing with his general education peers was essential to these. She knew that the influence of friends using speech was the best incentive for Makana to speak. Palapala shared what Makana's inclusion meant for other children with disabilities. *Makana was now officially in a fully inclusive classroom in the island! He was the only child with a developmental disability to be included in the general education classroom. My husband and I were asked to give a presentation on inclusion at a local conference in Hawai'i. But I took ill suddenly so Toni and Jessi took my place and presented at the conference.*

During observations of Makana in his new fully inclusive classroom, his teacher, EA, and Palapala noted that Makana was happy, played with his friends during recess, and understood the rules of the class. He had an EA and, with accommodations and modifications in the curriculum and instructions, he was an active and fully accepted member of his class.

The End of Makana's Full Inclusion in 3rd Grade: It All Began with a Resistant Teacher

Makana began 3rd grade with a teacher named Sheri who was resistant to having children with disabilities in her class. Sheri and her EA had no knowledge, training, or experience in special education. Palapala observed Sheri and noted that she lacked classroom management skills, and did not know how to modify the curriculum to allow Makana to partici-pate. Makana had begun displaying oppositional behaviors (e.g., running around, talking loudly) that distracted his peers from learning. To address these problems Sheri would put Makana's desk outside his classroom and have him and his EA sit out there.

Palapala recalled an incident where Sheri would not allow Makana to participate in the May Day (Lei Day) celebrations. On this day the school cel-ebrates the culture of Native Hawaiians. Sheri believed that Makana would run around and disrupt her class performance. Despite Palapala's offer to help, Sheri was adamant that Makana not participate in the performance with the 3rd-grade students. This caused Palapala a lot of pain. When Palapala informed another educator at the school about this predicament the educator then talked with the 3rd-grade teachers, asking how they would feel if their own child was not given the opportunity to participate with other children in these celebrations. Sheri relented. Makana enjoyed himself, moving to the rhythm of Hawaiian songs and dance. "Did fantastic" were the words used by his mother and the educator to describe Makana's performance.

Nonetheless, Sheri continued to be resistant to Makana's inclusion in her classroom. Moreover, no other 3rd-grade teachers came forward to have Makana in their classrooms. Toward the middle of 3rd grade, Palapala was forced to relinquish her commitment to his placement in the general educa-tion classroom, because she did not want him to be in a classroom where he was not wanted by the teacher. Palapala grew tired of fighting because at each IEP meeting she gave all that she had and the strain was taking a toll on her health. Furthermore, Lana, the special education resource teacher, who was Palapala's strongest supporter, had retired, so Palapala felt alone on the battleground: *So, I pulled him out [of the general education classroom]. I consoled myself by focusing on Makana's inclusion in Hawaiian studies, music, computer, and other non-academic courses with his peers without disabilities. I thought, at least I got him in the Hawaiian class to learn our Hawaiian language and practices with the Kupuna [Hawaiian teacher] and he got to be with other non-disabled children in the 3rd grade. I made sure that Makana participated in general education for at least part of his school day, in non-academic subjects such as Hawaiiana [Hawaiian studies], com-puter, music, library, recess, and lunch with his regular education peers.*

The reality of the extent of inclusion for Makana in non-academic subjects was that lunch and recess were the only everyday inclusionary experience for him. The remaining non-academic subjects occurred twice a month.

Intermediate School and High School

When Makana transitioned to intermediate school Palapala again advo-cated for Makana's rights to be included in the general education. Palapala attended a re-evaluation meeting that re-certified Makana as eligible for special education services. Palapala said that she did not value the results of the assessments used to qualify students for special education. She provided her reasons: *Makana has Down syndrome. I accept that he has mental retardation. I do not need a standardized test to tell me my son's IQ or his academic ability. I wanted his teachers to acknowledge his strengths such as the use of computer technology and his good sense of humor. Makana likes using the computer; he learns so fast on it. I knew that Makana needed to learn life skills such as grooming, shopping, and ordering food at a restaurant but I also thought that now Makana needed to be included in directing his own education. It's what he expects that matters. He needed guidance but he also needed to be involved and I wanted the education professionals to listen to him. I wanted Makana to participate in classes that included Native Hawaiian cultural practices.*

Palapala spoke about how the family spoke to Makana in Hawaiian and he responded. At home he participated in all of his Hawaiian cultural practices with his family. His brother, Jessi taught him Hawaiian words, songs, and dances that he learned in his Hawaiian immersion school. Palapala said that that when Makana completed his education he would continue living with his family and that he would be responsible for contributing to the family using his "gifts." However, Palapala wanted Makana's adolescent years at school to prepare him for life after school and this would include Native Hawaiian cultural practices as well as technology.

Palapala did not succeed at convincing the administrators to fully include Makana with his general education peers in intermediate and high school. He continued his education on life skills in a classroom with other adolescents with disabilities over the next ten years. Palapala's health prevented her from using her knowledge of Makana's legal rights and the strategies that had been effective when Makana was younger. But she continued to ensure that Makana participated in Native Hawaiian cultural practices by continuing to teach him Hawaiian language and Hawaiian practices such as hula and making different instruments at home.

THEIR SPIRITS LIVE ON: PALAPALA AND MAKANA'S LEGACY FOR FUTURE GENERATIONS

Palapala passed away in 2005 when Makana was 16 years old. Sadly, Makana passed away at the young age of 19. He was still attending high school, in a fully self-contained classroom with children with severe disabilities.

Does the passing of Palapala and Makana end the move towards including children with developmental disabilities in the general education classroom? We think not. Instead we posit that as long as special education professionals do their work with their consciences guiding them, the aspirations and dreams of parents like Palapala are a guiding star for generations of Native Hawaiian families who have children with disabilities. We also posit that a lack of compassion, ethics and an understanding of best practices when working with Native Hawaiian families are the roots of the ills in special education services.

In the end, when you reflect on Makana's education, he was in an inclusive setting for a very brief period of his short life. He was seen as the problem when the problem was in fact outside of him. It seems incredibly unfair. How could this have happened despite his mother's extraordinary efforts? The answer lies in the actions of the educators who resisted every inclusionary attempt of Palapala and who blocked or tried to block any possibility of inclusive schooling for Makana. A question worth asking is how special education professionals can do right by the next Native Hawaiian child with a disability and his family. Next, we outline best practices when working with Native Hawaiian families with children with disabilities, showcasing these using Palapala's experiences to illuminate how things could have been very different for the Kauahi family.

BEST PRACTICES WITH NATIVE HAWAIIAN FAMILIES WITH CHILDREN WITH DISABILITIES

There are key cultural values that are vital to understand and incorporate in practice when working with Native Hawaiian families. First, Palapala was not included as a collaborative partner in the development of Makana's initial IEP when he transitioned from early intervention to special education. The IEP was developed prior to the meeting; the trust between Palapala and the professionals had been broken. Palapala found herself constantly advocating for Makana's educational rights without any attempt by the professionals to regain her trust. Perhaps this occurred because they did not know Palapala, her cultural background, and strategies for collaborating with families, in particular families who are Native Hawaiian. It is not uncommon to find a disconnection between teachers and families when attempting to collaborate across cultures. Even though some teachers may be Hawaiian, they may defer to western interventions and pedagogy that they had been taught in their teacher training programs.

NATIVE HAWAIIAN PRACTICES AND THEIR APPLICATION

'Ohana Conference

'*Ohana* conferencing is an approach where families develop a plan to address a specific social issue that involves family members. It has been used effectively to build collaboration and partnerships between social agencies and Hawaiian families (Walker, 2005). This is done by providing a process that is grounded in Hawaiian values and supports the family as they develop a plan that can ensure the safety and well-being of the family while keeping the family intact. If the professionals developing Makana's IEP had been aware of 'Ohana conferencing, they could have used that process to develop a trusting and collaborative relationship with Palapala and her family. Fundamental to 'Ohana Conferencing is the belief that the family is competent and capable of making decisions regarding their child. The process provides the family members with an opportunity to (a) voice their thoughts and feelings regarding their child to professionals, and (b) develop a plan for their child within guidelines provided by the professionals. There are three phases: preparation—inviting the participants (e.g. family and friends, relevant professionals, facilitator); conference—stating the purpose for the meeting (usually to solve a problem); setting guidelines for discussion that might include pertinent questions that need to be answered; discussing this purpose (e.g., suggestions for solving the problem); making a decision collaboratively with family (e.g., an action plan which is reviewed by professionals; and monitoring (e.g., identifying individuals responsible for different parts of the plan and establishing dates for reconvening to monitor it). 'Ohana conferencing would have ensured Palapala that the professionals had Makana's best interests in mind because they had allowed her to take the lead in planning his education.

Ho'oponopono: Repairing a Broken Trust

Ho'oponopono, meaning "to set right", is a Hawaiian family centered process that focuses on empowering families, solving problems, and restoring harmonious relationships. Kupunas (elders) or kahunas (religious leaders) play a vital role in guiding, facilitating, and mediating harmonious relationships (Mokuau, 1990; Shook, 1985). Shook (1985) outlined four basic phases of Ho'oponopono: pule (prayer), kukulu kumuhana (statement of the problem), discussion, and pani (closing). However, the value of Ho'oponopono is untapped if one does not explicitly use the structures inherent in this problem-solving process, which promote open communication and collaboration to achieve positive resolution. The use of Ho'oponopono requires that individuals have a deep understanding for this cultural practice; simply using features of this practice should not be identified as the practice itself. Ground rules are often established to ensure that there is a feeling of trust, safety, and care (Chun, 2011). If the professionals working with Makana had used a strategy such as ho'oponopono to address the trust that had been broken with Palapala and restore the essential collaborative relationship, it is possible that Palapala could have become a strong ally and support to special education professionals.

CONCLUDING THOUGHTS

It is our hope that by sharing Palapala's story, we may convince education professionals to reflect deeply on their practices. We hope that, if they see themselves acting in some way similar to those professionals who contributed to Palapala's trials and tribulations in acquiring services and placements for Makana, they may make a concerted effort to get to know each family they work with. We have provided several strategies that can be used to include Native Hawaiian families as equal partners in collaborative relationships to develop an educational plan for their children. It is our sincere hope that professionals will utilize those strategies and include Native Hawaiian families in educational planning; this would be a tribute to Palapala and her struggle to ensure that Makana receive an education that supported his Native Hawaiian culture. Palapala worked hard for many years ensuring that Makana was included with his peers and had access to Native Hawaiian cultural practices at school. If just one child like Makana benefits from Palapala's story, then her struggle will not have been in vain.

In memory of Palapala and Makana
May their spirits continue to guide special educators to fully
embrace children with disabilities
A Hui Ho ~ Till we meet again

ACKNOWLEDGMENT

We would like to thank Kaleʻa Silva for providing Hawaiian translations and for information on Hawaiian views on children with disabilities.

REFERENCES

Blaisdell, K., & Mokuau, N. (1991). *Kanaka Maoli:* Indigenous Hawaiians. In N. Mokuau (Ed.), *Handbook of Social Services for Asian and Pacific Islanders* (pp. 131–154). Westport, CT: Greenwood Press.

Chun, M.N. (2011). *No nā mamo: Traditional and contemporary Hawaiian beliefs and practices.* Honolulu: University of Hawaiʻi Press.

Data Accountability Center (2011). Retrieved from https://www.ideadata.org/TABLES35TH/B1–15.pdf

Education for All Handicapped Children Act of 1975. PL94–142. (Renamed the Individuals with Disabilities Education Act in 1990).

Handy, E.S.C. & Pukui, M.K. (1972). *The Polynesian family system in Kaʻu, Hawaiʻi.* Rutland, VT: Charles E. Tuttle Company.

Heward, W.L. (2009). *Exceptional children: An introduction to special education* (9th ed.). Upper Saddle River, NJ: Merrill/Prentice Hall.

Individuals with Disabilities Education Act (IDEA), 1990. Reauthorized as the IDEA of 2004. PL 108–446, 20 USC §§ 1400 *et seq.*

Jung, A. (2011). Individualized education programs (IEPs) and barriers for parents from culturally and linguistically diverse backgrounds. *Multicultural Education, 19*(3), 21–25.

Jegatheesan, B., Sheehey, P., & Ornelles, C. (2011). *Teaching for transformation: Preparing teacher candidates to work with Asian American and Pacific Islander students with disabilities and their families.* Council for Exceptional

Children (CEC). Monograph, Knowledge, Skills and Dispositions for Culturally Competent and Inter-Culturally Sensitive Leaders in Education.

Jegatheesan, B. (2009). Cross-cultural issues in parent-professional interactions: A qualitative study of perceptions of Asian American mothers of children with developmental disabilities. *Research & Practice for Persons with Severe Disabilities, 34*(3–4), 123–136.

Jegatheesan, B, Fowler, S & Miller, P (2010). From symptom recognition to services: How South Asian Muslim immigrant families navigate autism. *Disability & Society, 25*(7), 797–811.

Kanahele, G. (1986). *Kū Kanaka: Stand tall.* Honolulu: University of Hawai'i Press and Waiaha Foundation.

Matayoshi, K. (2013). 2012 superintendent's annual report (Report No. 23). Hawaii: Systems Accountability Office. Retrieved from Hawaii Department of Education website: http://arch.k12.hi.us/PDFs/state/superintendent_report/2012/AppendixCDataTbl12.pdf

Mokuau, N. (1990). A family-centered approach in Native Hawaiian culture. *Families in Society: The Journal of Contemporary Human Services, 70,* 479–487.

Mokuau, N., & Tauili'ili, P. (1998). *Families with Native Hawaiian and Samoan roots.* In E.W. Lynch & M.J. Hanson (Eds.) *Developing cross-cultural competence: A guide for working with children and their families* (pp. 409–440). Baltimore, MD: Brookes.

Mokuau, N., Lukela, D., Obra, A. & Voeller, M. (1997). *Native Hawaiian spirituality: A perspective on connections.* Honolulu: University of Hawaii School of Social Work.

Ogata, V., Sheehey, P., & Noonan, M.J. (2006). Rural Native Hawaiian perspectives on special education. *Rural Special Education Quarterly, 25*(1), 7–15.

Park, J., & Turnbull, A (2001). Quality of partnerships in service provision for Korean American parents of children with disabilities: A qualitative inquiry. *Journal of the Association of Persons with Severe Disabilities, 26*(30), 158–170.

Pukui, M.K., Haertig, E.W., Lee, C.A., & McDermott, J. (1979). *Nānā i ke kumu: Look to the source: volume II.* Honolulu, HI: Hui Hānai.

Sheehey, P. (2006). Parent involvement in educational decision making: A Hawaiian perspective. *Rural Special Education Quarterly, 25*(4), 3–15.

Sheehey, P. (2001). *Hawaiian families' involvement in special education: A cultural perspective.* Doctoral dissertation. University of Hawai'i. *Dissertation Abstracts International, 6*(10), 3349.

Shook, E.V. (1985). *Ho'oponopono.* Honolulu: University of Hawai'i Press.

United States Census Bureau. (2010). *State and county quick facts.* Retrieved from http://quickfacts.census.gov/qfd/states/15/15001.html

Vaughn, S., Bos, C.S., Harrell, J.E., Lasky, B.A. (1988). Parent participation in the initial placement/IEP conference ten years after mandated. *Journal of Learning Disabilities, 21*(2), 82–89.

Walker, L. (2005). A cohort study of 'ohana conferencing in child abuse and neglect cases. *Protecting Children, 19,* 36–46.

14 School Culture Matters

Enabling and Empowering Native American Students in Public Schools

Zoe Higheagle Strong and Brinda Jegatheesan

The National Indian Education Study (NIES),[1] which is a part of the National Assessment of Educational Progress (NAEP) report card under the National Center for Education Statistics (Institute of Education Sciences, U.S. Department of Education), conducts a survey every two years that extends beyond the traditional NAEP standardized testing to measure other factors important to American Indian and Alaska Native education (AI/AN) (Stancavage, Mitchell, Bandeira de Mello, Gaertner, Spain & Rahal, 2006). The NIES 2011 report highlights the help seeking patterns for AI/AN students in grades 4 and 8. The majority of grade 4 students (73%) reported asking for help from family members at least once a week and more than half sought help from teachers (63%) (National Center for Education Statistics, 2012). In grade 8, the family members and teachers remained key relationships within which to discuss educational issues (National Center for Education Statistics, 2012). In Native American communities, immediate family members often include aunts, uncles, and grandparents. Furthermore, Bock (2006) found that Native American students were shown to care deeply about teacher support and approval, even more than peer support. Teachers identified as mentors because they personally help students beyond the usual capacity have also been shown to be vital for disadvantaged minority youth to improve academically (Erickson, McDonald & Elder, 2009). Teacher relationships that support culturally responsive practices are especially effective.

CULTURALLY RESPONSIVE MENTORING FOR NATIVE AMERICAN STUDENTS

Mainstream studies identify mentoring relationships as an effective approach to bridging the gap between minority communities and schools, specifically benefiting at-risk students. Klinck, Cardinal, Edwards, Gibson, Bisanz, and Costa (2005) defined mentors as adults who "provide friendship, guidance, and support for children and youth outside of their own immediate families" (p. 110). In a meta-analysis of 73 mentoring programs, DuBois, Portillo, Rhodes, Silverthorn, and Valentine (2011) stated that mentoring has the ability to help students improve "outcomes across behavioral, social, emotional, and academic domains of young people's development. The most common pattern of benefits is for mentored youth to exhibit positive gains on outcome measures while nonmentored youth exhibit decline" (p. 57). Culturally responsive mentoring is one key to supporting minority youth development effectively (Klinck et al., 2005; Spencer, 2006, 2007; Strong, 2013); yet there are few studies that provide research and practice guidelines on mentoring individuals from specific ethnic cultures such as Native American youth.

Culturally responsive mentoring can empower Native American students to cultivate a sense of school belonging and positive identity in public schools (Strong, 2013). In a study on Navajo youth identity and psychosocial wellbeing, Jones and Galliher (2007) concluded that "as living and being successful in traditional ways of life become more difficult, feelings of commitment and belonging to one's ethnic group may be instrumental in overcoming negative effects of acculturative stress" (p. 692). Native American students continually undergo acculturative stress as they strive to meet mainstream education standards that poorly reflect their own cultural values and practices. Human beings also have a tendency to develop their personal identity by evaluating themselves through another's perceptions, consequently a negative social mirror is found to adversely affect academic engagement (Suárez-Orozco, 2004, p. 184) and influence achievement and performance (Whitesell, Mitchell, & Spicer, 2009). Native American students' cultural values and behavior can often be misinterpreted in public schools and perceived as noncompliant, disrespectful (Huffman, 2010), not engaged, or uninterested (Powers, Potthoff, Bearinger, & Resnick, 2003). Cultural understanding and positive interactions from school administration and teachers can promote positive identity for Native American youth.

Public schools and supplemental education services could benefit from developing mentoring programs that include immediate and extended family and teachers in a less formal approach. Native American students tend to seek help differently than mainstream students.

THE PUBLIC SCHOOL EXPERIENCES OF TATIANA AND KIA

Tatiana and Kia are fifteen-year-old 10th-grade Native American girls in two different predominately non-Native public schools.[2] They are from two-parent households and attended different public schools on or near their tribal community. Both girls are registered tribal members from the same tribe in the Pacific Northwest of the United States. Both girls stay connected to their tribal youth programs. They live on or close to their tribal land that is surrounded by an urban city. Tatiana attended a predominately non-Native public school all of her middle school years, while Kia attended the first half of middle school at a Bureau of Indian Education (BIE) school operated by her tribe, and then transitioned to a non-Native public middle school. Even though they attend different public schools, they described themselves as friends based on participating in periodic tribal activities together.

A PUBLIC SCHOOL EDUCATION AND THE MEANING OF ACADEMIC SUCCESS

Education in a public school was viewed as a cognitive, goal-oriented approach. Together they defined success this way: *Staying focused on your grades and keeping up on everything. It's like figuring out your goals in life and like pursing those goals until you achieve them.* Both girls believed that educational success did not differ between Native American versus non-Native American students. They explained: *Everyone practically belongs to the same school. Everyone wants to succeed in each different race. Everyone wants to succeed in something. No one wants to fail. Educational success is defined similarly for every student with no cultural differences. If a student wants to achieve, they will work for it and succeed.*

ACADEMIC SUPPORT

Tatiana and Kia stated that at the BIE schools, they were both getting better grades because of lower academic rigor and expectations. Kia explained her transition to a public school this way: *So like when I go to public school it was harder but I can still do it. So it's more like a challenge. When I go to BIE school, I feel like I am not doing anything there. . . . At BIE school the work was really easier work. I was like in gifted and talented. I started there since Kindergarten then to end of 6th grade.*

Kia described the public school academic support she received this way: *They have programs at my high school called, college bound scholarship, career cruising, and just teachers supporting me, too. You can sign up for college bound and they are just always there. They help keep you organized, and help you start looking for colleges. So that kind of helps, too. My parents didn't really have that. They just show that I need to take advantage of that stuff. Go to college and be what I want to be, I guess . . . But in middle school they had college bound scholarship as well, but it was different from what's from high school, because in high school it's like this class. They lay out different careers, they show you what you need to do to get to that career, where in middle school it was just like a scholarship that they paid*

*for and I wanted to do it too, but my mom told me that my tribe already
paid for college so she really didn't see use in it, so now they have this other
program where it shows different careers and things. She wants me to join
that. That's pretty cool.*

MENTORING RELATIONSHIPS AND SUPPORT

The primary mentoring relationships that supported Tatiana and Kia at
school appeared to be teachers. Peer relationships were noted as mostly
negatively influencing their school experience and performance. However,
the teacher relationship was valuable in helping the girls achieve academically and enjoy learning. The girls described additional attributes such as
the personality characteristics (e.g., funny, nice, personable) that helped
connect them to a teacher, motivated them to learn, and pushed them to
do well. For example, both found humor, sharing personal thoughts or discussing non-academic topics, one-on-one conversations, and after school
meetings with the teacher valuable. Both looked forward to attending
school because such a relationship with the teacher made their schooling
experience enjoyable. Kia explained: *I have better relationships with teachers that have more humor, so like when I can joke around with my teacher,
I can do better in the class and work more. I keep my grades up and I ask
more questions and everything. It's enjoyable when teachers get out of the
box of academics and converse with us and care about us.*

Tatiana described her views this way: *I just feel like the teachers that
are like funnier, nicer, that they care a lot more than the teachers that are
just straight up mean.* Tatiana also explained the teacher/tutor qualities
that helped her focus on her learning and performance: *She (tutor) helped
me with math and I didn't really need help in math. So she (mom) like
got me another tutor and all the sudden my grades got better and better
because she started helping me in science and English, which actually
is what I needed help in. . . . the first tutor we didn't connect, like she
barely ever talked and like I didn't really get help when we didn't have a
relationship like me and my new tutor. It's a lot more helpful when you
have a relationship with someone. The relationship and the ability to
talk about life outside of tutoring improved my performance.*

When these two students received personal invitations to participate in
extracurricular activities and to try something beyond their comfort zone,
they accepted and gained valuable skills and experiences. Tatiana remem-
bered one such example: *The teachers that were the leaders of ASB (Associated Student Body) were the ones that chose me to give the speech, so I
thought, oh that's cool, I might as well and that's awesome, so um, so
I guess I have learned to be more confident in myself and talk a lot more
in front of people.*

PEER FRIENDSHIPS

Kia and Tatiana also discussed the issues girls face in middle school that require additional support. They witnessed a change in the girls' relationship with each other that they described as "drama." They attributed this drama to peer pressure, the focus on boys, drugs, and cattiness. They felt that boys tend to get cooler and more bonded to each other, while girl relationships grow further apart. They were discussing these relationship patterns at school, where students are primarily non-Native. Kia described the mentoring support needed in this environment: *Somebody that we are really close with that has a good head on their shoulders, really good at what they are doing or something. Someone who can keep us out of trouble...We need to be surrounded by good influences.*

Kia and Tatiana described relationships with girls as something that negatively impacted their school performance. They said the following: *Friendship with girls is drama. The avoidance or loss of these friendships helped us to achieve more in school. Female friendships were mostly distracting and negatively influenced our learning. Male friendships have less drama but do not help us academically.*

However, the importance of peer relationships was acknowledged. Kia explained: *If the girls were academically focused...if you have a friend and you both have good grades, then, why not. So like, more kids that have better grades, then, if they are all in the same class, then it's easier. My girlfriends were holding me back. I lost a lot of friends, so I think it kind of affects me positively. In a way I think some of my friends were holding me back from my potential, 'cause um, I really had a 2.5 when I had all those friends, then towards the end of the year my GPA started going up and started getting better. I get along with guys better than girls, just 'cause guys have sports to keep them on the right track and everything rather than girls, most girls just don't care anymore.*

Tatiana and Kia appear to have rejected conforming to the "drama" relationship dynamic found among the predominately non-Native girls at their school. In fact, they withdrew from these types of relationships to the point of alienation from other peers. Conversely, they held each other in high regard and sympathized with each other on the struggle of developing peer friendships with girls.

ACADEMIC ACHIEVEMENT

Succeeding in academics takes motivation and inspiration. Tatiana and Kia displayed positive self-esteem. Their relationships and past academic achievement appeared to contribute to their positive self-esteem. When the girls were asked to think about a time they felt successful in school, Tatiana discussed a memory of when she got to skip a math test because she was ahead. She stated, *I just really like math. Math comes really easy to me. I just always had an "A" in math. My confidence grew once I got to know people better.* Taking classes aligned with her talents helped boost her self-esteem.

Kia's self-esteem increased through leadership opportunities and academic success in her early middle school years. Kia entered into middle school as a shy girl, afraid to talk in front of a group. In 8th grade she was asked by the Associated Student Body (ASB) teacher to give a speech, and she did so successfully. She stated, *I think it's 'cause I've learned to be more confident in myself, just 'cause I have accomplished so much since 6th grade, 'cause I was a leader and everything in middle school.* Middle school transition had its ebbs and flows for both students. Tatiana described it this way: *I ended up just slacking because it was really easy at first. So I didn't think I had to do that much, so the first semester of ninth grade I completely slacked and only got a 1.7 and it kind of scared me. So, like the next semester, I ended up getting a 3.1 at the end. I just focused more and realized I actually have to try.*

In order to succeed educationally, Kia and Tatiana explained it this way: *It takes inspiration. Because most people in my life, my tutor, my mom and friend have all inspired me to get better grades* (Kia). *It takes motivation. Like having one thing that will always keep you focused and keep you on the right track* (Tatiana).

LACK OF NATIVE AMERICAN CULTURAL REPRESENTATION IN PUBLIC SCHOOL AND KNOWLEDGE OF NATIVE HISTORICAL EXPERIENCES

Tatiana and Kia have been active within their tribal community from a young age. Now that the girls attend a primarily non-Native public school, some of their experiences appear to have negatively shaped their perspective on Native identity and school belonging. According to the girls, the public school's effort to promote diversity was providing a multicultural week or day where all ethnicities had an opportunity to share their culture. They said, *everyone did what their culture does. They showed a little bit of their culture.* Kia's school only dedicated one day to honor different cultures, whereas Tatiana's school continued for a week. Kia described the multicultural focus as "really weird." Yet she was excited to see other ethnicities sharing their culture. Unfortunately, both of the girls expressed their disappointment that the Native American culture was not represented at either of their schools during the multicultural celebration. They did not seem to place the responsibility on the school; instead Kia seemed to blame the other two Native American students who were in the Native Club for not sharing their culture. Kia summed up: *When I was at the BIE school it was more about just Natives and when I went to public it was more about all the cultures.*

At the school level, they received minimal opportunities to celebrate their culture even during multi-cultural days or weeks. At Kia's school, they had an Indian club, but because of sports she was unable to attend. Tatiana said they did not have an Indian club at her school. The girls shared their disappointment at the lack of Native American representation in their schools' multicultural celebrations. Kia had a lot of views that were also supported by Tatiana: *There were no Natives. There was just clubs at my school. They have Korean club, Polynesian club, Spanish club and stuff like that. But there was a Native American club, like two people in it. They didn't do anything. It's kind of like, I was disappointed. Because if I had time to do it, I would like to show something from my culture and to have the confidence to talk about something, and sing a song like the other clubs. I mean the people who were in it didn't do anything. I thought, 'Are you not proud or something?'* (Referring to the two Native Americans in the club). *It just like disappointed me.*

Kia did not seem to be bothered that the school did not represent or teach about Native culture. She stated: *It doesn't bother me 'cause Natives have their own school where they learn about their culture. So if I really wanted to know about my culture, I could just go back to the BIE school.*

Kia also discussed the major cultural differences she experienced between attending BIE school and public school: *The BIE school is more about just Natives and when I went to public it was more like about all the cultures. It was, yeah, very weird. . . . when I went to (BIE school) they were all about like Native beliefs and everything, but public school like we had this day where Asians, they showed what their culture is about.*

Tatiana agreed with Kia and then furthered the views by discussing the lack of cultural mentoring opportunities at public school. She put it this way: *Multi-cultural week . . . The same with my school, except throughout the whole week there was like a different culture each day and they would have to dress up if you wanted to. And the last day of the week, there would be a big assembly for half of the day and they would just like do a dance or they sang or something like that. So it is kind of weird though 'cause at my school they are not really that many Natives so it was just like the Natives had nothing to do with it.*

Tatiana and Kia also expressed limited knowledge of Native historical experiences. The girls' lack of positive Native cultural representation at school and minimal knowledge of the implications of historical trauma and colonization seemed to partially contribute to their negative views towards Native Americans. Kia said, *I don't think Natives achieve that much because they are lazy. Natives get handed everything to them.*

CONCLUSIONS ABOUT CULTURAL MENTORING

When addressing educational issues for Native American students, such as narrowing the achievement gap in public schools, the lens of analysis should be through Native American cultural values and practices. Tatiana and Kia shared a more mainstream ideology of educational success by describing success in terms such as "thought out" and "being goal oriented." The public school culture shaped their views on academic success. According to Garrett et al. (2003), mainstream ideology takes a more individualistic and future-time orientation to achievement, while traditional Native values consist of cooperation and present-time orientation. Both girls are embedded in the cultural practices within their tribe, but it is apparent that the school played a predominant role in shaping perspectives on educational success. A key concern in their public schools was the lack of Native cultural representation and education on historical experiences. This had an impact on the students' cultural identity. Although Tatiana and Kia had many rich cultural experiences in their tribal community, they used many negative terms when describing other Native American students, as noted earlier. Both girls had limited knowledge of Native historical issues and expressed disappointment in the lack of Native American representation in public school. Whitbeck, Hoyt, and Stubben (2001) discussed the relationship between Native American identity and educational success from the perspective of the enculturation hypothesis: "Traditional culture imbues children with pride in cultural heritage and gives them the direction they need to negotiate their way though the cultural contradictions inherent in their contacts with European American society" (p. 6). The reinforcement of cultural values, practices, and historical education can cultivate positive cultural identity and cognitive strategies.

Both girls identified a teacher who played a supplementary role as "mentor". These teachers, who were well regarded by the students, were noted to use culturally responsive practices that enhanced their self-esteem and academic performance while studying in their public school. The teacher's impact on Native American student achievement has been well researched (Castagno, 2008; Cleary, 2008; Cleary & Peacock, 1998). The key attributes that impacted Tatiana and Kia were relationship-oriented, humor, talking in depth, cooperation, personable (sharing personal information), and willing to meet "one on one." These attributes enhanced Kia and Tatiana's self-esteem and academic performance. The findings support Erikson et al.'s (2009) study that identified the vital importance of teacher-mentors on academic achievement for minority youth.

INNOVATIVE OUTREACH TO NARROW ACHIEVEMENT GAP FOR NATIVE AMERICAN STUDENTS

TEAM-WORKS

The first author, a Nez Perce tribal member, spent over ten years working as Executive Director and program developer for the Washington Chapter of HOPE *worldwide*. She contributed to Native American education by developing culturally responsive mentoring and tutoring programs and started her own Foundation in partnership with her husband Mack Strong, a former National Football League player for over 14 years. Their TEAM-WORKS Foundation, a 501c3 nonprofit, provides culturally supportive youth mentoring programs to assist Native and urban at-risk youth to develop strong minds, strong bodies and strong character in order to succeed academically and in life. Their programs, which provide numerous supplemental education programs, serve over 350 Native and at-risk youth annually through summer workshops and camps on tribal reservations and Alaska Native villages, and throughout the Northwest through urban school and after-school academies. The main components in all programs are culturally responsive mentoring coupled with customized curricula that holistically address education, health and wellness, and character/social development. The following highlights successes and lessons learned during program and partnership development on Native land and urban areas.

Lesson Learned

Native students are often in learning environments that do not reflect their own cultural values or practices. Supplemental education programs and schools that embrace and support the Native communities' vision and goals for their own kids will provide meaningful, long-lasting learning experiences. The TEAM-WORKS programs offers Sports, Leadership and Culture Camps in Native communities and provides overall organizational structure and support to equip community elders, leaders, and mentors to teach their children.

One of the core values in Native communities is generosity and giving back. There has never been a shortage of community volunteers when we have respectfully invited and welcomed partnerships and discarded the attitude of "this is our program, and we will run it how we best see fit." Even as a Native educator, Zoe is amazed at the cultural differences and the richness that each community brings as they teach the staff how to best serve their children. When entering a Native community, it is always beneficial to first connect with Native elders, government council, and youth education leaders to determine if your program and ideas are needed or wanted in the community. If so, ask them to direct you on forming an advisory and planning committee to ensure that their cultural values and practices are properly implemented. When possible, make personal invitations to each person, not a general impersonal request. Establish your committee meetings in a relaxed, family-style environment by providing meals or snacks, share your heart for the community, seek guidance and enjoy the relationships without taking yourself too seriously.

Example of a Successful Program Partnership

Recently TEAM-WORKS conducted an annual Sports, Leadership and Culture summer camp in a small northwest tribal community. They brought in nine coaches and staff to provide skills development in football, basketball and volleyball for 140 students in grades 3 through 8. They had over 40 community volunteers who served in various capacities: elders teaching lessons, the language and cultural department teaching the language and cultural arts and games, local athletes assisting in the coaching sessions, and administrative support helping with registration and food organization. The TEAM-WORKS non-Native coaches and mentors modeled respect for the community's tribal culture by learning the language, standing for the drum and singing, and embracing the cultural practices. Native students often hear negative stereotypes about their culture and their cultural practices are often dismissed for mainstream ways. On the end of camp survey, students expressed a sense of cultural pride, stating that they learned, "my tribe's pride songs," "how to shoot a bow and arrow," "to try harder and respect my family" and "to respect and honor my elders." Other students made key decisions about life and school: "I will stop bullying," "I won't do drugs," and "I will have a response, to work hard" and the importance of education.

Lessons Learned

Early on, Zoe failed to develop relationships with council members and elders and to include local tribal culture from the onset of the program. She was invited into the community to develop an after school tutoring/mentoring program and eventually learned that she should have extended the planning phase to include more community members in the development process. Now she recommends taking the time to build those relationships first and solicit community feedback from tribal council, elders and families to ensure their own tribal values and practices are respectfully incorporated into programs. When serving Native students in urban areas, the TEAM-WORKS mentoring programs have been most effective when there are strong partnerships with Native communities and public schools. In urban public schools Native students are often disconnected from their school and non-Native peers. Inviting the Native community to serve in some capacity at the school and/or in programs helps Native students to feel less alienated and to gain a positive identity when they see positive Native role models.

The greatest student academic and socio-emotional gains occurred through in-school interventions paired with a teacher identified as a "teacher-mentor." These teachers go beyond the usual, visiting the student homes, making regular phone calls, initiating special family gatherings, and seeking outside services to support students' needs on multiple domains. TEAM-WORKS partners with these teacher-mentors who lead learning strategies for special needs and at-risk population classes with Native students (Native American/Alaska Native, Pacific Islander, American Samoan, and Native Hawaiian); they also work with other cultures by providing additional trained mentors and after-school family dinners and celebrations to help bridge the gap between the students' families and school.

Examples of Student Success Stories

Kilani, an American Samoan 8th-grade student whose grades drastically increased and behavioral referrals decreased within one year, said, "My grades and behavior got better since last year. Last year I had 63 referrals, and all F's." Now, he has no referrals and all A's. When asked what motivated the change, he replied, "I realized school helps a lot and in life you get more options with education." He then shared his experiences of reluctantly transitioning into the American school system in 2007 as a 4th-grade student. He explained that in Samoa, there was no black or white in school; they called everyone brother. Here he finds the school too competitive. His stated educational goals are to finish school and get a good job so that he can "go back home." The teacher-mentor also noticed he had a backpack filled with candy, chips, and caffeinated sodas that he ate each day. She helped him change his diet and his behavior changed in the classroom.

In another classroom, two Native American students appeared to be quiet and disconnected from class. After Zoe shared about her Nez Perce culture and experiences during a character education class, James, a Native American 7th grader, approached her and spoke proudly about his Native culture. Later that year James came into the classroom clenching his fists, shaking with anger, and not paying attention. He had long hair and said, "There are boys calling me a fagot in the halls and it broke out into a fight." Zoe empathized with him and offered him coping skills for dealing with his anger and conflict; he calmed down and re-engaged in class. Theresa, a 7th-grade Native girl, would not speak in large or small group discussions at school, yet when a mentor would sit with her individually in class when the rest of the students were meeting in groups, she was not afraid to share her insights and ask questions.

In order to successfully serve Native, minority, and at-risk youth and families, educators need to expand their learning and preparation beyond formal education to becoming a student of the community they intend to serve. Often Native and minority communities will embrace educators who are genuinely inquisitive about learning their culture. Furthermore, a strong partnership with the school administration and supplemental education program is important. The administration needs to be well informed of supplemental education programs goals and activities. Supplemental education can help bridge the cultural gaps between mainstream schools and communities. Academic and behavioral issues should also be addressed holistically through caring relationships. Some of the students highlighted were known as defiant, hard to reach students by teachers, but made incredible gains through nurturing relationships. For Zoe and Mack's contributions in serving Native and at-risk communities through TEAM-WORKS programs, they have won several awards including the 2009 Mark Matthews Service to Children Award, 2011 Washingtonian of the Year award from the Association of Washington Generals, and the 2012 Seattle Indian Health Board's Adeline Garcia Community Service Award.

EDUCATIONAL APPLICATIONS TO NARROWING THE ACHIEVEMENT GAP SUPPORTING NATIVE AMERICAN STUDENTS IN PUBLIC SCHOOLS

Public schools can support Native American students by interacting with the families of those students, with local tribal communities, and Native organizations to discuss meaningful approaches to include Native American cultural teachings and cultural practices. Inviting tribal elders and leaders into classrooms to discuss historical trauma and implications of the boarding school era, watching documentaries, and/or taking field trips to visit cultural sites are all valuable strategies that bring awareness and an understanding of historical trauma and cultural values and practices. During multi-cultural celebrations, teachers and administrators can also invite Native American representatives to share their culture if the students do not take initiative. This coming together of members of the community helps identify existing mentoring relationships that Native American students have within their families or tribal communities that enable teachers to collaborate in their efforts to support students' academic learning.

RELATIONSHIPS

Teacher relationships can be vital in helping Native American students succeed in their education by extending friendship, teaching them like family, determining student needs and developing a culturally supportive plan. Jegatheesan, Sheehey, and Ornelles (2012) argue for pedagogical practices nested within students' own cultural and social systems. They summarize three dimensions that teachers need to pay attention to: the personal dimension speaks to the need for teachers to understand how students' culture, social realities and history of colonization inform and impact their learning; the instructional dimension speaks to how compatible pedagogical practices contribute to a high quality of education, reduce inappropriate referrals for special education and prevent school failure; and lastly the interpersonal dimension emphasizes the need for skills such as compassion, patience, flexibility, and nurturance that facilitate healthy and trusting relationships, particularly among vulnerable populations.

TAILORING TO SPECIFIC TRIBES

Tatiana and Kia represent one geographic area in the Northwest. Each tribal community has different cultural practices and resources. Additionally this chapter only addresses two girls who attend public schools. According to Faircloth and Tippeconnic (2010), there are approximately 644,000 American Indian/Alaska Native students in the entire school system and approximately 92% of those students attend public schools. The school culture impacts the overall educational experiences of Native American students. In public schools that serve numerous different cultures and ethnic backgrounds, incorporating culturally responsive strategies in mentoring programs and/or improving teacher-student relationships is a viable school intervention for Native American student achievement. Tatiana and Kia have each spoken to the positive impact that culturally responsive mentoring and teacher relationships had on their development. Teachers who go beyond the call of duty in working with Indigenous students have the ability to unlock hidden potential in their students.

NOTES

1. The NIES was initially funded by the Office of Indian Education (OIE) and the first report began in 2005. The reports are only highlights of a large data set. More information on NIES/NAEP, on receiving training, and accessing the secondary data set is available on line: http://nces.ed.gov/nationsreportcard/nies/
2. Participants were given pseudonyms and their tribal affiliation was kept anonymous for confidentiality purposes. Consent from parents and assent from students were obtained prior to data collection.

REFERENCES

Bock, T. (2006). A consideration of culture in moral theme comprehension: Comparing Native and European American students. *Journal of Moral Education*, 35(1), 71–87. doi:10.1080/03057240500495310

Castagno, A.E., & Brayboy, B.M.J. (2008). Culturally responsive schooling for Indigenous youth: A review of the literature. *Review of Educational Research,* 78(4), 941–993. doi:10.3102/0034654308323

Cleary, L.M. (2008). The imperative of literacy motivation when Native children are being left behind. *Journal of American Indian Education,* 47(1), 96–117. Retrieved from http://jaie.asu.edu/

Cleary, L.M., & Peacock, T.D. (1998). *Collected wisdom: American Indian education.* Boston: Allyn & Bacon.

DuBois, D.L., Portillo, N., Rhodes, J.E., Silverthorn, N., & Valentine, J.C. (2011). How effective are mentoring programs for youth? A systematic assessment of the evidence. *Psychological Science in the Public Interest,* 12(2), 57–91. doi:10.1177/1529100611414806

Erickson, L.D., McDonald, S., & Elder, G.H. (2009). Informal mentors and education: Complementary or compensatory resources? *Sociology of Education,* 82(4), 344–367. doi:10.1177/003804070908200403

Faircloth, S.C., & Tippeconnic, J.W.,III. (2010). *The dropout/graduation crisis among American Indian and Alaska Native students: Failure to respond places the future of Native peoples at risk.* Los Angeles: The Civil Rights Project/ Proyecto Derechos Civeles at UCLA. Retrieved from www.civilrightsproject. ucla.edu

Garrett, M.T., Bellon-Harn, M., Torres-Rivera, E., Garrett, J.T., & Roberts, L.C. (2003). Open hands, open hearts: Working with Native youth in the schools. *Intervention in School & Clinic,* 38(4), 225.

Huffman, T. (2010). *Theoretical perspectives on American Indian education: Take a new look at academic success and the achievement gap.* Lanham, MD: Alta-Mira Press.

Jegatheesan, B., Sheehey, P., & Ornelles, C (2011). *Teaching for transformation: Preparing teacher candidates to work with Asian American and Pacific Islander students with disabilities and their families.* Monograph: Knowledge, Skills and Dispositions for Culturally Competent and Inter-Culturally Sensitive Leaders in Education. Arlington, VA: Council for Exceptional Children.

Jones, M.D., & Galliher, R.V. (2007). Ethnic identity and psychosocial functioning in Navajo adolescents. *Journal of Research on Adolescence (Blackwell Publishing Limited),* 17(4), 683–696. doi:10.1111/j.1532–7795.2007.00541.x

Klinck, J., Cardinal, C., Edwards, K., Gibson, N., Bisanz, J., & Costa, J. (2005). Mentoring programs for aboriginal youth. *Pimatisiwin: A Journal of Aboriginal and Indigenous Community Health,* 3(2), 109–129.

National Center for Education Statistics. (2012). *National Indian Education Study 2011: The educational experiences of American Indian and Alaska Native students at grades 4 and 8.* NCES 2012–466. Washington D.C.: National Center for Education Statistics. Retrieved from http://nces.ed.gov/pubsearch/ pubsinfo.asp?pubid=2012466

Powers, K., Potthoff, S. J., Bearinger, L. H., & Resnick, M. D. (2003). Does cultural programming improve educational outcomes for American Indian youth? *Journal of American Indian Education,* 42(2), 17–49. Retrieved from http:// jaie.asu.edu/abstracts/abs2003

Spencer, R. (2006). Understanding the mentoring process between adolescents and adults. *Youth and Society,* 37(3), 287–315. doi:10.1177/0743558405278263

Spencer, R. (2007). 'It's not what I expected' A qualitative study of youth mentoring relationship failures. *Journal of Adolescent Research,* 22(4), 331–354. doi:10.1177/0743558407301915

Stancavage, F.B., Mitchell, J.H., Bandeira de Mello, V.P., Gaertner, F.E., Spain, A.K., and Rahal, M.L., (2006). *National Indian education study, part II: The educational experiences of fourth- and eighth-grade American Indian and*

Alaska Native students (NCES 2007–454). Washington D.C.: U.S. Department of Education, Institute of Education Sciences, National Center for Education Statistics. Government Printing.

Strong, Z. (2013). *Native youth voices on success, identity, and cultural values: Mentoring middle school Native American students for educational success.* (Unpublished master's thesis). Seattle: University of Washington.

Suárez-Orozco, C. (2004). Formulating identity in a globalized world. In M.M. Suárez-Orozco, & D.B. Qin-Hilliard (Eds.) *Globalization: Culture and education in the new millennium.* (pp. 173–202). Berkeley: University of California Press.

Whitbeck, L.B., Hoyt, D.R., & Stubben, J.D. (2001). Traditional culture and academic success among American Indian children in the upper Midwest. *Journal of American Indian Education, 40*(2), 48–60. Retrieved from http://jaie.asu.edu/v40/V40I2A3.pdf

Whitesell, N.R., Mitchell, C.M., & Spicer, P. (2009). A longitudinal study of self-esteem, cultural identity, and academic success among American Indian adolescents. *Cultural Diversity and Ethnic Minority Psychology,* 15(1), 38–50. doi:10.1037/a0013456

Part III Commentary
Reflections

Linda Sue Warner

Part III of this volume focuses primarily on the diversity of American Indian student populations, instructional approaches, and research. For this section, perspectives were provided by collaborations among Lois A. Yamauchi, Rebecca Lunning, and Kristin Begay; Patricia Sheehey and Brinda Jegatheesan; and Zoe Strong and Brinda Jegatheesan.

To reflect on these perspectives, I bring nearly forty years' experience working with American Indians/Alaska Natives/Native Hawaiians as both a teacher and a student. I also had the privilege of knowing William Demmert's work and more recently have become acquainted with the work of Denny Hurtado. Over these years, I met William Demmert on numerous occasions and my earliest memory of him was a telephone conversation initiated by his brother Leroy Demmert, who had been my supervisor while I taught at Mt. Edgecumbe School in Alaska. When we had that conversation, William "Bill" Demmert was the Director of the Office of Indian Education Programs in Washington D.C. for Department of Interior. He was actually my boss's boss's boss. The fact that he would take the time to talk to me about a pursuing my degree tells you a lot about Bill Demmert. He had not met me previous to this point, but I recall, very explicitly, one thing he said to me: "The Bureau of Indian Affairs should be in the business of helping Indians." I never forgot that he tried to create a "can do" organization out of one of the most dysfunctional agencies to ever exist in the federal government. He reinforced what I believed about students—and what these authors suggest as well—that they deserve quality and care in both instruction and organization.

In Chapter 12, Yamauchi, Luning, and Begay discuss both research and practice that engages American Indian students through Instructional Conversation (IC). Instructional conversation, they write, was promoted by Bill Demmert as a way of connecting both teachers and students from separate communities, creating collaboration across cultures. The authors use their experiences in Hawaii and provide examples from the Hawaiian Language Immersion program. Because IC has a solid research foundation, its application to day-to-day instruction is easily adaptable to using Native language in the classroom. The authors also discuss the use of IC on the Navajo reservation at Rough Rock, one of the premier non-traditional instructional settings in Indian Country. While the results varied, the use of IC also can be linked to other Indigenous groups, and Demmert did exactly that by introducing the strategy to Indigenous educators worldwide through his chairing of the Circumpolar North group. This, again, is a testament to his vision and his continuing belief that students deserve strategies that promote success.

In Chapter 13, Sheehey and Jegatheesan share best practices developed from work with special populations. The authors' discussion of traditional beliefs and practices within the Hawaiian culture assure us that they too heard Demmert and Hurtado's admonition to classroom instructors of Indigenous students that they honor the knowledge and skills that students bring to a classroom in the creation of learning objects that will best serve their students. These authors know from field experiences what Demmert and Hurtado professed most often: "Native Hawaiians' learning and communication are informed by their traditions." Traditions for tribal communities that have been isolated or have resisted assimilation present a more focused challenge in the face of high stakes testing. Tribal traditions, in this case Hawaiian traditions, of community and the values and relationships associated with community do not easily lend themselves to mainstream education practice where students receive lectures while sitting in neat little rows. I found it particularly insightful that the authors note that there is no common usage or terminology for "disabilities" or "special needs" in the Hawaiian language. I think this is likely true in many more Indigenous cultures, where relationships trump individual acknowledgement. Such interrelatedness connects these students to their communities, which are now connected to a better understanding of teaching and learning. This interrelatedness is the heart of the message from Demmert and Hurtado as they influenced work that reaches out through these chapters to teach us now. This chapter also provides a close look at the stories of children—stories that speak to those of us who are teachers as examples in a clearer way than statistics or test scores. This chapter provides strong evidence that lessons learned from tribal or Indigenous peoples can provide a roadmap for all students and are especially helpful to teachers in schools where communities need to be empowered to change the opportunities for their students.

The third chapter in this section, provided by Strong and Jegatheesan, looks at American Indians in public schools and addresses the need for culturally responsive mentoring. It reminds me of the first time I met Rosemary Christensen, a lady I consider an exemplary teacher and mentor because when we first met, someone introduced me to her as Dr. Warner. I think we both learned something in that meeting because she eschewed my title and asked me if I had a first name and I remember sharing with her that I used the title because I wanted the students I worked with to understand that it is possible to be an American Indian, a woman, *and* a Ph.D. Additionally, this chapter reminds me that mentoring is not about age in tribal cultures.

I have had mentors who are younger than I and I have mentored individuals who are older. Mentoring, as exemplified by Bill Demmert and Denny Hurtado is about trust and responsibility; it is one of the reasons that we so elaborately introduce ourselves. Indian Country is small, and introducing yourself by explaining your family links you to others in that community and establishes the lines of responsibility.

These forty years have taught me a lot through my listening to previous teacher/mentors and my reading and reflecting on the current work, such as the chapters here. Culturally responsive mentoring comes from Donald Willower's[1] definition of a teacher, one with "a good heart." For me it is summed up as I paraphrase the following from one of Willower's lectures on The Great Law:

As teachers, we are mentors of our students for all time.
We labor to stand against anger, sadness, criticism, and defeat.
Our hearts shall be full of peace and our minds filled with an
    urgency for the welfare of our students.
With endless patience, we embrace our duty.
Our firmness shall be tempered with tenderness.
Our words and actions shall be marked by calm deliberation.

NOTES

1. Donald Willower was a highly respected teacher and education administrator as well as faculty member. His archived papers can be accessed at http://www.libraries.psu.edu/findingaids/732.htm

15 Visions for the Future of Indian Education

Thoughts to Guide Ongoing Work at the Intersection of Evidence-Based Practice and Culturally Sensitive Education

Peggy McCardle and Virginia Berninger

In this volume we draw upon the insights of Native American educators to offer practical, evidence-based, culturally sensitive practices for narrowing the achievement gap for Native Americans in the U.S. and paying the educational debt for the way they have been mistreated and underserved. These practices include storytelling, both personal and cultural, in the oral tradition and through digital narratives and talking circles. These practices may be in science, technology, math, history, geography, art, music—every aspect of education both in and out of school. But they all include the importance of respect for culture, acknowledgement of Native traditions and cultures, and the importance of family and extended family/tribal involvement in education. Acknowledgment of the importance of learning and teaching others of the cultural histories of Indigenous peoples is strongly woven through these chapters. The authors highlight the importance of relationships, and this principle underlies both education and policy, as they describe collaborations and relationships within and among legal, educational, and tribal bodies. The organization of the volume provides a schema for assisting educators in drawing upon these culturally sensitive practices both in implementing them and in gathering evidence of their effectiveness in the classrooms, schools, and communities in which they educate Native Americans.

Part I of this volume addresses literacy and social studies instruction for Native students. The chapters offer varying approaches to using culture and traditional ways of knowing to guide instructional approaches, to adapt proven educational practices to make them more communicative, motivating, and relevant to Native students. Beltran, Olsen, Ramey, Klawetter, and Walters (Chapter 2) address student empowerment through narrative. They cite evidence that past and ongoing trauma and stress can be mediated through the development of strong cultural identity, which can also enhance opportunities for academic success. Giving students a safe, accepting environment in which to practice cultural traditions and using traditional practices as part of the education process have been shown to be successful for Indigenous students (Riggs, 2003). For example, Beltran et al. cite literature highlighting the importance of storytelling and oral tradition in preserving historical records, cultural traditions, and identity. Beltran et al. as well as Braine and Segundo (Chapter 11) offer examples of how video and mixed media technologies can and are being used to help preserve these traditions and to offer authentic lessons to today's students. Beltran and colleagues caution that issues such as confidentiality and staying true to the flexibility of storytelling tradition require vigilance in using digital storytelling as an educational activity and tool, but they see the empowerment it offers students as worth that additional effort.

Washington State's Sovereignty Curriculum is a model for Native education. In Chapter 3, Brown offers her perspective on how the curriculum came about, a personal narrative that is a story of becoming—at once her own story of becoming and the story of the development of this curriculum, *Since Time Immemorial*, which provides information on Native history and culture for teachers and students, whether Native or non-Native, to learn a true history of their country. Brown illustrates through her own learning the importance and empowerment of learning about, living with and through cultural traditions and values, and making them available—in a modern way via the world wide web—without losing the value and flexibility of the story telling traditions, of the honoring and involvement of tribal leaders, and of being open to continuing adaptation as Native groups from other regions are invited to adapt the curriculum to their own ways and histories. Taken together, Beltran et al. and Brown's chapters illustrate the importance of cultural sensitivity to education and also to the research that we hope will continue to contribute to a melding of evidence and culture as bases for new effective and innovative educational approaches.

Craig (Chapter 4), who works in school settings serving Native Americans, lays out the three theories underlying Culturally Based Education (CBE) as identified by Demmert and Towner (2003), and links them to current reality in schools and classrooms. Through his descriptions of including community members as cultural guides to help teachers learn about Native culture, Craig shares both the process and its impact on teachers. We hope that other educators, working in partnerships with researchers, will implement such practices and gather data for evaluating the effectiveness of their implementation of these cultural guides in their own educational settings. French and Harper (Chapter 5) likewise describe professional development efforts for teachers at an Ojibwe language immersion school. Their approach to this professional development is grounded in decolonization theory and seeks to invoke in teachers a deeper understanding of and a will to work toward ending colonization. They seek to strengthen the school team's integration of cultural practice and curriculum, to have all content areas taught in the Native language, to document outcomes for both academic and social skills, and to create assessments that can document levels of student language development in the Native language. This ongoing work illustrates how teachers can learn about and support Native culture in their educational practice. The assessments being developed will provide important documentation of the effect of this work and will be instrumental in convincing other schools of the success of intensive teacher preparation and support in contributing to positive student outcomes.

The last two chapters in this section, by Hurtado and Leary (Chapters 6 and 7, respectively), illustrate how two states—Washington and Wisconsin—have implemented policies based on legislation, to improve education for Native students and to heighten knowledge and awareness across each state of Native history, culture, and traditions. Hurtado's story traces his work on House Bill 1495, and the development of both a literacy curriculum for young children and the development of the state Sovereignty Curriculum, *Since Time Immemorial* (STI), emphasizing that no such activity can succeed or even happen without strong collaborative relationships. (Note that the logo prior to Chapter 6, developed by Native artists, represents the collaboration among the 29 tribes in the state of Washington who worked together on House Bill 1495 and on the STI curriculum.) This curriculum can serve as a model for other states, in both the process that was followed in its development and in the nature of the curriculum itself, which is modular and flexible, allowing any tribe or group to adapt it and insert its own cultural content, its own treaty histories, etc. within the framework of the overall curriculum. The pilot testing done as part of the curriculum development is also a model of both community involvement with and commitment to the curriculum and of the importance of integrating research into the process. The reciprocity of having real schools pilot the curriculum, making necessary changes based on what was learned from the piloting, and collecting actual data on children in schools to demonstrate the acceptability and success of the curriculum are important illustrations of the potential for practice-research partnerships.

In Part II, a developmental approach to merging the two education traditions, evidence-based practice and culture-based education, is provided. Lockard and deGroat (Chapter 8) offer a history of Navajo Head Start immersion. When the U.S. government required that all Head Start programs adopt a research-based curriculum, the Navajo Nation merged their Diné language curriculum with a research-based curriculum to create the Ade'e'honiszin Curriculum, which infuses the Diné language and culture in the daily classroom experiences of the children. This wonderful example of the merging of the two traditions will hopefully inspire others to implement comparable programs and collect data on their effectiveness for children graduating from their programs: for example, whether and to what degree they enable the children to continue to develop fluency in their heritage language and succeed in the mainstream educational program in which English is the language of instruction. Similarly, Notari-Syverson and Coolidge explain the importance of understanding culture in early oral language development through the early grades as it impacts the development of written language literacy. They cite evidence that integrating cultural knowledge with educational approaches from early in a child's educational experiences does make a difference seen as late as adolescence. These authors highlight early childhood evidence-based programs that have been adapted for use in Native preschools and Head Start programs, but note the ongoing need for more evidence-based curricula that are culturally and linguistically appropriate and the need to prepare teachers to teach Native children with understanding and respect for the sovereignty of tribes and the right of tribes to be involved in the development of such programs.

Porter, Dill, Masutani, Goya, and Perry (Chapter 10) address the development of Native Hawaiian children in preschool and family education programs, including a creative program for homeless families. These programs, developed by a public not-for-profit foundation, have collected data which indicate positive effects; all three programs include an early childhood education curriculum, and their 'graduates' have scored at the highest levels in the state on school readiness assessments. They also report positive effects on caregiver skills, and success in moving homeless families into shelters, when government agencies have consistently failed in efforts to work with this group. They attribute their success and national recognition for innovation to their multigenerational family-oriented approach, which incorporates the culture and family values of Native Hawaiians. The programs of this foundation can serve as a model for research-practice partnerships, which others can implement and document, to build the evidence base for effective culturally sensitive programs.

Finally, Braine and Segundo (Chapter 11) in their innovative, hybrid print-plus-web-video chapter, take us further up the developmental continuum to middle school, high school and college. As they trace their own stories, they also offer stories of their students, and offer a model for the mentoring, recruitment and retention strategies needed to increase the number of Native students not only succeeding educationally in middle school and high school but also entering higher education and even perhaps research and academic careers themselves. Both increasing the number of Native teachers and researchers and educating non-Native students about Native cultures are important.

Part III, the final section of this book, addresses culturally sensitive instructional approaches implemented with Hawaiian and American Indian students, in the context of community-school and family-school relationships. After a brief overview of the research on instructional conversation, Yamauchi, Luning and Begay (Chapter 12) offer an example of their adaptation of this approach in a Hawaiian language immersion classroom of first graders, explaining how this program was molded to be compatible with the collective, holistic learning approach of Native Hawaiian culture.

They also address use of this adapted approach with other Indigenous cultures. Given the utility of instructional conversation for a variety of Indigenous cultures, additional research documenting the elements of its success in these various settings is needed. Sheehey and Jegatheesan (Chapter 13) also present a Native Hawaiian example, this time in special education. They highlight the clash between the standard approach to special education and the Native Hawaiian culture's values and beliefs about disability, a clear example of qualitative research offering a deeper cultural understanding that can enable care providers to adjust their approach so that children, Indigenous and non-Indigenous, can benefit. While family involvement is important in education in general, and highlighted in early childhood programs, a deeper understanding of the values and beliefs of a culture and how these guide or restrain certain levels of involvement in such programs can be critical to the successful implementation of the programs and to the successful education of the children in those programs—and it can be done without sacrificing a commitment to instructional excellence and evidence-based practice.

The final chapter (Strong and Jegatheesan) also highlights the value of more deeply understanding a student's culture. Through the examples of the TEAM-WORKS supplemental programs for youth, the authors highlight the value of students having pride in and receiving respect for their Native cultures in preparing these students to better succeed in traditional educational programs, as well as the value of having those students bring to educational settings some of their own cultural values and practices. TEAM-WORKs is currently collecting evidence on the effectiveness of their practices in local schools.

In 1999, Demmert wrote about his personal observations to that date—of legislation, of progress toward greater recognition of the importance of language and culture, of a vision of better schools and better teacher training and a more accurate representation of America's early history for all public school students in the U.S. He called for more work toward this in the new millennium, and in fact in 2005 he co-led a major symposium funded by the Federal government in collaboration with the Santa Fe Indian School, on improving academic performance among Native American students. This effort was an educational experience for the non-Native researchers and federal officials involved, raising awareness to a new level and hoping to build greater research and practice collaborations with Native scholars. Two resulting special issues of the *Journal of American Indian Education* focused on programs and practices (McCardle & Demmert, 2006a) and research (2006b). However, as we have tried to highlight in this volume and as Demmert made continually clear throughout the symposium, the two cannot in reality and should not be separated. At that meeting, and in the final paper of the second issue (Demmert, McCardle, Mele-McCarthy, & Leos, 2006), it was clear that the recommendations from the original *Indian Nations*

At Risk Task Force Report (U.S. Department of Education, 1991) were still appropriate and should be expanded and pursued. Indeed, the guiding principles for researchers—to consider the culture, values, and priorities of the student's family and community in planning, designing and conducting research, and defining desired outcomes of education programs—clearly have not changed. They are more commonly acknowledged by many, but are not nearly widespread enough. The "Blueprint" representing the collective wisdom of the symposium participants (Demmert et al., 2006), laid out the many types of research needed. These too remain important and relevant—all too few have been accomplished. Recommendations included using varied methodologies, mixed methods (integrating qualitative and quantitative studies), conducting exploratory studies, taking advantage of natural experiments, and using extant data from large national studies; we are gratified to see indications of these approaches in this volume, although as always more is needed. Demmert et al. also called for using culture-based methodologies to enable the study of effectiveness, and using social science methods where appropriate and adapting them as necessary. They called for a focus on measurement, to ensure that appropriate measures are developed that can identify those who need intervention and to monitor student progress; as Sheehey and Jegatheesan make very clear in their chapter in this volume, even with such measures, and even with culturally appropriate measures, the planning for and implementation of interventions must be embedded in culturally appropriate practices with family involvement and respect for the family's values and beliefs.

In the research Blueprint, there were also calls for more work on Culture-Based Education as a concept, and for materials to be developed that would embody the concept. The curricula and programs that have been developed and are shared in this volume provide evidence that this is happening.. While there is always room for more work, making this work even more widespread, and continuing to study the impact of these programs across various groups of students, it is gratifying to see that so much progress has been made. There was also a call for clarification of what would constitute cultural competence in teachers, which is a difficult concept to clearly define (although see Bettancourt, Green, Carrillo, & Ananeh-Firempong, 2001; National Alliance for Hispanic Health, 2001; National Center for Cultural Competence, 2014; Office of Minority Health, 2013). Nevertheless, there are clear indicators in the chapters in this volume that teachers can develop it, and those who do learn and understand the impact of Indigenous peoples' histories, respect the cultural beliefs and values of these cultures, and no longer hold a deficit view of those unlike themselves (see e.g., Powell, 1998; Flores, Cousin, & Diaz, 1998), are on their way to demonstrating cultural competence. The better we demonstrate the differences this makes in the lives of students, the more powerful the argument that all teachers must learn to embody this concept.

Language has also been a major focus of attention—in the Blueprint, in Demmert's earlier personal narrative (Demmert, 1999), and in the Native community generally over many years (Fillmore, 2011). The recognition of the power and importance of language as an integral part of cultural identity is increasingly being recognized, along with an increase in bilingual programs, Native language immersion programs, and language revitalization programs. (See e.g., Grergory & Garcia, 1022; Grounds, 2011; Nicholas, 2011; Wyman, Marlow, Andrew, Miller, Nichaolai & Rearden, 2011; Reyhner, 2011; and Mauelito, Bird & Belgard, 2011, as well as chapters in this volume.) However, states passing laws to restrict the use of any language except English for primary instruction have had a deleterious effect, despite research on bilingualism that supports the value of knowing additional languages (e.g., Alladi et al., 2013; Barac & Bialystok, 2012; Kroll & Bialystok, 2013; also see Chapter 12, this volume). Reporting on schooling of Indigenous Mexican students in the U.S., Ruiz and Barajas (2012) point out that it is critical for teachers to understand these students and families' Mexican-origin migration, in order to understand why families make the choices they do to have their children in bilingual classes where the children are taught in Spanish, but are learning English, when neither language is their home language. These authors note the dearth of research on Mexican Indigenous students, and call for additional research to be done in collaborative teams of researchers and teachers to explore how and why these families make program choices and the impact that being in a bilingual school has on Indigenous students' educational success, especially if we are to avoid deficit perspectives, racial discrimination and ineffective education.

There is little research on the specific immersion programs and heritage language programs in place in Native communities, but we urge teachers to collaborate with researchers to document these programs. For many immigrant communities, immersion programs in their Native language or bilingual programs to help children maintain their Native language are threatened by the legal status and education policies of the public schools (Wright, 2007). However, American Indian and Alaska Native communities have a different status, and under the most recent Executive Order (No. 13592, 2011) the federal government is committed to working with tribes to preserve and revitalize Native languages. There is therefore an opportunity to implement and research these various language programs, when it may be much more difficult to implement and research language programs in immigrant communities. Still, this will not be an easy task, for Native communities too face major challenges due to national and state policies. In addition, as Manuelito et al. (2011) note, "the balance between education programs that prepare Native American children for opportunities outside the community are constantly weighed against those that are important to the maintenance and survival of their community and way of life" (p. 318). But the two need not be incompatible;

and we believe that research examining the impact of such programs on students' motivation and overall educational success could be very important to the future of such programs.

The 2005 Blueprint (Demmert et al., 2006) ended with five priorities: (1) increasing the number of Native researchers; (2) making research more community-based, with greater participatory involvement, and with varied methodologies; (3) defining, examining, and addressing the achievement gap; (4) comparing CBE to existing instruction; and (5) focusing on early childhood. Most of these priorities remain, almost a decade later. There are more Native researchers now, thanks to efforts such as those of many of this volume's authors—Hurtado, Braine, Segundo, Leary, and of course the late Bill Demmert. And many of the other authors are young Native researchers. But we need to continue to recruit and mentor Native students in colleges and universities, and to encourage them to engage in research. It is hard to gauge whether research is more community-based and participatory, but in recent years there has been general move in in this direction for some research funding agencies (NIH Office of Behavioral and Social Sciences Research [OBSSR], 2008).[1] The message seems clear as a theme running through all of the chapters in this volume that community and family involvement in educational programs and research involving students is critical to success, as Native American cultures are holistic, collective, and collaborative; and approaches to education should honor and accommodate these traditions and ways of knowing and learning. We are just beginning to address the achievement gap for Native students, but we have the tools to do so if we will only use them. The key is melding evidence-based practices with culture-based education, with respect for and understanding of cultural differences.

Our vision is built upon the legacy of the late William Demmert and his colleagues, and the voices and contributions of the authors in this volume to pay the educational debt (Ladson-Billings, 2006). That vision includes not only educating Native students but also educating non-Natives about the numerous contributions of Native Americans and Indigenous Peoples to world civilization (Keoke, & Porterfield, 2003; Phillips, 2010). These include outstanding Native Americans such as Sequoyah, who at age 50 created the syllabary for a written language to preserve the oral language of the Cherokee (Rumford, 2004), so that that story of Native contributions could be shared with non-Natives. It also includes the five nations council of the Iroquois (Levine, 1998) that served as the model for the American Constitution for governing the land that originally belonged to them. That vision is one of free public education for all children, based on evidence of effective instructional practices and designed and implemented with knowledge and understanding of the culture and traditions of the students to whom it is offered. That vision, if we are to pay the educational debt, must be directed to all, both Native

Americans and non-Natives, and must include students, teachers, families, and community in the contemporary world.

NOTES

1. Although the program announcement for National Institutes of Health funding, which involved multiple NIH Institutes, is no longer active, it is hoped that this remains a priority for this and other funding agencies. The definition and a note on continued support is still cited on the OBSSR web page at http://obssr.od.nih.gov/scientific_areas/methodology/community_based_participatory_research/index.aspx

REFERENCES

Alladi, S., Bak, T.H., Duggirala, V., Surampudi, B., Shailaja, M., Shukla, A.K., Chaudhuri, J.R., & Kaul, S. (2013). Bilingualism delays age of onset of dementia, independent of education and immigration status. *Neurology, 8122)*: 1938–1944.

Barac, R. & Bialystok, E. (2012). Bilingual effects on cognitive and linguistic development: Role of language, cultural background, and education. *Child Development*, 88(2): 413–422.

Bettancourt, J.R., Green, A.R., Carrillo, J.E. & Ananeh-Firempong, O. (2003). Defining cultural competence: a practical framework for addressing racial/ethnic disparities in health and health care. *Public Health Reports, 118*(4): 293–302.

Demmert, W.G. (1999). Indian education revisited: A personal experience. *Journal of American Indian Education*. 38(3): *Special Issue 1,* 5–13.

Executive Order 13592, 3 CFR. (2011). Improving American Indian and Alaska Native Educational Opportunities and Strengthening Tribal Colleges and Universities. Sec. 3, White House Initiative on American Indian and Alaska Native Education.

Demmert, W., McCardle P., Mele-McCarthy, J., & Leos, K. Preparing Native American children for academic success: A blueprint for research. *Journal of American Indian Education,* 45(3): 92–106.

Flores, B., Cousin, P.T., & Diaz, E. (1998). Transforming deficit myths about learning, language, and culture (pp. 27–38). In M.F. Optiz (Ed.) *Literacy instruction for culturally and linguistically diverse students.* Newark, DE: International Reading Association.

Gregory, G.A. & Garcia, L. (2011). Keeping language alive in an urban setting: the cases of Nahuatl and Cherokee (pp. 65–82). In M. Romero-Little, S. Ortiz, T. McCarty, with R. Chen. (Eds) *Indigenous languages across generations—strengthening families and communities.* Tempe: Arizona State University Center for Indian Education.

Grounds, R. (2011). Youth bridging the gap: The hope for Native language revitalization (95–107). In M. Romero-Little, S. Ortiz, T. McCarty, with R. Chen (Eds) *Indigenous languages across generations—strengthening families and communities.* Tempe: Arizona State University Center for Indian Education.

Jackson, F. (1994). Seven strategies to support a culturally responsive pedagogy. *Journal of Reading* 37(December 1993-January 1994): 298–303..

Keoke, E., & Porterfield, K. (2003). *American Indian contributions to the world. 15,000 years of inventions and innovations.* New York: Checkmark Books.

Kroll, J. & Bialystok, E. (2013). Understanding the consequences of bilingualism for language processing and cognition. *Journal of Cognitive Psychology*. 25(5). doi: 10.1080/20445911.2013.799170

Ladson-Billings, G. (2006). From the achievement gap to the education debt: Understanding achievement in U.S. schools. *Educational Researcher*, 35(7), 3–12.

Levine, E. (1998). *If you lived with the Iroquois*. Illustrated by Shelly Hehenberger. New York: Scholastic.

Manuelito, K.D., Bird, C.P., & Belgarde, M. In M. Romero-Little, S. Ortiz, & T. McCarty; with R. Chen. (Eds). *Indigenous languages across generations—strengthening families and communities* (pp. 303–320). Tempe: Arizona State University Center for Indian Education.

McCardle, P. & Demmert, W. (2006a) Report of a National Colloquium, I—Programs and Practices. *Journal of American Indian Education*, 45(2), 1–5.

McCardle, P. & Demmert, W. (2006b) Report of a National Colloquium, II—Research. *Journal of American Indian Education*, 45(3), 1–4.

National Alliance for Hispanic Health (2001). *A Primer for cultural proficiency: Towards quality health care services for Hispanics*. Washington, D.C.: Author.

National Center for Cultural Competence. (2014). Definitions of cultural competence. Curricula enhancement module eeries. Washington, D.C: Georgetown University Center for Child and Human Development. Retrieved from http://www.nccccurricula.info/culturalcompetence.html

NIH Office of Behavioral and Social Sciences Research. PAR-08-074. Community participation in research. Retrieved from *http://grants.nih.gov/grants/guide/pa-files/PA-08-074.html*. See also "Community-Based Participatory Research", at http://obssr.od.nih.gov/scientific_areas/methodology/community_based_participatory_research/index.aspx

Nicholas, S.E. (2011). Prospects and processes for heritage language revitalization: Lessons from Hopi (pp. 106–128). In M. Romero-Little, S. Ortiz, T. McCarty, with R. Chen (Eds) *Indigenous languages across generations—strengthening families and communities*. Tempe: Arizona State University Center for Indian Education.

Office Minority Health. (2013). What is cultural competency? Washington, DC: Office of Minority Health. U.S. Department of Health and Human Services. Retrieved from http://minorityhealth.hhs.gov/templates/browse.aspx?lvl=2&lvlID=11

Phillips, C. (2010). *The complete illustrated history. Aztec & Maya. The greatest civilizations of ancient Central America with 1000 photographs, paintings, and maps*. New York: Metro Books.

Powell, R.G. (1998). Johnny can't talk, either: The perpetuation of the deficit theory in classrooms (pp. 21–26). In M.F. Optiz (Ed.) *Literacy instruction for culturally and linguistically diverse students*. Newark, DE: International Reading Association.

Reyner, J. (2011). Healing families and strengthening communities through language revitalization (pp. 281–303). In M. Romero-Little, S. Ortiz, & T. McCarty; with R. Chen (Eds) *Indigenous languages across generations—strengthening families and communities*. Tempe: Arizona State University Center for Indian Education.

Ruiz, N.T. & Barajas, M. (2012). Multiple perspectives on the schooling of Mexican indigenous students in the U.S.: Issues for future research. *Bilingual Research Journal: The Journal of the National Association for Bilingual Education*, 35(2): 125–144. doi: 10.1080/15235882.2012.703639

Rumford, J. (2004). *Sequoyah. The Cherokee who gave his people writing*. Translated by Anna Sixkiller Huckaby. Boston: Houghton Mifflin.

U.S. Department of Education. (1991). *Indian Nations At Risk: An Educational Strategy for Action*. Final Report. ERIC Number: ED339587. Washington, DC: U.S. Department of Education.

Wright, W. (2007). Heritage language programs in the era of English-only and No Child Left Behind. *Heritage Language Journal*, 5(1): 1–26.

Wyman, L., Marlow, P., Andrew, C.F., Miller, G., Nicholai, C.R., & Rearden, Y.N. (2011). Focusing communities and schools on Indigenous language maintenance: A Yup'ik example (pp. 262–281). In M. Romero-Little, S. Ortiz, T. McCarty, with R. Chen (Eds) *Indigenous languages across generations—strengthening families and communities*. Tempe: Arizona State University Center for Indian Education.

Contributors

Kristin Kawena Begay is a school psychologist who is keenly interested in effective teaching practices for Indigenous populations. She has worked as a classroom teacher on the Navajo reservation in New Mexico, as a school psychologist on the Tulalip reservation in Washington, and as a school psychologist and counselor with native Hawaiian students in Hawai'i. Her research has focused on outcomes of using effective teaching strategies with Hawaiian immersion students.

Ramona Beltrán, Ph.D., MSW is Assistant Professor at the University of Denver Graduate School of Social Work. She is of Mexican and Yaqui descent. Her scholarship focuses on the intersections of historical trauma, embodiment, and environmental/social determinants of health as they affect health and risk behaviors in Indigenous communities. She specializes in using decolonizing theories and methodologies with an emphasis on qualitative and innovative geo-spatial and photographic technologies in community-based research and practice.

Virginia Berninger, Ph.D. Psychology (Johns Hopkins), formerly on Harvard and Tufts New England Medical School faculties and since 1986 University of Washington Educational Psychology Faculty, has worked with diverse populations in her clinical work, general and special education teaching, and research (Principal Investigator, NICHD-funded cross-sectional and longitudinal studies of typically developing oral and written language learners, instructional studies for at risk readers and writers, and Interdisciplinary Research Center on Learning Disabilities—genetics, brain imaging, assessment, and instruction). She is committed to optimizing Native American achievement and educating non-Natives about the many contributions of Native Americans to world civilization.

Iisaaksiichaa (Good Ladd) **Ross A. Braine** is the Tribal Liaison for the University of Washington. He is an enrolled member of the Apsaalooke Nation, a Big Lodge Clan member, and a part of the Nighthawk Society. He is the first full-time Tribal Liaison for the UW and is currently working on the construction of wəɬəbʔaltxʷ—Intellectual House, longhouse style building on campus. He also spends much time in the community developing and strengthening relationships between tribes and the university. He is currently enrolled in the UW Information School—Master of Science in Information Management graduate program and will graduate in 2015.

Shana Brown, a descendant of the Yakama Nation, is a trainer for Washington State's Office of Native Education in addition to being their co-author of *Since Time Immemorial: Tribal Sovereignty in Washington State.* She has written curriculum for the Washington State Historical Society and the University of Montana's Regional Learning Project *Tribal Perspectives of History in the Northwest.* Currently she is writing Common Core State Standards aligned curriculum for the National Park Service's *Honoring Tribal Legacies Along the Lewis and Clark National Historical Trail.* Shana lives in Seattle with her husband and two children and teaches full time in Seattle Public Schools.

Rosemary Ackley Christensen, Ojibwe, Associate Professor Emerita University of Wisconsin, Green Bay was born in the Bad River Ojibwe Nation, Odanah, the village of her mother, in Wisconsin and enrolled in the Band of her father at Mole Lake (Sokaogon). She holds an Ed.M. from Harvard University (1971) and was a cohort member of the *Leadership Academy* at the University of MN where she completed her Ed.D. (1999). Her dissertation is entitled: *Anishinaabeg medicine wheel leadership: The work of Dave F. Courchene Jr.* She is an experienced curriculum developer, planner, trainer, writer, evaluator, researcher, and an advocate and practitioner of culturally-based teaching methods. Christensen is a founding member of the National Indian Education Association, and is interested in and works on projects focusing on systemic change.

Jane Coolidge, M.A., CCC-SLP, is a speech-language pathologist specializing in emergent literacy, language, and dyslexia. She has worked with the Muckleshoot Tribe in Auburn, Washington, the American Indian Head Start Quality Improvement Center, University of Oklahoma, and as National Literacy Specialist for American Indian/Alaska Native Head Start technical assistance system. In 2011, at the National Center for Quality Teaching and Learning, Coolidge trained Tribal Head Start early childhood teachers. She has served as adjunct faculty for Northwest Indian College and Antioch University, in Washington State, has worked on culturally appropriate interventions in literacy, and currently works in Georgia on diagnosis and treatment of dyslexia.

Anthony B. Craig is an elementary principal in the Marysville School District, which serves students from the Tulalip Tribes. He is a member of the Yakama Nation. He received his Ed.D. in educational leadership and policy studies from the University of Washington. His work has focused on collaborating with members of the tribal community and educators in schools to develop school systems that leverage the strengths of tribal culture(s) as a foundation for school improvement. He believes that schools must be culturally based in order to strengthen students culturally and lead to excellent academic achievement.

Jennifer deGroat (Diné) is a Senior Lecturer in Bilingual Multicultural Education at Northern Arizona University and teaches at the University of Arizona–Tuscon. She teaches bilingual methodology, multicultural education, and bi-literacy. Originally from the Eastern Navajo Agency, she holds an M.A. from the University of New Mexico and is pursuing a doctorate; current studies include biliteracy and language immersion. She has taught in Bureau of Indian Education schools, coordinated Navajo language immersion camp for Navajo families, and is a member of the National Council of Teachers of English, the Dine' Language Association, the Indigenous Bilingual Education/ National Association for Bilingual Education, and the National Indian Education Association.

Jan Dill founded Partners in Development Foundation in 1997 and has served as President and Chairman of the Board since January 12, 2001. Jan's passion and focus is to strengthen Hawai'i's children and families and promote environmental stewardship. He received an M.A. in Law and Diplomacy degree in economic development and an M.A. in international affairs and successfully completed oral exams for the doctoral course program from the Fletcher School of Law and Diplomacy at Tufts University. He earned a B.A. degree in political science/philosophy from Beloit College in Wisconsin. Jan is married with five children and 14 grandchildren.

Kristen French (Blackfeet/Gros Ventre) is currently Associate Professor of elementary education and Director of the Center for Education, Equity and Diversity at Western Washington University. Mentored by Dr. William G. Demmert, Jr., French's return to WWU provided an opportunity to honor Demmert's work and 'give back' to the university and students where her journey began. In 2012, she received the Ken Gass Community Building Award for outstanding contributions to children, youth, and families, the WWU's Women of Color Empowerment Award, and the WWU's Excellence in Teaching Award. Her engaged scholarship includes multicultural teacher education, Indigenous education, decolonizing theory, and critical performative pedagogy.

Danny "Ka'eo" Goya is the Project Director for the Ka Pa'alana Traveling Preschool and Homeless Family Education Program. Danny has a Bachelors degree in History and a Minor Studies Certificate in Hawaiian Ethnic Studies from the University of Hawai'i at Mānoa, where he also earned his Post-Baccalaureate Certificate in Secondary Education (PBCSE). He has over 15 years of experience teaching K-12 in the Hawai'i State Department of Education, Hawai'i Association for Independent Schools (HAIS), and the school system in Japan. Danny is one of two active NCFL (National Center for Family Literacy) Certified Trainers in the nation focused on homeless families. He and his family reside in Pālolo.

Leslie Harper (Ojibwe) is Director of the Niigaane Ojibwemowin Immersion School located on the Leech Lake Reservation in Minnesota. Since 2003, Niigaane has been featured at the National Museum of the American Indian, Cultural Survival, and recently featured in the regional Emmy-award winning documentary, First Speakers: Restoring the Ojibwe Language. In 2009, Niigaane received the prestigious National Indian Education "William Demmert Cultural Freedom Award" for "extraordinary and courageous work that celebrates the right to freedom of Native language, culture, and educational excellence." Because of Leslie's successful leadership, she was honored with the 2012 Minnesota Indian Education Association Award for Outstanding Administrator.

Denny Hurtado (TacH Mi acH t3n) received his master's degree in school administration from California State University Humboldt. Retired Director of Indian Education, Washington State Office of the Superintendent of Public Instruction and former chair of the Skokomish Tribe, he also is the 2014 Charles E. Odegaard Award recipient. For decades, Hurtado has advocated for Indian rights and education throughout Washington and the U.S. working with 29 tribes. He led the creation of groundbreaking curricula geared to K-12 educators; the curriculum, *Since Time Immemorial: Tribal Sovereignty in Washington State*, was developed in response to House Bill 1495 passed in 2005 to better educate, all students, teachers and administrators about tribal history and Sovereignty in Washington. His life reflects his strong commitment to social equity and education.

Brinda Jegatheesan is Associate Professor of Educational Psychology at the University of Washington. She has been a bilingual special education teacher in India, Singapore, and Hawaii'i. Her research focuses on ethnomedical beliefs/practices and the linguistic socialization of children with severe disabilities from Asian American Pacific Islander backgrounds. Another strand of her research involves animal-assisted therapy and activities with children in the US and Asia. Her research has a biocentric approach to the scientific inquiry of child development.

Susanne Klawetter, LCSW, is a doctoral student at the University of Denver's Graduate School of Social Work interested in examining social determinants of maternal and child health disparities. She is currently a JFK Partners Leadership Education in Neurodevelopmental Disabilities (LEND) Fellow with the University of Colorado, School of Medicine

J P Leary (Cherokee/Delaware) is Assistant Professor of Humanistic Studies-First Nations Studies at the University of Wisconsin–Green Bay. He previously served as the American Indian Studies Consultant at the Wisconsin Department of Public Instruction from 1996–2011 where his primary responsibilities related to professional development and curriculum development for Act 31 implementation. In 1997, he co-founded, with Ronald N. Satz, the American Indian Studies Summer Institute, and he remains a staff member. He continues to work with tribal communities and school districts across Wisconsin and continues to research and write about Act 31 and related issues.

Louise Lockard is a Clinical Associate Professor of Bilingual Multicultural Education at Northern Arizona University where she coordinates the Master's Program in Bilingual Multicultural Education and teaches courses in the foundations and assessment of bilingual and second language programs. She holds a Ph.D. in Language, Reading, and Culture from the University of Arizona. Her research has focused on the history of Navajo education and she directed the Title VII Learn in Beauty Project, 1998–2003. She currently directs a Professional Development Project with forty Navajo language teachers earning Master's degrees and preparing to teach in Navajo language immersion and dual language classrooms in Arizona public schools.

Rebecca J. 'Ilima Luning is an Educational and Cultural Specialist in the Department of Educational Psychology at the University of Hawai'i at Mānoa. She is a Native Hawaiian scholar born and raised in Kailua, O'ahu. She is a fluent speaker of the Hawaiian language and a proponent for culture-based education through research and work with Ka Papahana Kaiapuni (Hawaiian language immersion program). Her doctoral research in developmental psychology in the Department of Psychology at the University of Hawai'i at Mānoa is focused on ascertaining a Hawaiian ethnotheory of learning through analyzing Hawaiian cultural practitioners' and classroom educators' teaching philosophies.

Alison Masutani is the Vice President of Operations and Project Director for the Tūtū and Me Traveling Preschool. Prior to joining PIDF in 2003, Alison worked in the banking industry for 15 years, focused on private and business banking. She left to start up a technology company, then co-founded security system businesses and provided organizational management services. Alison received her B.B.A. in Finance from the University of Hawai'i at Mānoa. She currently resides in Kāne'ohe with her family; her interests include music, international cuisine, and cooking.

Peggy McCardle, Ph.D., M.P.H., is a private consultant/editor in areas related to learning, literacy and learning disabilities. She worked at the National Institutes of Health for more than two decades, during which she developed literacy initiatives including support for research on bilingualism, biliteracy, and English-learners. She holds a Ph.D. in linguistics and master's degree in public health. McCardle has been a classroom teacher, speech-language pathologist, and has held faculty and clinical positions. She has taught scientific and technical writing, and has experience developing and co-editing volumes and thematic journal issues.

Angela Notari-Syverson is a Curriculum Specialist in the College of Education at the University of Washington in Seattle. She has extensive experience and expertise in early language and literacy development as well as in assessment. She has authored books and journal publications in these areas. Dr. Notari-Syverson has directed federal projects on early literacy curriculum involving collaboration with Native American preschool programs in the state of Washington. She also worked as a Speech Language Pathologist in the Seattle Public Schools. She has a Ph.D. in Early Childhood Special Education from the University of Oregon.

Polly Olsen, BA is Community Relations & K-12 Education Director for the Indigenous Wellness Research Institute at the University of Washington, School of Social Work. She is a member of the Yakama Nation in Central Washington. She is the Principal Investigator/ Program Director of the Native Youth Enrichment Program, which focuses on providing culturally responsive science, technology, engineering, and mathematics training for Native youth.

Lora Perry is the Project Director of the Nā Pono No Nā 'Ohana Program. She has devoted her life to education and is an active NCFL (National Center for Family Literacy) trainer. Lora is a member of the State of Hawai'i Governor's Early Learning Advisory Board and the Collective Impact Early Childhood Group. Lora has a Bachelors Degree in Organizational Management from Hawai'i Loa College and Masters Degree in Early Education from the University of Hawai'i at Mānoa. Her master's thesis was *First Year Outcomes of a Native Hawaiian Family Education Program.*

Toni Porter is a Senior Researcher in Innovation, Policy, and Research at Bank Street College of Education. Her work focuses on early care and education issues. Porter has served as the principal investigator on two national research projects related to family, friend and neighbor child care—*Supporting Quality in Home-based Child Care,* and *The Child Care Assessment Tool for Relatives,* a measure to assess quality in relative child care. She has been the lead investigator on several evaluations of child care initiatives, and is currently a key consultant on the *Family-Provider Relationship Quality.*

Anastasia Ramey, MSW is Research Coordinator for the Native Youth Enrichment Program and Center for Indigenous Child & Family Research at the Indigenous Wellness Research Institute at the University of Washington, School of Social Work. She is of Turtle Mountain Chippewa descent.

David Rose, Ph.D., is Director of *Reading to Learn, a* program to train teachers (primary, secondary, and university) in a unique methodology for integrating literacy in teaching practice (www.readingtolearn.com. au). An Associate of the School of Letters, Arts, and Media, University of Sydney, his work has been particularly concerned with Indigenous Australian communities, languages, and education programs. He is a speaker of Pitjantjatjara, a language of Australia's Western Desert, and an initiated member of the Western Desert Indigenous ceremonial Law. His books include *The Western Desert Code: an Australian crypto-grammar.* Canberra: Pacific Linguistics, 2001, and with J.R. Martin, *Learning to Write, Reading to Learn: Genre, knowledge and pedagogy in the Sydney School,* London: Equinox, 2012.

Glaadai Tommy Segundo (Thomas Segundo III), an enrolled member of the Haida tribe of Southeast Alaska born and raised in the Seattle area, considers himself an "Urban Indian." A 2006 graduate of the University of Washington in Sociology, he is currently Native American/Alaska Native Recruitment Coordinator for the UW-Seattle campus. He has over eight years of experience in Indian Education and working with Native youth at the Seattle Indian Health Board, Huchoosedah Indian Education Program, United Indians of All Tribes, and now UW. Passionate about Indian Education, he plans to earn a masters degree in educational psychology and continue to work on narrowing the educational achievement gap for Native youth.

Patricia Sheehey is an Associate Professor in Special Education at the University of Hawaii Manoa. Her areas of research include culturally and linguistically diverse families of children with disabilities, early childhood special education, and children with severe disabilities. Patricia shares Palapala's passion for including Makana with his same-age peers and for struggling to advocate for him every day of her life. She, too, had a son much like Makana that she wanted included with his peers.

Zoe Higheagle Strong, M.Ed. and doctoral student at the University of Washington in Educational Psychology. She is a Nez Perce tribal member. Currently, she is the Vice President of Strong Alliance, an educational consulting company, and a Cofounder of the Mack Strong TEAM-WORKS Foundation. Her work and research focuses on developing culturally responsive youth mentoring programs that holistically address the educational and social-emotional needs of children in Native and at-risk communities. More recently, she has expanded her research and program evaluation work on preferred practices and preparation for early learning childhood educators serving in Native communities.

Karina Walters, Ph.D., MSW, is Director of the Indigenous Wellness Research Institute and Associate Dean of Research at University of Washington School of Social Work. She is an enrolled member of the Choctaw Nation of Oklahoma. Her research focuses on historical, social, and cultural determinants of physical and mental health among American Indians and Alaska Natives. She serves as principal investigator on several groundbreaking studies associated with health-risk outcomes among American Indian individuals, families, and communities funded by the National Institutes of Health.

Linda Sue Warner, a member of the Comanche Tribe of Oklahoma, holds a masters degree in education administration from Pennsylvania State University and a Ph.D. in general administration with emphasis in personnel from the University of Oklahoma. Warner began teaching in 1970 and has held various teaching and administrative positions across the U.S. Her honors include being appointed by the White House to the National Advisory Council of American Indian Education; she has also served on the Board of the Foundation for Excellence in American Indian Education in the Department of Interior and the Negotiated Rule-Making Committee for Highly Qualified Teachers in Department of Education. She has two sons, one grandson, and two granddaughters.

Julie A. Washington, Ph.D. is a Professor in the Department of Educational Psychology and Special Education-Program in Communication Disorders at Georgia State University. Dr. Washington's work has focused on understanding cultural dialect use in young African American children with a specific emphasis on language assessment and academic performance. In addition, her work with preschoolers has focused on understanding and improving the early literacy and language skills necessary to support later reading proficiency in high-risk groups, including African American children growing up in poverty. Dr. Washington's research is funded by the National Institutes of Health-National Institute on Deafness and Other Communication Disorders and by the U.S. Department of Education.

Lois A. Yamauchi is a Professor in the Department of Educational Psychology at the University of Hawai'i at Manoa in Honolulu, Hawai'i. Her research has focused on innovative approaches to education for Native Hawaiians and other Indigenous groups. She has conducted education research in the Zuni Pueblo, New Mexico, and has consulted with the country of Greenland regarding their reform of preschool education to be more culturally relevant for Greenlandic children.

Index

CPSIA information can be obtained
at www.ICGtesting.com
Printed in the USA
FFOW03n1411200418
46319359-47871FF